# Biliteracy from the Start
## Literacy Squared in Action

# Biliteracy from the Start
## Literacy Squared in Action

Kathy Escamilla

Susan Hopewell

Sandra Butvilofsky

Wendy Sparrow

Lucinda Soltero-González

Olivia Ruiz-Figueroa

Manuel Escamilla

**Caslon Publishing**
Philadelphia

Caslon, Inc.
825 N. 27th St.
Philadelphia, PA 19130


caslonpublishing.com


9 8 7 6 5


Library of Congress Cataloging-in-Publication Data

Escamilla, Kathy.
Biliteracy from the start : literacy squared in action / Kathy Escamilla, Susan Hopewell, Sandra Butvilofsky, Wendy Sparrow, Lucinda Soltero-Gonzalez, Olivia Ruiz-Figueroa, Manuel Escamilla.
    pages cm
Includes bibliographical references and index.
ISBN 978-1-934000-13-7 (pbk. : alk. paper)   1. Bilingualism.   2. Literacy.   3. Language acquisition.   4. Education, Bilingualism.   I. Title.

P118.7.E83 2013
306.44'6071—dc23                                                              2013026179

Literacy Squared is a registered trademark.

 Box 2.9 is used with permission from Arte Público Press, the oldest and largest publisher of U.S. Hispanic books.


The poem in Table 5.2 is from *Angels Ride Bikes and Other Fall Poems* by Francisco X. Alarcón. Copyright © 1999 by Francisco X. Alarcón. Permission arranged with Children's Book Press, an imprint of Lee & Low Books, Inc., New York, NY 10016. All rights not specifically granted herein are reserved.


Printed in the United States of America.

# About the Authors

**Kathy Escamilla** is a professor in the Division of Educational Equity and Cultural Diversity at the University of Colorado, Boulder. Her research interests center on biliteracy for Spanish-English emerging bilingual children in U.S. schools. Her career in education spans 41 years and she has been a teacher, resource teacher, bilingual program director, and professor.

**Susan Hopewell** is an assistant professor of education in the Division of Educational Equity and Cultural Diversity at the University of Colorado, Boulder. She is interested in issues of language, culture, equity, and identity—especially as they affect, or are affected by, (bi)literacy practices. Her K–12 public school teaching experience includes eight years as a classroom teacher in a dual language elementary school and four years as the literacy coach in a maintenance bilingual program.

**Sandra Butvilofsky** is a research associate with the BUENO Center for Multicultural Education at the University of Colorado, Boulder. Her interests are in classroom-based research, with a focus on the biliterate writing development of simultaneous bilingual children in elementary schools. Her elementary teaching experience includes five years as a bilingual classroom teacher and five years as a trained *Descubriendo la lectura*/Reading Recovery teacher. She has been involved in the Literacy Squared research project since 2006.

**Wendy Sparrow** is a professional research associate at the University of Colorado, Boulder. Her research interests include the bilingual literacy development of Latino elementary school children and fidelity of program implementation in bilingual and dual language programs and interventions. Before becoming involved in research, she spent seven years as a bilingual elementary classroom teacher and Title I literacy instructor in the public school setting.

**Lucinda Soltero-González** is an assistant professor of education in the division of Educational Equity and Cultural Diversity at the University of Colorado, Boulder. She was an elementary school teacher and a bilingual special education teacher for over seven years before earning her doctorate in language, reading, and culture from the University of Arizona. Her research interests include the development of bilingualism and early biliteracy in young Spanish-speaking children and biliteracy practices in U.S. schools.

**Olivia Ruiz-Figueroa** worked in Tucson Unified School District for 22 years as a classroom bilingual education teacher, Title 1 reading teacher, and a *Descubriendo la lectura*/Reading Recovery teacher leader. She was one of the original authors of the Spanish reconstruction of Marie Clay's Reading Recovery program. Growing up in a bilingual/bicultural home, she continues to focus on assessment, instruction, and cultural equity for emerging bilingual students being educated in the United States.

**Manuel Escamilla** earned a Ph.D. in curriculum and instruction, with an emphasis in early childhood education, from the University of Kansas. He has been a Head Start program director and has spent most of his professional life working with parents to improve the higher-education opportunities for their children. He is a project director for the BUENO Center for Multicultural Education at the University of Colorado, Boulder.

# Preface

This book is for teachers, administrators, instructional leaders, curriculum developers, professional development providers, assessment and evaluation specialists, policymakers, and advocates who expect their emerging bilingual students to develop biliteracy. It is grounded in ten years of research, instruction, assessment, and professional development in elementary school bilingual programs that serve emerging bilingual students from Spanish-speaking homes. The holistic biliteracy framework at the center of this work can be adapted and applied to any context that provides instruction through two languages with the explicit goal and anticipated outcome of biliteracy for all students.

## History and Development of Literacy Squared

In 2004, two of the authors conducted an intensive session at the National Association for Bilingual Education Conference in Albuquerque, New Mexico. The title of the session was, "Transitions to Biliteracy: Structures and Strategies." Our primary purpose was to argue that transitions in bilingual and dual language programs should emphasize transitions to *biliteracy* rather than the more typical transitions to *English*. A secondary purpose was to discuss how to develop cross grade-level trajectories to ensure successful transitions, preferably to biliteracy, but also to English medium classrooms. More than 350 educators, including practitioners, researchers, and school administrators attended the session, and we engaged in a dialogue about the state of the field. Together, we concluded that issues in transition were among the most challenging in all program models, including bilingual education, dual language, and English as a second language (ESL). Specifically, we noted the following:

- Transition is somewhat of an oxymoron; children are in bilingual or ESL programs with native language support one day and in all English instruction the next. Many schools have transition criteria (e.g., test score cutoffs, time in program). However, they lack transition strategies for teachers to implement or mechanisms to monitor and guide these transitions. There is, in fact, no true transition between languages (August & Shanahan, 2006; Goldenberg, 2008).
- There are few, if any, transitional curriculum materials and/or assessments, particularly in literacy, to assist teachers in helping children transition from one language to another (August & Shanahan, 2006).
- Teachers do not feel prepared to adequately address transition issues (Gersten, 1996), and transitional classrooms are places where children report feeling a great deal of stress (Pappamihiel, 2001).
- Transition frequently means transition to English, with little or no emphasis placed on transition to biliteracy (August & Hakuta, 1997; August & Shanahan, 2006).
- Little research is available to guide practice with regard to transitioning children from one language to another (Gersten, 1996; Saunders, O'Brien, Lennon, McLean, 1998).

In short, we concluded that while the concepts of transition and transfer had been discussed abstractly in the field, they had not yet been operationalized adequately in schools and classrooms. We recognized a dire need to help children and teachers make more successful transitions between languages both in instructional practices and assessment. As we complete this book in 2013, we note that this continues to be a critical issue (Beeman & Urow, 2013).

In 2004, we agreed to develop a research plan, along with an instructional model and assessment plan, to examine how programs of bilingual and dual language education could enhance the development of trajectories toward biliteracy. We were further motivated when some of the educators in the audience volunteered their schools and districts to be participants in any research related to the development of the proposed project.

In the fall of 2004, we convened a group of researchers and practitioners to conceptualize Literacy Squared and its four components: research, assessment, professional development, and the holistic biliteracy instructional framework. As we met and planned we conducted an extensive review of literature that led us to create a model that challenges some of the traditionally held paradigms about language and literacy instruction in bilingual/ dual language and ESL programs. Our holistic biliteracy framework was novel in its paired literacy focus, connected literacy environments, and goal of biliteracy development rather than transition to English. Our framework demanded that assessments of emerging biliteracy be aligned with the holistic biliteracy framework and we achieved this through the development of novel ways of interpreting existing reading and writing assessments in English and Spanish.

Further, we agreed that a new instructional and assessment model for building trajectories toward biliteracy had to be comprehensive. The formal name for this project and this book, *Biliteracy from the Start: Literacy Squared in Action,* has been chosen because it captures our belief that best practice involves building trajectories toward biliteracy using both Spanish and English, beginning in kindergarten. The word "squared" indicates the exponential potential of literacy in two languages.

This book is the result of the past decade of research, professional development, and classroom implementation of Literacy Squared. Over the course of the past nine years, we have created a theoretical framework for developing biliteracy via paired literacy instruction; conducted an extensive review of literature to examine the most current research on transition and transfer; concluded a pilot study to examine the potential of the holistic biliteracy framework; completed two different longitudinal studies, each three years in length, to examine the reading and writing development and outcomes for children participating in Literacy Squared classrooms; developed an observational matrix for assessing fidelity of implementation of the model in research classrooms; and initiated a third phase of research and implementation. Participating school districts have included three districts in Texas, one district in Oregon, four districts in Colorado, and, most recently, a district in Washington. Over time, the project has involved over 6,000 children and 300 teachers. Our work is ongoing and iterative. Research informs practice, practice informs professional development and research, and all partners learn from and with each other.

## How to Use This Book

Teachers and administrators in any type of bilingual program (e.g., transitional, dual language) or native/home/heritage language arts classes (e.g., Spanish language arts) can use the following features from *Biliteracy from the Start: Literacy Squared in Action*:

- The innovative holistic biliteracy instructional framework for grades K–5 to strengthen biliteracy development for emerging bilingual students
- Paired literacy instruction and assessment
- Empirically based biliterate reading trajectories, benchmarks, and zones that offer concrete biliteracy targets and anticipated outcomes for students from Spanish-speaking homes in well-implemented bilingual programs
- Assessment practices and techniques to monitor and document children's trajectories toward biliteracy
- A curriculum development process to create units for biliteracy instruction that align with state content (e.g., Common Core) and language development standards (e.g., English- and Spanish-language development standards; new and home language arts progressions)

When educators use the holistic biliteracy framework, with its focus on paired literacy instruction and assessment, they can expect to transform teaching and learning effectively at the classroom and program levels.

The biliterate reading trajectories, benchmarks, and zones can also be used by dual language educators. However, educators cannot uncritically assume the same numerical values because of the differences in their target populations (e.g., two-way dual language programs include students from monolingual English-speaking homes) and their content and language allocation plans (e.g., dual language programs offer may more instructional time in Spanish). Therefore, dual language educators need to develop empirically based biliterate reading trajectories, benchmarks, and zones based on longitudinal evidence of how their students (from monolingual English-speaking homes, bilingual homes, or monolingual Spanish-speaking homes) develop reading in two languages over time using DRA2, EDL2, or other appropriate measures. Given that, by definition, dual language programs provide a minimum of 50% and a maximum of 90% of content-area instruction in the partner language (e.g., Spanish), we should expect to find stronger outcomes for all students over time.

Educators working to develop a coherent and coordinated Common Core–aligned language arts block that has allotted time dedicated to English language arts, native or home language arts (e.g., Spanish, Mandarin, Arabic), and ESL can use the holistic biliteracy framework to inform their language policy, structure their programs, align curriculum development across languages, stimulate creative ways to team-teach, and document student trajectories toward biliteracy. Teachers can use language development standards or progressions to differentiate instruction and assessment for the emerging bilinguals in their classes.

## Special Features

This book has many features that make the Literacy Squared holistic biliteracy framework accessible and practicable, including the following:

- A model for paired literacy instruction—learning to read and write in two languages, beginning in kindergarten
- An expanded definition of literacy instruction that includes oracy and metalanguage as well as reading and writing
- Authentic methods to interpret the development of Spanish and English reading and writing
- Clear content- and language-allocation policy recommendations for an elementary school language arts block with dedicated time allotted to authentic Spanish literacy and literacy-based ELD
- Guidance for teachers in how to make explicit and direct connections between Spanish and English literacy environments
- Innovative Literacy Squared teaching approaches, including Lotta Lara, theDictado,* and *así se dice*
- Lesson plans, activity structures, instructional routines, student work, and assessment practices that illustrate Literacy Squared in action
- Detailed analyses of student writing side by side using the Literacy Squared writing rubric that provides strong models of paired literacy instruction and assessment across grade levels
- Literacy Squared observation protocol template that educators can use to monitor, evaluate, and strengthen implementation of instructional and assessment approaches.

The Literacy Squared writing rubric, observation protocol, and lesson planning template can also be found at casloncommunity.com/Biliteracy-from-the-Start/.

Overall the purpose of this book is to celebrate biliteracy, and to provide educators with strategies and structures to improve the biliteracy potential of Spanish-speaking children in U.S. schools.

---

*We invented the term "theDictado" to reflect the bilingual focus of this method in Literacy Squared.

# Foreword

## Squaring Literacy through Biliteracy

Education in the United States is dominated by discourse surrounding the poor performance of American students, especially emergent-bilingual Latino students, on high-stakes standardized exams in English. The Common Core State Standards, which have been adopted by 46 states and the District of Columbia at the time of this writing, have been one response to the weak performance of American students in international competitions, such as PISA (Program for International Student Assessment).

Kathy Escamilla and her coauthors start the conversation about the education of Latino bilingual students from an alternative angle. *Biliteracy from the Start: Literacy Squared in Action* doesn't apologize for the use of Spanish in the rigorous education of young Latino children to meet literacy standards. Instead, it points to the potential of biliteracy in squaring gains for Latino children whose bilingualism develops as they enter U.S. schools. In addition to changing the conversation about teaching young, Latino bilingual students by insisting that literacy in English and Spanish be squared (i.e., the role of literacy in two languages has equal sides and dimensions, thus multiplying itself and its effects), this book leads to action by educators, as the subtitle suggests. The squaring potential of this book lies not only in the approach to teaching biliteracy that it promotes but also, as I will point out, in the alternative conceptualizations about the instruction and assessment of biliteracy that it presents. Furthermore, the practices have been squared to potential through a multiple approach that has included longitudinal research, as well as implementation of the model in various locations—Texas, Oregon, Colorado, and Washington—with 6,000 children and 300 teachers who have participated in professional development. Thus, the book is not only a how-to-book for teachers; it also makes an important contribution to the field of biliteracy.

The book challenges some of the traditional assumptions that have been made about bilingual students, as well as biliteracy. It focuses not on immigrant children who are often sequential bilinguals, but on those the authors call "the new normal"—bilingual children born in the United States who are developing bilingualism simultaneously as they live in homes and communities where English and Spanish is heard, spoken, and performed. These young bilinguals often have attended preschools where, unfortunately, English is the only language of instruction. Thus, they enter kindergarten with varying degrees of proficiency in English and Spanish, falling at different points of a bilingual continuum. For these children, traditional models of sequential biliteracy, as used in many bilingual education programs, do not make any sense; for, as Merrill Swain pointed out in 1972, bilingualism (and not English or Spanish) is their first language.

This increase of young, simultaneous-bilingual children is a global phenomenon, as witnessed by the attention that Bilingual First Language Acquisition (BFLA) has received among international scholars. However, BFLA has not been studied appropriately in U.S. children, mostly because of our fear as Americans that bilingualism could be a native, and not a foreign, phenomenon. This book is unique in pointing out the importance of native-born American bilinguals and the shift in education paradigms that must occur to meet their needs.

In the last decade or so, the concept of superdiversity proposed by Steven Vertovec has persuaded many that efforts to educate for bilingualism and biliteracy were worthless. Escamilla and colleagues remind us that biliteracy is worthwhile and important, especially for young, Latino bilingual children who continue to be the majority in many U.S. regions. Leaving behind the traditional concept of sequential biliteracy acquisition, this book shows teachers how to engage in what they call "paired literacy," a concurrent approach to biliteracy instruction in both English and Spanish that mirrors the children's simultaneous bilingual acquisition. What makes the approach rich and complex is that although it recognizes the importance of what I have called "translanguaging" (the importance of drawing on all the children's bilingual competencies and engaging in cross-language connections), paired literacy encourages holistic biliteracy instruction and assessment. Holistic in this book refers to the integration of oracy, reading, writing and metalanguage, as well as to seeing biliteracy itself as a distinct system. Holistic also refers to a combined approach—specifically designed for young bilingual students—that provides authentic Spanish literacy instruction and literacy-based English language development. Escamilla and colleagues show that a sheltered English approach simply is insufficient to teach literacy to young, bilingual children. The book guides teachers in making literacy instruction for young, Latino bilingual children explicit while de-emphasizing independent reading. The approach offered for biliteracy instruction is novel and goes beyond traditional approaches that have been proposed specifically to teach emergent bilinguals or monolingual students.

Escamilla and colleagues also demonstrate the relevance of the holistic biliteracy framework for assessment by establishing biliterate reading zones and proposing rubrics that help teachers fully assess bilingual children's biliteracy. The book also guides educators through lesson planning and creating units that enable children to make connections between Spanish and English literacy, as they draw from each to build their holistic biliteracy.

There is much in this book for teachers, administrators, and scholars. For teachers, in addition to the points mentioned previously, the book contributes original strategies for biliteracy, such as Lotta Lara, *así se dice*, and anchor charts for cross-language connections. For administrators and literacy coaches, the book also includes an observation protocol. For scholars, the book corrects myths about American bilingualism; young, Latino bilingual children; and biliteracy. The holistic approach to teaching and assessing Spanish and English literacy that the book proposes, accompanied by many authentic examples from children and templates for teachers, makes *Biliteracy from the Start* the beginning of a new discourse and new action that will benefit Latino bilingual children.

—Ofelia García, Graduate Center, City University of New York

# Contents

PART II

## ASSESSMENT
Monitoring Trajectories for Biliteracy in Reading and Writing

PART III

## LESSON PLANNING
Creating Holistic Biliteracy Lessons and Units

# Biliteracy from the Start
## Literacy Squared in Action

# What Is Literacy Squared?

*The roots of the term education imply drawing out children's potential, making them more than they were; however, when children come to school fluent in their primary language, and they leave school essentially monolingual in English, then our schools have negated the meaning of the term education, because they have made children less than they were.*

Mary Ashworth, as cited in Cummins, 1989

## Key Terms

| | |
|---|---|
| **Bidirectional transfer** | **Holistic biliteracy framework** |
| **Bilingualism** | **Late-exit transitional bilingual program** |
| **Biliteracy** | **Limited English proficient** |
| **Biliteracy zones** | **Literacy Squared** |
| **Concurrent translation** | **Metalanguage** |
| **Cross-language connections** | **Model** |
| **Dual language program** | **Oracy** |
| **Early-exit transitional bilingual program** | **Paired literacy instruction** |
| **Emerging (emergent) bilingual** | **Simultaneous bilinguals** |
| **English language learner** | **Trajectories toward biliteracy** |

## Guiding Questions

- How does a holistic biliteracy perspective challenge the way schools structure literacy programs for emerging bilingual students?
- How does a focus on qualities of instruction shift the debate about effective practice in the bilingual education field?
- How can the notion of trajectories toward biliteracy inform the ways we teach the increasing numbers of simultaneous bilinguals in U.S. schools?

In virtually every corner of the world, **bilingualism** and **biliteracy** are valued and deemed to be advantageous to individuals, communities, and to the economic and cultural future of nations. The ability to read, write, speak, and negotiate life in more than one language is deemed an attribute of well-rounded and highly educated people in any country.

Even in the United States, long known for its stubborn adherence to English monolingualism, there is a growing interest in the development of bilingualism. This interest is fueled by the fact that there are upwards of 10 million children who enter U.S. schools speaking languages other than English, of whom 80% are Spanish speakers. Current estimates put this number at about 1 in 10 students in U.S. schools. The language, culture, and funds of knowledge that these emerging bilingual children bring to school constitute a huge and often untapped national resource. Bilingualism and biliteracy can and should be outcomes of schooling for these children. Spurred by changing demographics, as well as by the globalization of business and commerce, there is also growing interest in the development of bilingualism and biliteracy for students who enter school as monolingual English speakers. The focus of this text is on biliteracy, including but not limited to, reading and writing in two languages.

## An Innovative Approach

This book presents an approach to instruction and interpreting assessments for emerging bilingual children called "**Literacy Squared**." The approach was conceived and developed as an innovative **holistic biliteracy framework** that could be used to nurture and develop bilingualism and biliteracy in the millions of Spanish-speaking students in U.S. public schools. During its development and refinement over the last decade Literacy Squared has comprised four components (Figure 1.1):

1. *Instruction*: a framework for what we have labeled "holistic biliteracy instruction," which includes recommended teaching approaches and time allocations across the grades intended to foster development and learning in two languages through **paired literacy instruction**. This instructional framework is unique in that it intentionally and purposefully connects Spanish and English literacy environments.
2. *Assessment*: recommended procedures, including formative and summative measures, for monitoring students' progress on what we have called "**trajectories toward biliteracy**." The assessment framework is a holistic framework for observing and measuring the development of reading and writing in Spanish and English.
3. *Professional development (PD)*: the PD component of Literacy Squared is closely aligned to our ongoing research, and involves our work with the schools who have adopted and are fully implementing Literacy Squared as their **model** for the education of emerging bilingual learners. This book is, of course, a PD book, in that it is intended for use by teachers and school leaders. It is *not*, however, about the training we do to insure fidelity of implementation in every aspect of the model and to feed the research on Literacy Squared.
4. *Research*: while not the topic of this book, the research that underlies and supports the Literacy Squared approach is a driving component of the work. We are encouraged by the positive findings thus far in the cohorts under study, and our team is engaged in ongoing, longitudinal research to confirm and extend the evidence of its effectiveness for student achievement in biliteracy.

While instruction is at the center of Literacy Squared, we emphasize that improving instruction is dependent on the creation of new assessment systems to interpret the literacy development of emerging bilingual children. Improving instruction and assessment requires PD programs that are iterative in nature and that inform research as well as practice. The entire project needs to be part of ongoing research efforts to document empirically all that is Literacy Squared.

The major focus of this book, then, is on the first and second of these components: the instructional elements, lesson plans, and assessment strategies that comprise the Literacy Squared model as implemented in classroom practice. However, it is important for readers to be aware of the research we have undertaken in the development of this model, and to understand that full, successful implementation of Literacy Squared is best accomplished in tandem with a comprehensive PD program. Therefore, in the last sections of this first chapter we include a brief discussion of the research and PD aspects of Literacy

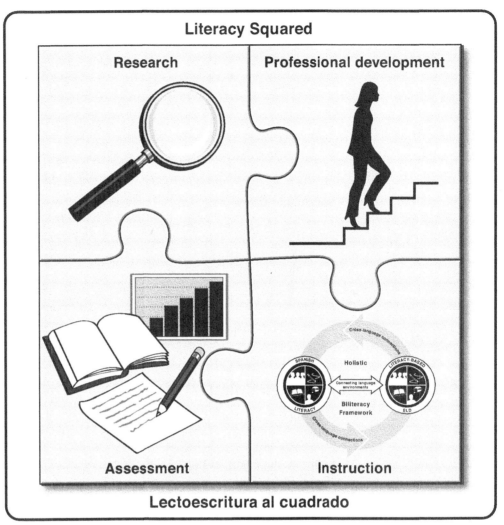

**Figure 1.1** Literacy Squared overview.

Squared, and provide additional materials online (casloncommunity.com/Biliteracy-from -the-Start) for those readers who are inclined to delve further.

The primary purpose of this book is to provide schools and teachers with the following:

- An innovative instructional framework for grades K–5 designed to enhance the development of biliteracy for emerging bilingual students.
- Assessment practices and techniques developed to effectively monitor and document children's trajectories toward biliteracy.
- A process to create units for biliteracy instruction, including sample lesson plans and planning documents.

As we have developed Literacy Squared, we have also become aware of the potential applications of this work for **dual language programs** that include monolingual English speakers. Our book, like most dual language programs in the U.S., focuses on developing bilingualism and biliteracy in Spanish and English. However, we believe the theory and practices presented in the book can be applied in contexts where languages other than Spanish and English are being utilized as instructional media. The book was written to serve the needs and interests of bilingual and dual language teachers, program coordinators, and administrators of bilingual/dual language programs, especially in elementary schools.

**TABLE 1.1**

Unique Features of Literacy Squared

| Literacy Squared | Traditional Bilingual Programs (early and late exit) |
|---|---|
| Paired literacy instruction beginning in kindergarten | Sequential literacy instruction beginning in L1 (dominant language) followed by L2 (secondary language) |
| Literacy-based ELD—ELD instruction includes reading and writing beginning in kindergarten | ESL/ELD instruction focuses on listening and speaking in grades K–2; reading and writing are added in grade 3 |
| Spanish literacy instruction and literacy-based ELD continue through grade 5 | Children transition out of Spanish literacy and ESL/ELD (Spanish literacy and ESL cease) |
| Spanish and English literacy environments are connected in concrete ways to facilitate cross-language learning | Spanish and English literacy have separate themes and topics |
| Has time allocations across grade levels attached to specific pedagogical approaches | Has time allocations across grade levels with no specific pedagogical approaches |
| Emphasizes direct and explicit teaching methods with a focus on modeled, shared, and collaborative approaches | Emphasize indirect, process approaches with lots of time devoted to independent work |
| Includes a robust approach to the teaching of biliteracy including oracy, reading, writing, and metalanguage | Emphasize reading and writing |
| Explicit teaching of cross-language connections | Strict separation of languages |
| Trajectories toward biliteracy assessment protocols | Literacy development assessed separately in English and Spanish |

## What Makes Literacy Squared Unique?

We have frequently been asked if Literacy Squared is just another late-exit transitional bilingual program with a new label. Or whether it is a curriculum, a program, or a collection of strategies with a research base.

We believe that Literacy Squared differs from other bilingual and dual language programs in at least three major ways:

1. It is a biliteracy model developed for children who are simultaneous emerging bilinguals, and demonstrates the potential of paired literacy instruction (rather than sequential instruction) in English and Spanish.
2. It shifts the debate in the field from a narrow focus on the language of instruction to include the qualities of instruction. That is, the instructional framework we have developed provides guidance to teachers, in the form of pedagogical methods, about how to maximize the **bidirectional transfer** of students' knowledge and skills from Spanish to English and English to Spanish. The framework for holistic bilingual instruction emphasizes the importance of **oracy** and metalinguistic skills, in addition to reading and writing, for the development of biliteracy.
3. The Literacy Squared approach also includes formative and summative assessment procedures that are designed to foster the development of biliteracy, to examine this development using a holistic bilingual lens, and to enable teachers and schools to monitor student progress via the interpretation of trajectories toward biliteracy.

Table 1.1 provides a summary of the distinctive features of Literacy Squared, which are discussed further in the sections that follow.

## Biliteracy Framework for Emerging Bilinguals

The instructional approaches, strategies, and assessment practices in this book are meant to align and address the language resources and strengths of the millions of children who enter school with nascent knowledge of linguistic systems and literacy in two languages. Like others in the field (García, 2009; Reyes, 2006; Ruiz, 1988) we view these languages as resources to be nurtured and developed in school. As a beginning to this development, we suggest that schools, teachers, and researchers develop a positive discourse for discussing the attributes and characteristics of these children.

One part of that discourse is the labels we use. **English language learner (ELL),** the term most often used to describe students who are acquiring English as a second language (ESL), has largely supplanted the more deficit-oriented term **limited English proficient (LEP).** A newer term, **emerging or emergent bilingual,** emphasizes the development of bilingual competencies in children whose native language is other than English. And, finally, the term **simultaneous bilinguals** denotes children who are developing two languages at the same time, and applies to an increasingly large proportion of emerging bilingual children.

## Simultaneous Emerging Bilingual Children: The New Normal

Before detailing the instructional components of our framework, it is important to describe more fully the population of students who are most likely to be in classrooms where this approach is adopted. Simultaneous bilingualism is a concept that is neither well understood nor widely used in the United States in the development and implementation of either bilingual or dual language programs; yet it is a term that fits a vast majority of emerging bilingual children. Briefly defined, simultaneous bilinguals are children who begin to acquire two languages between the ages 0–5 (Baker, 2001). Emerging bilingual children who were born in the United States are likely to be simultaneous bilinguals because many live in homes where two languages are used and/or come from monolingual Spanish homes and have attended preschools where English is the medium of instruction. The Urban Institute reports that 77% of the emerging bilingual children in grades K–5 and 56% in grades 6–12 were born in the United States and are likely simultaneous bilinguals (Capp, Fix, Murray, Ost, Passel, & Herwantoro, 2005). For these children, bilingualism is their dominant language. With the exception of the work of Ofelia García (2009), there are few, if any, biliteracy programs designed for simultaneous emerging bilingual children. We suggest that these children represent the "new normal," and Literacy Squared was created with their needs in mind. Table 1.2 contrasts the characteristics of simultaneous bilinguals (the new normal) with those of sequential bilinguals.

## Paired Literacy: Two Languages from the Start

While there is still a lot to learn about bilingual reading instruction, research over the past four decades has concluded definitively that teaching emerging bilingual students to read in Spanish as well as English promotes both biliteracy and higher levels of reading achievement in English (August & Shanahan, 2006; Genesee, Lindholm-Leary, Saunders, & Christian, 2006; Goldenberg, 2008; Greene, 1997; Rolstad, Mahoney, & Glass, 2005; Slavin & Cheung, 2005). What is most compelling about this body of evidence is that in no case did positive results from an English-only literacy program exceed those from a bilingual program (Slavin & Cheung, 2005). This large and growing body of research establishes that bilingual reading approaches are effective in helping children learn to read and write in two languages.

While language of instruction arguments have established definitively that the use of a child's non-English language is a benefit in learning to read or write, these studies are

**TABLE 1.2**

### Simultaneous and Sequential Bilingual Children

| Simultaneous | Sequential |
|---|---|
| Exposed to two languages between ages 0–5 | Exposed to a second language after age 5 |
| May not have a clearly dominant language (L1) | Has a clear L1 |
| May know some concepts in one language and others in another language | Clearly knows concepts only in L1 |
| Is often labeled as a child with "low" levels of language proficiency in two languages | Is labeled as "Spanish dominant" |
| Has language skills in two languages that can be used to develop biliteracy | Has language skills in one language that can be used to develop biliteracy |

based largely on sequential bilingual paradigms. They offer little guidance to teachers on instructional strategies for simultaneous emerging bilinguals.

In the Literacy Squared approach to holistic biliteracy instruction, we maintain the attention on language of instruction and enhance this focus by attending to methods and goals of instruction that better align with the linguistic characteristics of simultaneous emerging bilingual children. Slavin and Cheung (2005) concluded that paired literacy instruction, in which students learn to read and write in both languages at the same time, in bilingual programs seemed to hold great promise, although such programs were not commonly implemented. However, the potential was clear: paired literacy instruction, if used with fidelity and quality across grade levels, can enhance and accelerate literacy development in both languages.

As we developed an instructional framework, our focus on paired literacy instruction enabled us to sidestep the cumbersome transition guidelines and policies about instructional language used by many schools and districts, and instead to implement instruction that capitalizes on student strengths in both of their languages. Within a paired literacy approach, English literacy instruction is not delayed while children are learning to read and write in Spanish. It is also unnecessary to cease Spanish literacy instruction once children reach a certain reading level in Spanish. The Literacy Squared framework emphasizes building trajectories toward biliteracy, with sustained language and literacy development in both languages. Within this approach, the teaching of Spanish literacy begins in kindergarten along with English language development (ELD) instruction; such paired instruction continues through grade 5. Figure 1.2 is a graphic representation of the paired literacy instructional framework we have developed, showing the equal attention given to Spanish literacy and literacy-based ELD instruction. Notice also the icons within the smaller circles

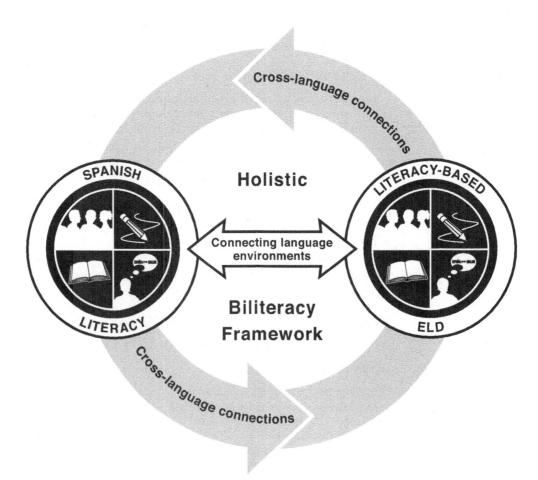

**Figure 1.2** Holistic biliteracy framework.

on both sides of the diagram, which represent the four elements of literacy—oracy, reading, writing, and **metalanguage**—that are addressed in paired literacy, within both Spanish literacy and ELD instruction.

## Qualities of Instruction for Holistic Biliteracy Development

The holistic biliteracy framework defines "holistic" as relating to or concerned with complete systems rather than with their analysis, treatment, or dissection into parts. In this book we use holistic in two senses. First, we use it with regard to our literacy framework and recommend that literacy instruction should be viewed broadly, as a system that includes oracy, reading, writing and metalanguage. (Too often, literacy is narrowly defined as reading and writing.) We also use the word holistic with regard to the development of bilingualism and biliteracy. Rather than viewing the development of biliteracy in Spanish and English as separate linguistic and cognitive systems, we believe that biliteracy develops as an integrated system that should be studied holistically. The goals and methods of holistic biliteracy instruction discussed in the following sections represent our view of biliteracy as a complete system. These goals and methods focus not only on the language of instruction but on the qualities of instruction within each language.

### Authentic Spanish Literacy Instruction

In a departure from traditional **early- or late-exit transitional bilingual programs**, and in keeping with a paired literacy approach, children never transition out of Spanish literacy instruction in our framework. Instead, Spanish/English paired literacy instruction is maintained through grade 5. While we have not worked directly with secondary schools, we would strongly recommend that school schedules at these levels allow for children to continue to take language and literature classes in Spanish as well as English in order to continue biliteracy development. Further, to the extent possible, we ensure that instruction in each language is as authentic as possible. Too often within U.S. bilingual and dual language classrooms, Spanish literacy instruction is modeled on English literacy instruction with little or no attention to how literacy practices and development in Spanish differ from those in English.

We believe that teaching children to read and write in Spanish and English involves some of the same methodologies and strategies. However, methods and strategies should also consider how the internal structure of each language is different, especially when utilizing part to whole strategies (Beeman & Urow, 2013; Escamilla, 2000; Freeman & Freeman, 2006; Izquierdo, 2010; Vernon & Ferreiro, 1999). Following are just a few examples:

- Syllable awareness emerges before phoneme awareness in Spanish and is a stronger predictor of reading success. The role of syllabification in English is not as strong as in Spanish.
- Vowels are the first building blocks of Spanish literacy, consonants the second. In contrast, the building blocks of English are the names and sounds of each letter.
- In English, children start by learning consonants, but in Spanish they start by learning vowels. Learning letter names in Spanish is less important than matching vowels to consonants to form syllables.

Thus, in Literacy Squared classrooms, teachers are encouraged to adapt and utilize methods of literacy instruction that have been demonstrated to be effective in Mexico and other Central and South American countries, rather than directly applying strategies for English literacy to the teaching of Spanish literacy (Smith, Jiménez, & Martinez-León, 2003).

### Literacy-based ELD Instruction

Within the Literacy Squared approach, the development of literacy in English is especially designed for emerging bilingual students. It is text based, and includes, but is not limited to, the development of listening and speaking. (By contrast, in traditional bilingual programs, instruction in Spanish focuses on reading and writing to the exclusion of oracy and metalanguage. And in traditional ESL instruction, reading and writing in English is not introduced until grades 2 or 3.) Literacy-based ELD instruction begins in kindergarten and continues through grade 5, as does Spanish literacy instruction; both include oracy, reading, writing, and metalanguage from the outset.

Our approach to literacy-based ELD instruction is founded on research demonstrating that methods appropriate for developing first language literacy differ from those that are most effective for developing second language literacy. For example, teachers may need to explicitly explain the cultural content of some text material to second language learners when such content would not need to be explained to native speakers. (E.g., when reading a story about a child getting an allowance, teachers may have to explain what the concept of an allowance is to children from cultures where allowances are not given.) Idiomatic expressions or figurative language may also require explanation for students who may be reading at the word level but do not understand the text at the phrase level. (E.g., in the sentence, "Grandma used elbow grease to get the table clean," children need to understand how the idiomatic expression "elbow grease" is different at the phrase level than the words "elbow" or "grease" used separately [Bernhardt, 2003; Grant & Wong, 2003].) The literacy-based ELD lessons we have developed consider what children already know about how to read and write in Spanish, and do not reteach concepts—such as directionality; using context clues to figure out unknown words; decoding concepts (breaking words down into parts); and that letters make words, words make sentences, sentences make paragraphs, text has meaning—that children already know. Instead, the lessons teach children how what they know can be applied to reading and writing in English, and further develops their knowledge of how it is different from reading and writing in Spanish.

## Equal Attention to Oracy, Reading, Writing, and Metalanguage

The holistic biliteracy framework also differs from other bilingual/dual language programs in that it includes equal amounts of instructional time devoted to oracy, reading, writing, and metalanguage. The strong emphasis on development of oracy (the language needed to interact with texts) and metalanguage (the language used to talk about language) are unique features of Literacy Squared. The explicit teaching of these underemphasized literacy skills is critical to the implementation of a robust biliteracy program for emerging bilingual children. Teaching oracy fosters the development of expressive language through structured and planned dialogue, the rehearsal of selected language structures, and the refinement of vocabulary. Reading and writing instruction in Spanish and English are needed to develop decoding, fluency, and comprehension skills in both languages. Metalanguage or metalinguistic awareness is needed for children to develop an understanding of and ability to talk about language both within and across language systems. Chapters 2 through 5 provide more detailed discussions of the instructional components of our biliteracy framework within oracy, reading, writing and metalanguage.

## Cross-Language Connections

Note that the graphic representation of the Literacy Squared instructional framework in Figure 1.2 is surrounded by arrows referring to **cross-language connections**. We have incorporated this instructional feature into our program to ensure that teachers provide direct and explicit attention to developing children's metalinguistic awareness about how Spanish and English are similar and different. Within Literacy Squared, we use two types of cross-language connections. The first refers to specific methods that the model has adapted from Mexico and modified for use in U.S. English/Spanish literacy programs. The second focuses on teaching children the metacognitive linguistic skills of cross-language expression in reading and writing (Escamilla & Hopewell, 2007).

Cross-language strategies are a defining feature of Literacy Squared and should not be confused with **concurrent translation**. Concurrent translation involves continuous and direct translation of statements, instructions or concepts from one language to another, which often results in students tuning in only to the language in which they are most proficient. Making cross-language connections is a strategic method used by a teacher to help students connect what they know in one language with what they are learning in another.

## *Time Allocations and Teaching Approaches by Grade Level*

While most bilingual/dual language programs include language allocation charts to show how teaching in each language is distributed across the curriculum, Literacy Squared has enhanced the time allocation chart by adding recommended pedagogical approaches for the development of Spanish literacy and literacy-based ELD at each grade level. Table 1.3 shows the recommended time allocations and teaching approaches; notice that the time alllocated for Spanish literacy instruction decreases through the grades, while the time for literacy-based ELD instruction increases. With regard to Table 1.3, it is important to note that dual language programs have the advantage of being able to maintain a 50/50 time allocation from grades 3–5; this is a luxury that we wish were available also to more transitional bilingual program models.

## *Emphasis on Explicit Instruction and Collaborative Approaches*

The approaches listed in Table 1.3 place particular emphasis on modeled, shared, and collaborative teaching approaches throughout all of the instructional components. Our work and the work of others has led us to conclude that modeled, shared, and collaborative approaches, which tend to involve more direct and explicit instruction, are the most effective and at the same time the most culturally responsive approaches to biliteracy development for Spanish/English emerging bilingual children. We know that for most learners interactive learning enhances cognitive development because "concepts first learned through social interaction become internalized and made one's own" (Klingner & Vaughn, 2000, p. 70). Also, as Genesee and Riches (2006) state, "interactive learning environments are especially relevant to ELLs because of the diverse sociocultural background of these students and because interactive learning decreases student anxiety" (p. 116). With regard to writing in particular, Ammon (1985) and Genesee and Riches (2006) found that frequent writing for second language learners, unaccompanied by direct and explicit instruction, did not increase accuracy in writing.

The Literacy Squared framework emphasizes the sociocultural nature of learning and language acquisition by encouraging grouping structures that include collaborative work and direct and explicit instruction, rather than isolating students via long periods of independent practice. In Table 1.4 the descriptors attached to the reading and writing approaches in Table 1.3 to indicate grouping structures from whole class to independent work—modeled, shared, collaborative, teacher-led small groups, independent, and performance—are more fully described. Together, the charts in Table 1.3 and 1.4 illustrate a pedagogical model for biliteracy development, showing how the Literacy Squared instructional framework implements paired literacy; includes oracy, reading, writing and metalanguage across grade levels and across languages; and incorporates explicit instruction and group work in both Spanish literacy and literacy-based ELD instruction. We want to emphasize that while particular pedagogical approaches to biliteracy instruction are highly recommended within the Literacy Squared framework, these recommendations do not limit the choice of texts; teachers and schools are free to utilize any materials they feel are appropriate or are mandated to use.

## Assessment Strategies to Build Trajectories toward Biliteracy

As we create new instructional models for simultaneous emerging bilingual children, we must also develop new and different methods for assessing biliterate development. In this book, we propose a new assessment paradigm that can be used to build what we call trajectories toward biliteracy. We consider trajectories toward biliteracy to be a procedure to examine positive and measurable progressions over time toward the goal of biliteracy in Spanish and English. We suggest that these trajectories can be utilized in schools and by teachers to create a new and more positive discourse about biliteracy development in emerging bilingual children. The assessment protocols we've developed, which are unique to Literacy Squared, involve the reinterpretation of reading and writing assessments to better understand how the development of biliteracy is different than the development of either Spanish or English monoliteracy. The resulting system of biliterate assessment

**TABLE 1.3**

Literacy Squared Language Time Allocations and Grade Appropriate Instructional Approaches

| Grade | Spanish Literacy | Literacy-based ELD |
|---|---|---|
| K | **2 hours (1 hour for ½ day kindergarten)**<br>Reading: Modeled, shared, teacher-led small groups<br>Writing: Modeled, shared, collaborative, independent<br>Oracy<br>Spanish Dictado (Jan.) | **45 minutes (30 minutes for ½ day kindergarten)**<br>Reading: Modeled, shared<br>Writing: Modeled, shared<br>Oracy<br>Cross-language connections |
| 1 | **2 hours**<br>Reading: Modeled, shared, Lotta Lara, teacher-led small groups, collaborative, independent<br>Word work<br>Writing: Modeled, shared, collaborative, independent<br>Oracy<br>Cross-language connections<br>Spanish Dictado | **60 minutes**<br>Reading: Modeled, shared, Lotta Lara, collaborative<br>Writing: Modeled, shared, collaborative<br>Oracy<br>Cross-language connections<br>English Dictado |
| 2 | **90 minutes**<br>Reading: Modeled, shared, Lotta Lara, collaborative, teacher-led small groups, independent<br>Word work<br>Writing: Modeled, shared, collaborative, independent<br>Oracy<br>Cross-language connections<br>Spanish Dictado | **60 minutes**<br>Reading: Modeled, shared, Lotta Lara, collaborative<br>Writing: Modeled, shared, collaborative<br>Oracy<br>Cross-language connections<br>English Dictado |
| 3 | **60 minutes**<br>Reading: Modeled, shared, Lotta Lara, teacher-led small groups, collaborative, independent<br>Word work<br>Writing: Modeled, shared, collaborative, independent<br>Oracy<br>Cross-language connections<br>Spanish Dictado | **90 minutes**<br>Reading: Modeled, shared, Lotta Lara, teacher-led small groups, collaborative, independent<br>Word work<br>Writing: Modeled, shared, collaborative, independent<br>Oracy<br>Cross-language connections<br>English Dictado |
| 4 | **45 minutes**<br>Reading: Modeled, shared, collaborative (literature, genre/author studies), independent<br>Writing: Modeled, shared, collaborative, independent<br>Oracy<br>Cross-language connections (e.g., cognate studies)<br>Spanish Dictado | **2 hours**<br>Reading: Modeled, shared, Lotta Lara, teacher-led small groups, collaborative (literature, genre/author studies), independent<br>Word work<br>Writing: Modeled, shared, collaborative, independent<br>Cross-language connections (e.g., cognate studies)<br>Oracy<br>English Dictado |
| 5 | **45 minutes**<br>Reading: Modeled, shared, collaborative, (literature, genre/author studies), independent<br>Writing: Modeled, shared, collaborative, independent<br>Cross-language connections (e.g., cognate studies)<br>Oracy<br>Spanish Dictado | **2 hours**<br>Reading: Modeled, shared, Lotta Lara, teacher-led small groups, collaborative (literature, genre/author studies), independent<br>Word work<br>Writing: Modeled, shared, collaborative, independent<br>Cross-language connections (e.g., cognate studies)<br>Oracy<br>English Dictado |

acknowledges children's developing skills in Spanish and English as intertwined rather than belonging to separate linguistic systems. We agree that developing trajectories toward biliteracy involves interplay between both languages, not merely one language influencing or transferring to another (Bialystok, 2007). Only through bilingual assessments can we approximate an accurate understanding of the language and literacy development of emerging bilingual students. To that end, we have created what we term **"biliteracy zones"** for reading and writing: suggested targets for teachers working with emerging bilinguals.

The protocols and rubrics developed for Literacy Squared can easily be adapted and used by teachers in any bilingual or dual language program. Similarly, although the bi-

**TABLE 1.4**

## Pedagogical Model for the Development of Biliteracy

| Spanish Literacy | Teaching/Learning Approaches | Literacy-based ELD |
|---|---|---|
| Teacher reads aloud and writes for children modeling the enjoyment, purpose, and process. The text and/or message is one that most of the children cannot read instructionally or independently. | **Modeled\*** <br> Model fluent reading and conventional writing and promote enjoyment of reading and writing. <br> Model metalinguistic cross-language connections. <br> Model language structures, new vocabulary and book-based dialogues. | Teacher chooses a text in English that can be made meaningful. The text is one the children have already read in Spanish, one in which the pictures can carry the meaning, or one for which teachers can use realia, gestures, or other types of comprehensible input to make the text understandable. Children may respond to text in Spanish. There is value in repeated text readings. Patterned text with useful language structures and vocabulary should be considered in text choice. Shorter texts may be more effective. |
| Teacher reads and writes with children, inviting them to join in and try out strategies by themselves with teacher support. Texts should be chosen so that children will come to control them through repeated readings and written experiences. Focus on developing decoding and comprehension skills. | **Shared\*** <br> Teachers read and write *for* and *with* children to scaffold literacy tasks. <br> Teachers engage children in structured dialogues to extend understanding of texts and to enrich oral and written language repertoire. <br> Teachers engage children in articulating cross-language connections. | Same as Spanish, except that the focus in English is on developing oracy and comprehension in English, with less emphasis on decoding. Focus on language structures, vocabulary expansion, and dialogue. Explicit cross-cultural dialogue in text analysis. |
| Children read and write with peers. Teacher creates opportunities and monitors children's interaction with text and other children. | **Collaborative\*** <br> Teacher structures additional opportunities for reading, writing, and oracy with peers. | Same as Spanish except that the focus is on oracy and comprehension in English. Oral rehearsal and language negotiation are fundamental to the reading and writing task. |
| Teachers group children by reading instructional level (in Spanish) in order to teach specific skills and strategies related to reading and writing. Grouping can also be based on background knowledge or area of interest. Children can read, write, speak, and listen across a range of levels related to a common theme. Teacher can provide multiple opportunities with one text rather than reading one text per day. | **Teacher-led small groups\*** <br> Address the specific skill needs and interests of children in small homogeneous groups. | Children's placement is based on levels of *Spanish* reading for the purposes of focusing on cross-language transfer and oracy development. Grouping can also be done based on background knowledge or area of interest. Children can read, write, speak, and listen across a range of levels related to a common theme. Teacher can provide multiple opportunities with one text rather than reading one text per day. |
| Children read and write by themselves. Teacher needs to provide opportunities to read a variety of texts and genres, and write on a variety of topics. | **Independent** <br> Sustained and expanded opportunities to read and write. | Children read and write by themselves. Teachers need to provide opportunities and encouragement to read a variety of English as well as Spanish texts. |
| The teacher makes observations and collects data to determine which skills and strategies children have mastered to make instructional decisions about how to provide continued support. Teacher monitors application of cross-language strategies. | **Performance** <br> Observe and document children's reading, writing, oracy, and cross-language behaviors and strategy repertoires. | Teacher makes observations and collects data about children's oracy development, in addition to literacy development, in English. Teacher monitors application of cross-language strategies. |

\*The emphasis of the Literacy Squared literacy instruction is in explicit and interactive approaches.

literacy trajectories were developed for Spanish and English emerging bilingual children, they can be adapted for other languages. In Part II of this book, we demonstrate how teachers and schools can use these trajectories as both summative and formative assessments in paired biliteracy programs and other types of bilingual and dual language programs. Our conceptual framework requires that children's growth in Spanish and English reading and writing be assessed annually and across time, to ensure children are on a trajectory toward biliteracy. Further, we suggest that children's progress be interpreted not by monolingual Spanish or monolingual English grade-level or benchmark standards, but rather by standards developed specifically to measure emerging biliteracy. Specifically, we ask teachers to analyze students' progress in relation to the trajectory, to determine whether or not they are in identified biliteracy zones, and to observe whether or not children's reading and writing in Spanish and English are being developed in parallel ways; it is important to be able to observe how children are using what they know in one language to help them learn to read and write in another. Further, we recommend that reading and writing outcomes are better understood vis a vis ranges rather than static cut scores.

## Professional Development

The success of Literacy Squared, as with other bilingual and dual language programs, depends on its consistent implementation within classrooms and across grade levels. Many researchers have concluded that if literacy/biliteracy achievement for emerging bilingual children is to be improved we must move beyond rhetoric and research about language of instruction and engage in conversations about the qualities of instruction (August & Shanahan, 2006; Gersten & Baker, 2000; Slavin & Cheung, 2005). Over the past decade, as we have refined our instructional framework and conducted the comprehensive PD done in conjunction with its development, we have become confident that, with proper support and guidance, schools and teachers can learn these structures and strategies. Further, if this model is implemented with fidelity, successful trajectories toward biliteracy will be the result. We reject the notion that "good teaching is good teaching" and instead suggest that school leaders work closely with teachers to help them design and deliver comprehensive biliteracy instruction that is coherent and coordinated across languages.

Attaining full implementation levels across all grades requires continued monitoring of these levels and provision of ongoing support and coaching for Literacy Squared teachers. In the schools that have participated in all aspects of Literacy Squared, there are structured and frequent PD opportunities for teachers and coordinators in order to develop shared understandings of the instructional framework, to coach and support teachers as they try out the recommended lessons and pedagogical approaches, and to help teachers and others learn to use the trajectories toward biliteracy assessment system. Our PD also includes sharing and discussing current research on biliteracy development.

In order to support schools and teachers using the Literacy Squared approach, we created an observation protocol to monitor the quality and fidelity of implementation of Literacy Squared. It is available at the end of the book or online (casloncommunity .com/Biliteracy-from-the-Start/). Entitled the "Literacy Squared Observation Protocol," it has eight domains that are aligned to the holistic biliteracy framework for comprehensive biliteracy instruction. The protocol was designed as a tool for teachers, coordinators, and administrators to better understand the Literacy Squared approach and instructional framework, and also as a tool for assessing fidelity of implementation. (The latter use is important to our ongoing research, mentioned in the following section of this chapter.)

As a formative tool, the Literacy Squared observation protocol can help determine PD needs, and can help teachers, researchers, coaches and coordinators better understand the successes and challenges that are faced when implementing Literacy Squared. Given the current accountability paradigm and the scapegoating of teachers in the public discourse, it is important to understand that this observation tool is not intended to be used punitively. Rather this tool, along with coaching opportunities, is meant to be part of a collaborative learning and inquiry approach, in which teachers and administrators support each other in the implementation of the holistic biliteracy framework for comprehensive biliteracy instruction. Using this tool, teachers and others have observed each other implementing recommended pedagogical approaches, and have used their observations to support each other in improving biliteracy instruction. Videotapes of lessons have been analyzed using the protocol, and have proven very valuable in helping to ascertain areas of teacher strength and need, and to help teachers and schools fully implement the Literacy Squared approach. In short, the observation protocol is meant to assess fidelity and to contribute to ongoing professional development in Literacy Squared schools, not to rank teachers.

## Research Support for Literacy Squared and the Framework for Holistic Biliteracy Instruction

From its inception the Literacy Squared project has devoted a great deal of time and energy to conducting research around program outcomes, to establishing trajectories toward biliteracy, and to addressing a variety of quantitative and qualitative research questions regarding the impact of Literacy Squared on schools, teachers, and students. It was always our goal that Literacy Squared would be research based and research tested. An exhaustive review of Literacy Squared–related research is beyond the scope of this chapter or this book. To date our research studies have involved over 4,000 children, 250 teachers, and research sites in five different states.

### Questions

When we began the project our research was designed to satisfy the concerns and curiosities of our research partners and our research team. Accordingly, we have conducted basic research examining the reading and writing outcomes in Spanish and English of students in our project addressing the following research questions:

1. What are Spanish reading and writing outcomes of students longitudinally and annually?
2. Does earlier instruction in English literacy impede acquisition of Spanish literacy?
3. What are the relationships between English and Spanish reading and writing across grade levels?
4. How do Literacy Squared children do on high-stakes tests?

### Findings to Date

Our findings have been documented in all our partner schools and districts (e.g., see Sparrow and Escamilla, 2012), and can be summarized as follows:

▨ **Research questions 1 & 2:** (1) What are Spanish reading and writing outcomes of students annually and longitudinally? (2) Does earlier instruction in English literacy impede acquisition of Spanish literacy?

Each year classroom outcomes are generally higher than they were in the previous year, for the cohorts participating in Literacy Squared. The mean scores for Spanish writing are generally higher than those in English, though over time students are making greater gains in English and their English achievement is approximating that of their Spanish achievement. This closing of the gap between student outcomes in Spanish and English is demonstrated across all of the cohort groups studied and in both reading and writing.

When looking across cohorts, students who are in Literacy Squared longer have higher outcomes. (E.g., those that started Literacy Squared in grade 1 had higher outcomes than those that started in grade 2; those that started in grade 2 had higher outcomes than those that started in grade 3.) Results show the benefits of teacher and student participation in Literacy Squared over time. While our research in this area is still ongoing, these findings suggest that paired literacy instruction is beneficial to students. The earlier introduction of reading in English does not impede Spanish literacy acquisition, and it concomitantly enhances English literacy acquisition.

▨ **Research question 3:** What are the relationships between English and Spanish reading and writing across grade levels?

A historical and ongoing question in the field of bilingual/dual language education has been to to examine the relationship between Spanish and English reading and writing outcomes to determine if, in fact, good readers and writers in Spanish are likely to become good readers and writers in English. As a part of our continuing research efforts, we run correlation coefficients annually that give us indications as to whether or not there is a positive correlation between ability to read and write in Spanish and subsequent ability to read and write in English.

Our data to date illustrate that Spanish/English reading and writing correlations are strong and significant, and that Spanish reading/writing and English reading/writing correlations are also strong and significant. The strongest relationships are Spanish/English reading and Spanish/English writing. We believe these findings—of strong and statistically significant relationships between student abilities to read and write in Spanish and subsequent development of reading and writing skills in English—confirm the value of developing biliteracy in both reading and writing. Moreover, that these relationships become stronger over time indicates the value of paired literacy instruction that begins in kindergarten and lasts at least through grade 5.

**Research question 4:** How do Literacy Squared children do on high stakes tests?

It is important to note first that our research team, along with many other researchers and practitioners in the field, acknowledges the problems inherent in the current high-stakes testing system, especially as it relates to emerging bilingual children in the United States. That said, because students in Literacy Squared schools are required to take high-stakes tests in whatever form they are administered in partner states, we have chosen to analyze the results of Literacy Squared students on these tests despite the problems involved in their construction and interpretation. We compare the results of Literacy Squared students to other emerging bilingual students in the state, as well as to all student outcomes.

To give an example of how the research is trending: the data for students in grades 3–5 who took the Oregon Assessment of Knowledge and Skills (OAKS) test (which assesses only reading outcomes) in 2010 and 2011 indicate that greater numbers and percentages of students in the Literacy Squared program were being assessed as proficient on the OAKS test than either LEP students in the state as a whole or other LEP students in Salem. (Note: the state of Oregon uses the term LEP in the calculation of the numbers of students who are ELLs taking the OAKS test, and we use it here to be consistent with state terminology.) In other words, a larger percentage of Literacy Squared students met or exceeded the state standard than LEP students in the state or district. Most impressive of all is the grade 5 data, where outcomes for Literacy Squared students in English reading in grade 5 far surpass those of LEP students in the state and district. In sum, the research conducted thus far shows the potential of Literacy Squared for developing biliteracy but also for accelerating literacy achievement in English for emerging bilingual students.

## A Word about Fidelity of Implementation

As mentioned in the foregoing PD section, fidelity of implementation is important to the research. We need to be certain that the pedagogical approaches in Literacy Squared are being consistently implemented in the cohorts under study so that outcomes, whether positive or negative, can be attributed to the model and not to extraneous variables. Inconsistent or incomplete implementation can significantly affect research findings and results. In our research in Literacy Squared, we have correlated higher levels of implementation with high student outcomes (Sparrow, Butvilofsky, Wiley, & Escamilla, 2012).

However, we also understand that some readers of this book may not be able to implement the Literacy Squared model in its totality. Some educators using this book may decide, for example, that they can only implement parts of the instructional framework (e.g., oracy, literacy-based ELD, theDictado). It may also be the case that in districts where language allocation times are mandated by central offices, teachers and schools will not have the freedom to fully implement the approach as designed. In this case, we suggest that fidelity is still important in monitoring and documenting program success. However, when the instruction and assessment framework is applied partially rather than fully, the school should use only the aspects of the protocol that are relevant to their own contexts and situations. We also suggest that there may be certain aspects or components of the model that can stand alone while schools build capacity, with the caveat that future research is needed to evaluate the efficacy of stand-alone components.

## Summary and Preview

This book is about developing biliteracy in Spanish/English emerging bilinguals. It provides a holistic biliteracy instruction framework that was developed specifically for contexts in which children are becoming biliterate, and recommends paired literacy instruction in Spanish and English beginning in kindergarten. Unlike others, this framework was not adapted from a model for monolingual English literacy development, and also unlike other instructional approaches in the ELL field, it assumes that children can learn to read and write in two languages at the same time. It provides strategies for assisting children in the development of two languages in ways that directly and explicitly connect Spanish and English within and across grade levels.

In Part I (Chapters 2–5), each aspect of the instructional framework is explained in detail along with sample instructional strategies for teachers to utilize as they implement lessons in oracy, reading, writing, and metalanguage.

Part II presents and details an innovative protocol for assessing children's progress toward biliteracy. Chapter 6 focuses on assessment in reading and Chapter 7 on assessment in writing. Contrary to other assessment systems, this protocol provides a mechanism for evaluating children's trajectories toward biliteracy in a holistic manner that measures how children's literacy is developing in reading and writing in Spanish and English and across languages. It is our hope that the discourse created by assessing children's progress toward biliteracy as suggested in this book will create more positive discourse about biliteracy development in emerging bilingual children.

Finally, in Part III, the work of comprehensive biliteracy instruction is illustrated at the curricular level, through the process of unit planning. Chapter 8 provides a discussion of the planning process and demonstrates the use of the Literacy Squared lesson plan template. Chapters 9 and 10 present fully developed examples, at the primary (kindergarten) and intermediate (grade 5) levels, of comprehensive biliteracy lessons that are designed to be implemented across multiple weeks and that illustrate how all of the components of the instructional framework can be applied in ways that concretely connect literacy environments in Spanish and English.

Biliteracy must be understood as a special form of literacy that is distinct from the literacy experiences and processes of monolinguals (Bauer & Gort, 2011). This book is an attempt to better understand biliteracy development and to create instructional environments that honor and nurture that development.

## Questions for Reflection and Action

- Which programs does your school offer for emerging bilinguals? Do you believe these programs are appropriate and effective? Why/why not? What concepts from the theories underlying Literacy Squared could you bring to a professional learning community or professional learning network conversation regarding best practices for emerging bilinguals?
- List all of the PD opportunities you have had in the past 2–3 years related to literacy.
  - What was the nature of the PD?
  - To what extent were topics focused on emerging bilingual learners?
  - Did the PD include writing and/or oral language?
  - Did the PD include modification for literacy instruction for emerging bilingual students?
  - What recommendations might you make to your principal for more comprehensive and focused professional development?
- How might you use the research designs and/or questions posed above to implement and examine a biliteracy program at your school?

# INSTRUCTION
# Teaching within a Holistic Biliteracy Framework

The Literacy Squared holistic biliteracy framework is comprised of four core instructional elements: oracy, writing, reading, and metalanguage. As the figure on the next page illustrates, all four elements are included in biliteracy instruction in both Spanish literacy and literacy-based English language development (ELD). In Part I, each of these elements is discussed in separate chapters; however, they are connected to one another during literacy instruction within and across language environments. In contrast to the artificial separation of reading and writing time observed in many schools, Literacy Squared recommends that they be integrated within the language arts schedule for each language. It is also recommended that teachers plan their literacy instruction in units of study to be carried out over the course of several sessions and sometimes weeks. This carryover facilitates a fluid and natural integration of the four instructional elements while allowing students and teachers to engage more deeply with texts. Additionally biliteracy instruction is interconnected, and children are explicitly taught to make cross-language connections. This connection of language environments avoids redundancy in teaching because the skills and knowledge taught in English build on what children know and can do in Spanish.

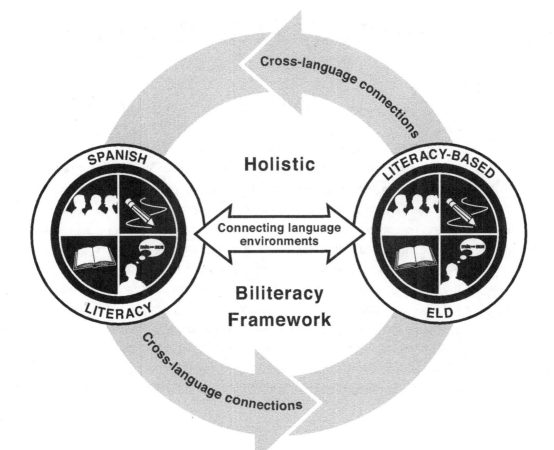

Holistic biliteracy framework.

# Oracy

*Oral language is the medium we use to make friends, earn a living and become partici-pating members of the community. It is through speech that we assimilate the thoughts and opinions, ideas, emotions, humour, wisdom, common-sense, even moral and spiritual values of those around us and it is through perceptive listening and courteous speaking that we move towards breaking down social, professional and racial barriers.*

Christabel Burniston, ORACY Australia

## Key Terms

| | |
|---|---|
| **Dialogue** | **Oracy** |
| **Echo, choral, and partner reading** | **Vocabulary** |
| **Language structures** | |

## Guiding Questions

- What is the difference between general oral language development and oracy?
- Why is oracy important in Spanish literacy?
- Why is oracy important in literacy-based ELD?
- What is the difference between oracy development in Spanish and English?

The holistic biliteracy framework (on the preceding page) establishes **oracy** as one of the four domains of language that are essential to the effective development of bilit-eracy in Spanish and English. In this chapter we discuss the oral language skills that con-tribute to the acquisition of literacy and provide examples of teaching strategies to develop those skills in bilingual learners.

The term "oracy" was coined in 1970 by Andrew Wilkinson, a British researcher and educator, in an attempt to draw attention to the neglect of the development of oral skills in education (MacLure, Phillips, & Wilkinson, 1988). Over the years, the influence that oral language can or should play in the development of reading and writing has fluctuated. From 1970–2000 it was generally accepted that well-rounded literacy instruction included attention to the development of oral language. With the publication of the National Insti-tute of Child Health and Human Development's National Reading Panel (NRP) Report in 2000, the role of oral language took a backseat to the development of phonemic aware-ness, phonics, fluency, vocabulary, and comprehension. It is important to note that the NRP research focused on monolingual English speakers and not emerging bilingual stu-dents. Six years later, August and Shanahan (2006) conducted a synthesis of research about emerging bilingual learners and they pointed to the importance of oral language in the development of English literacy for second language learners. This research became known as the National Literacy Panel (NLP). In our observations from our early work in Literacy Squared we noticed that while the results of the NRP had been taken up and implemented, the results from the NLP had not. As a result, emerging bilingual children had few opportunities to develop their oracy skills. In our work with Literacy Squared we emphasize that, for biliteracy, the development of oracy is necessary in both languages, and we propose that it constitute 25% of literacy instruction in both Spanish and English.

## Why Is Oracy Important? What the Research Says

Research has amply documented the important role that oracy plays in developing reading comprehension and written vocabulary. For example, Snow and Tabors (1993) demonstrated that children can sound out a written word more efficiently if they know what it is meant to sound like and if they know the meaning of words, they can predict what might occur in a text, thus increasing their ability to interact meaningfully with texts. Jennings (1991) found that children who had frequent oral encounters with stories are able then to make successful predictions when reading narrative. Cooper, Collins, and Saxby (1992) and Dyson and Genishi (1994) found that adding specific types of oracy activities to the literacy curriculum established not only an extensive oral language base but also contributed to the development of literacy skills such as word recognition, grammar, and comprehension. These oracy activities included vocabulary development via learning archaic expressions, puns, phrases, rhymes, chants, tongue twisters, metaphors, figures of speech, and revoiced dialogue.

The UK National Oracy Project (Norman, 1992) concluded that the importance of speaking and listening skills cannot be emphasized enough. Talk is rehearsal for writing; it is also an outcome in its own right, allowing students to extend and develop their thinking skills. Exploratory talk is an effective way of using language to think and is one of the key building blocks of literacy. The Project report recommends the following academic purposes for oracy instruction:

- Talk to engage, including brainstorming and reviewing existing knowledge.
- Talk to extend understanding and to explain or justify understanding.
- Talk to express learning, including presenting final outcomes.
- Talk to evaluate learning—in this case the authors suggest that talk is the end product.

The same authors conclude that discounting oracy development for academic purposes has negative effects on literacy.

The preceding research involved only monolingual English-speaking children; however, it is important to note that a parallel research base has established the importance of oracy in developing literacy in Spanish. Unlike the fluctuating emphasis placed on oral language development in English, the importance of oracy development in Spanish literacy in Central and South America has never been contested. Research by Ferreiro (2002) documented the connectedness between oracy (*oralidad*) and writing (*escritura*), with a caveat that the relationship is both dependent and independent and comprehensive literacy programs must pay attention to both oracy and writing. Further, the Mexican National Reading Program (*Programa Nacional para el Fortalecimiento de la Lectura y la Escritura Básica, PRONALEES, 2002*) emphasizes oral language development as one of its cornerstones and recommends the following types of oracy development: *conversación* (conversation), *descripción* (description), *situaciones comunicativas* (dialogue using different forms and functions of language), *dramatización* (dramatization), *historias cortas* (short stories), *entrevistas* (interviews), *adivinanzas* (riddles), *chistes* (jokes), *trabalenguas* (tongue-twisters), *poemas* (poems), *rimas* (rhymes), *canciones* (songs), *noticias* (relating news events), and *debate* (debate). This literature establishes the important role that oracy plays in the development of literacy in Spanish; but, again, it is important to note that the work has been done in Spanish with monolingual children.

What about the role of oracy in biliteracy programs? Research conducted on over 1,500 Spanish/English bilingual children in grades K–3 examined whether lexical, syntactic, fluency, and discourse measures of oral language collected under narrative conditions predict reading achievement both within and across languages (Miller, Heilmann, Nockerts, Iglesias, Fabiano, & Francis, 2006). Results demonstrated that Spanish and English oral language skills contribute to reading within and across languages. Similar results were found in studies examining the importance of oracy in the development of literacy in emerging bilingual students in biliteracy programs (Pollard-Durodola, Mathes, Vaughn, Cardenas-Hagan, & Linan-Thompson, 2006; Simich-Dudgeon, 1998). The research is clear on the need for oracy instruction in Spanish literacy, English literacy, and paired literacy programs.

## Oracy Objectives in Literacy Squared

Oracy is an integral part of paired literacy instruction, and we suggest that all Literacy Squared lessons have both literacy and oracy objectives. The literacy objectives drive the reading and writing aspects of the lessons, and the oracy objectives focus on the oral language needed to accomplish the literacy tasks. Both can and should be aligned to current state and district standards and to the newly developed national Common Core State Standards.

In our definition, oracy is an aspect of oral language, but it includes a *more specific subset* of skills and strategies within oral language that more closely relates to literacy objectives in academic settings. We suggest that teachers include three types of oracy components in their lessons: **language structures**, **vocabulary**, and **dialogue**. Table 2.1 provides brief purposes and descriptions for each oracy component. We emphasize the importance of including oracy objectives daily in both Spanish and literacy-based ELD lessons. It is often wrongly assumed that students do not need as much oracy development in Spanish as they do in English.

Oracy objectives should be different in each language, as they should address students' varying levels of proficiency in each language, and students' Spanish oracy skills may be at a slightly more elevated level than their English oracy skills. Teaching objectives for language structures, vocabulary, and dialogue should extend students' linguistic abilities and repertoires. When planning oracy objectives, we find it useful for teachers to ask themselves the following questions:

- What language is necessary to accomplish the literacy task?
- What language do students need to control to be able to communicate what they know and think?

**TABLE 2.1**

### Oracy Components for Spanish Literacy and Literacy-based ELD

| Oracy Component | Purpose | Should Be | Should Not Be |
|---|---|---|---|
| Dialogue | Ensure meaningful student participation in literacy related discussions | • Open ended<br>• A give and take conversation<br>• Connected discourse<br>• Student talking to students and teacher<br>• Problem solving and reasoning | • Haphazard conversation<br>• Unplanned questions and prompts<br>• Based on "right or wrong" answers |
| Language structures | Expand grammatical complexity of students' speech | • Rehearsed in context<br>• Comprehensible<br>• A means to expand students' linguistic repertoire | • Rote memorization of chunks of language<br>• Repetition of language students do not understand |
| Vocabulary | Refine and expand students' word and concept range | • Collaborative<br>• Contextualized<br>• Meaningful and comprehensible | • Isolated lists of words<br>• Decontextualized vocabulary work<br>• Copying definitions from a dictionary<br>• Writing unrelated sentences, each sentence using a different vocabulary word |

## Language Structures

Language structures serve as scaffolds to assist students in expanding their linguistic repertoires so that they can engage in complex tasks. Table 2.2 provides details about the oracy component of language structures, whose purpose is to assist in expanding students' grammatical complexity. While students may understand a particular text that they read, it does not mean that they have the language to discuss it, especially for different functions of language (e.g., predicting, inferring).

In providing language structures for students, teachers can help to ensure that they have the opportunity to engage in meaningful dialogue: language structures help students express their ideas more accurately, as well as in more complex ways. Students need to be provided with multiple opportunities to rehearse the language structures and use them for real purposes in structured dialogues. As teachers provide these opportunities, they need to be mindful of students' various levels of language proficiency because different students may be ready to take on more complex language. For example, in a kindergarten classroom we observed in Salem, Oregon, the teacher was teaching students to compare and contrast and had provided language structures that included words such as "and" and "but." After having students practice using those more basic words, the teacher introduced the words "whereas" and "however," and together all of the students practiced saying these words in context. While it may sound stilted for kindergartners to use this language, students take on the language we teach and school is the place where they are likely to be exposed to and learn this register. Why not start them early? When the students continued with the lesson, some students went back to the more basic words, while others incorporated the more complex words into their dialogue. By introducing language structures with different levels of complexity, the teacher provided students with the opportunity to use more complex language. Those who were ready could begin practicing the more complex language, and those who were not had other scaffolds in place, but were also exposed to the more complex language.

Further, we have noticed that rather than a spiraling curriculum, language structures are frequently repeated across grade levels. For example, in one of our schools teachers at various grade levels were teaching sequencing and summarizing, and at each grade level we observed that the vocabulary used to teach these skills was, "first, then, next, and finally/last." While this vocabulary is acceptable for students in grade 1, and may be appropriate for grade 2, by grades 3 and 4 students should be utilizing a greater variety of sequencing words and words with more complexity to create summaries. Such vocabulary might

**TABLE 2.2**

### Sample Goals for Language Structures

| Goal | Example |
| --- | --- |
| Expand grammatical complexity | • Expand statements using connected discourse<br>• Simple sentence<br>• Prepositions<br>• Conjunctions<br>• Relative pronouns<br>• Adverbial clauses |
| Provide opportunity for transformations | • Statements to questions<br>• Positive to negative statements<br>• Questions to statements<br>• Requests to commands<br>• Statements to exclamations |
| Make transformation with insertions | • Do insertion (John has a dog. Does he also have a cat?)<br>• Get insertion (I pay for my lunch everyday. I get paid for taking out the trash.) |
| Forms and functions | • Language to address various communicative tasks (e.g., agree/disagree, make a request, compare/contrast) |

Adapted from Gentile, L. (2004). *The oracy instructional guide*. Carlsbad, CA: Dominie Press.

**TABLE 2.3**

Criteria for Selecting Vocabulary

| Criteria | Descriptors | Examples |
|---|---|---|
| Importance and utility | • Words that will support academic learning<br>• Words that are characteristic of mature language users<br>• Words that appear across a variety of disciplines | Find<br>• Find the square root of ___.<br>• One of the findings from this study. . .<br>• We find that it is hard to. . .<br>Stage<br>• The play will be held on the stage.<br>• The stages of the water cycle are. . .<br>• They staged a walkout. |
| Instructional potential | • Words that can be worked in a variety of ways so that students can build rich representations of them and their connections to other words and concepts | Left<br>• Right vs. left<br>• Past tense of leave<br>• Remainder in math<br>Round<br>• It is a shape.<br>• A way to estimate<br>• A composition for multiple voices to sing<br>• To gather |
| Conceptual understanding | • Words that provide precision and specificity in describing a general concept that is already understood | • Easy/hard: simple/difficult; a breeze/challenging<br>• Chair, stool, bench<br>• Socks, stockings, tights, booties |

include, "in the beginning, subsequently, concluding with," and so forth. All oracy structures should become more complex as students progress across grade levels.

## Vocabulary

Vocabulary knowledge has been shown to be an important predictor of reading fluency and comprehension (Hickman, Pollard-Durodola, & Vaughn, 2004), and thus an essential component of oracy instruction. Our examination of lesson plans and observations in classrooms has led us to recognize that teachers have a tendency to focus on vocabulary words that are quite technical and not highly utilized. However, because emerging bilingual students need more exposure to vocabulary in order to refine and expand their knowledge of words and concepts, teachers need to consider high utility words that students are likely to see in different texts and contexts in addition to technical words that they need to understand a particular text. Also, it is important to select vocabulary words that will extend students' conceptual understandings (Table 2.3). Research demonstrates that if students are familiar with the 2,000 most frequently used English words, they will know a large percentage of words in spoken conversation (90%), fictional text (87%), newspapers (80%), and even college-level academic text (78%) (Nation, 2001).

## Dialogue

As illustrated by the sample goals outlined in Table 2.4, the component of dialogue is meant to ensure that students have the opportunity to engage in meaningful discussions about the text with which they are interacting. Dialogue goes far beyond the teacher simply asking questions that students answer; it entails the teacher fostering a conversation about the text among the students in the class, and eventually transferring the questioning and discussion to the students. Therefore, it is important that the teachers recognize the end goal for the dialogue and plan questions accordingly, in order to guide students' discussion in an appropriate way.

## Sample Oracy Objectives

In our experience with planning and implementing Literacy Squared lessons, we have observed that the creation of oracy objectives is one of the more difficult aspects of the

**TABLE 2.4**

Goals for Developing Dialogue

| Goal | Example |
|------|---------|
| Teach verbs that elicit dialogue | • Advocate<br>• Argue<br>• Articulate<br>• Clarify<br>• Debate<br>• Defend<br>• Discuss<br>• Explain<br>• Interpret<br>• Justify<br>• Negotiate<br>• Persuade<br>• Propose<br>• Respond |
| Encourage students to make personal connections with what they read | • Agree/disagree with an event/person (e.g., do you agree with how Robert solved the problem with his sister?)<br>• Respond to "what if" questions—What if you had been the girl in the story? What would you have done? |
| Encourage students to understand that not every question has a right/wrong answer | Respond to open-ended questions<br>• Can you tell me one thing you learned about ____?<br>• What were you thinking when you read about ____?<br>• What were you feeling?<br>• What was the most important thing you learned about ____? Why? |

program, especially in literacy-based ELD. For this reason we have provided examples to illustrate how oracy and literacy objectives are written within Spanish and literacy-based ELD lesson plans in Boxes 2.1 through 2.4.* It is important to note that oracy is meant to be used in the context of larger biliteracy units (see Chapters 8–10). We have separated them out here to illustrate the components of language structures, vocabulary, and dialogue. However, the examples are not stand-alone lessons.

## Recommended Resources

Various resources exist to help teachers in choosing questions to elicit dialogue and choose language structures and vocabulary (Box 2.5). For Spanish literacy, we recommend the materials available from the *Secretaría de educación pública* (SEP) *de México* curriculum, which is the equivalent of the Department of Education in Mexico. The lessons in the SEP curriculum include many aspects of oracy, such as questions that elicit dialogue and the use of high utility and conceptual words in context, helping to expand and develop students' Spanish vocabulary. Teachers can use or adapt these materials to meet their oracy objectives, and we encourage teachers to use these materials in planning the Spanish component of their biliteracy units. SEP materials are available online and bound copies may be available at no cost from your local Mexican Consulate. In considering planning and teaching English oracy, many commercially produced products are also available.

## Teaching Methods to Develop Oracy

As mentioned earlier, oracy instruction is an integral part of every Spanish literacy and literacy-based ELD lesson. From our work with teachers, we have found that two reading methods, Lotta Lara and readers theater, are excellent entry points for the planning and implementation of oracy objectives and instruction within paired literacy instruction. In the following sections both methods are described, as are the steps involved to imple-

*All boxes are at the end of the chapter in numerical order.

ment them. These are not the only ways to develop oracy, but we have found them to be effective.

## Lotta Lara

One method for the development of both oracy and reading is a Literacy Squared innovation, the Lotta Lara strategy. Lotta Lara focuses on two objectives: developing students' oral language skills (oracy) through explicit planning, and increasing reading fluency through repeated reading. The name for this strategy, Lotta Lara, is a play on words, but respectfully honors a colleague of ours, Estelle Lara, who applied the findings of research on Wide Reading (Kuhn, 2004; Pikulski & Chard, 2005) to her own first grade classroom. Estelle Lara created a six-week intervention where she grouped students heterogeneously to teach fluency by reading three different texts, three times. We then adapted the procedure by adding more readings of the same text, as well as oracy exercises, thus the term "lotta." Based on NRP's findings (2000), children's ability to read fluently increases their overall comprehension. Lotta Lara provides students with multiple opportunities to read developmentally appropriate texts and to participate in using oral language to communicate related understandings with appropriate scaffolds. As the NRP found, "guided repeated oral reading that included guidance from teachers had a significant and positive impact on word recognition, reading fluency, and comprehension across a range of grade levels" (p. 12). Our addition of oracy exercises to the Lotta Lara procedure ensures that children have ample opportunities to use oral language to express their comprehension of text, thereby integrating the teaching of reading strategies with oracy.

Many Literacy Squared teachers have had great success in implementing Lotta Lara and have seen their students' participation in reading and speaking increase. As a result, we feel this is one of the easier Literacy Squared strategies to implement, as long as an equal focus is placed on both oracy and the repeated reading.

In the following sections, we describe the steps involved in implementing Lotta Lara. In Literacy Squared, the Lotta Lara strategy is used in Spanish literacy in grades 1–3, and in literacy-based ELD from grade 1 through grade 5 (see the Time Allocations and Grade Appropriate Instructional Approaches in Table 1.3). One book or text is used three times in one week and is read by the students a total of nine times. While students will be reading to increase their reading fluency and comprehension, equal emphasis is placed on oracy through the use of connected discourse and the rehearsal of preplanned language structures. Twenty to forty minutes should be allotted to the Lotta Lara lesson on each of the three days.

**Select a Text.** It's important to pay careful attention to the selection of text for this strategy because students will be reading it nine times. To begin, the book or other text that is selected should complement the genre being studied in the biliteracy unit and be culturally and personally relevant to the students. Because the reading of the text is so highly scaffolded, we suggest a selection that is appropriate to the middle to upper reading abilities of your students. The language in the book/text should be appropriate to students' linguistic abilities, while at the same time providing opportunities to expand their linguistic repertoires. Texts may also be modified or adapted to address students' linguistic and literate strengths and needs. Additionally, it is important that all students can view the text, as they will be reading along with the teacher. We have seen teachers use multiple copies of trade books, make copies of texts, or use a document camera in order to facilitate this. We recommend Lotta Lara be used at the beginning of the year, with one book/text per genre unit.

**Preread and Plan Oracy Objectives.** Before beginning the Lotta Lara sessions, read the book thoroughly and identify specific vocabulary to teach students, language structures to promote comprehension of the text, and questions to encourage dialogue.

**Do Multiple Readings of the Text.** On the first day of Lotta Lara, introduce the book/text to the students by including attention to oracy. This can include activating background knowledge through engaging students in a dialogue by eliciting intrapersonal questions related to the text in either the text's target language or using Spanish strategically in literacy-based ELD, practicing targeted language structures, and introducing relevant vocabulary.

Next, provide the students with a general introduction of the text in one or two sentences and a brief picture/book walk, orienting the student to the whole book, while contextualizing the target vocabulary and providing students opportunities to view and practice specific structures from the text. For example, the introduction in the lesson, *My House is Your House* (see Box 2.7), would require students to practice saying the phrase, "Welcome. Please come in. My house is your house."

After the introduction, read the text aloud to the students in its entirety, before engaging students in repeated readings: echo, choral, and partner reading. The teacher reads the text aloud to the students on day 1 but *not* on days 2 and 3. This first reading by the teacher allows students to hear a complete fluent read of the text to more fully understand the text as a whole. On all three days, students partake in the repeated readings. **Echo reading** involves having the teacher read a phrase or sentence fluently and the students reread it using expression and intonation. It is important that the teacher read a bit more than the students can retain aurally, as the focus of the exercise is to have students reading and not relying on their memory alone. After the text has been echo read, the students and the teacher chorally read the text. **Choral reading** involves reading aloud in unison. As with the echo reading, the teacher monitors students to ensure attention to print and continuous reading of the text without pausing to ask questions or elicit input from students. Finally, the students engage in **partner reading**, in which pairs of readers alternate reading aloud, following a specific turn-taking procedure. Think strategically when pairing students and ensure they understand the procedure for partner reading. Consider student compatibility, seating arrangements, and structures for reading (e.g., seating students side by side, facing each other)

**Incorporate Explicit Oracy Instruction (throughout).** Once all three readings have occurred, it is time for oracy and comprehension extensions. Keep in mind that the oracy portion of the lesson is just as important as the repeated readings and should never be omitted. Boxes 2.6 and 2.7 show sample Lotta Lara lessons within Spanish literacy and literacy-based ELD that include oracy instruction. For days 2 and 3, the Lotta Lara session begins with a review of the target vocabulary and language structures and moves into the repeated readings (echo, choral, and partner) with time for explicit oracy instruction. The checklist in Box 2.8 can be used to guide appropriate use of the Lotta Lara strategy in the classroom.

## Readers Theater

Readers theater is a simple, effective, and risk-free way to get children to enjoy reading and to engage in repeated reading (Walker, 2012). It involves teaching children to read and speak by putting on a play; but unlike traditional theater, the emphasis is mainly on oral expression of the part. Readers theater involves children in understanding their world, reading aloud, performing with a purpose, and bringing enjoyment to both themselves and their audiences.

Readers theater scripts are adapted from literature children are reading and it requires no sets, costumes, props, or memorized lines. Instead of acting out literature as in a play, the performer's goal is to read a script aloud effectively, enabling the audience to visualize the action. Performers bring the text alive by using voice, facial expressions, and some gestures (Cornwell, 2012). Cornwell (2012) and Kimbell-López (2003) identify specific benefits to children of using readers theater in the classroom, including the following:

- Development of fluency through repeated exposure and reading of text
- Increased comprehension of text.
- Integration of reading, speaking, listening in an authentic context
- Enhanced engagement of students
- Increased motivation to read
- Confidence-building and improved self-image of students related to reading
- A real purpose for reading
- Concrete opportunities for cooperative learning

Readers theater is not a new strategy. However, we decided to include it in this chapter on oracy because it can be a powerful strategy to build fluency and expression in reading and can be used to engage students in oracy strategies that ultimately deepen their ability to interact with and comprehend text. Readers theater is another way to enhance text comprehension while building reading fluency and creating interest and enthusiasm for reading. The readers theater format provides an opportunity for students to develop fluency through multiple readings of the text and by using expressiveness, intonation, and inflection when rehearsing the text. As with all other strategies, we suggest that readers theater scripts be created in both Spanish and English.

**Creating the Scripts.** Readers theater may be performed with many kinds of literature: picture books, short stories, parts of novels, poetry, folk tales, works of nonfiction, newspapers, or magazine articles. Not all literature, however, makes a good readers theater script. We suggest that teachers look for literature that

- Is interesting or has compelling content
- Has a strong story line, interesting characters, conflict, plot action, humor
- Uses dialogue
- Is not filled with descriptive passages
- Flows at a steady pace

While teachers of students in upper elementary or middle school can and should encourage their students to create and write their own readers theater scripts, we suggest that teachers in K–3 create the scripts from books they are reading in either Spanish or English. It is not necessary to use a piece of literature in its entirety; in fact shortened versions and/or excerpts of texts can be especially effective in literacy-based ELD. However, the key is to be sure to keep in mind the reading level of the students when selecting a piece of text. Choose text they can read aloud successfully, given repeated practice. The following list is a basic sequence for creating and implementing a readers theater script:

1. Choose the piece of text you wish to adapt to script form.
2. Determine what portions of the text to leave in to be true to the story line, characters, or topic and which portions can be deleted.
3. Delete the less critical passages: descriptions, transitions, and so forth.
4. Rewrite or modify those passages that need to be included but require adaptation.
5. Keep speeches and narrative passages short.
6. Divide the parts for the readers.
7. Have children use highlighters to mark parts and demonstrate how to interpret the part and read expressively, how to hold the script, and when to assume various stage positions.
8. Give the students lots of time to prepare, practicing their roles in different ways: individually and in small groups, privately, and in front of others.
9. Send a copy of the script home for parents to read and practice with their children.
10. Rehearse with the readers, providing needed direction and support regarding their interpretation, pacing, expression, volume, positions, and motions.
11. Begin with short presentations.
12. Perform for an audience as often as possible.
13. Use props sparingly.

**Using Bilingual Books.** In order to illustrate how to use bilingual books to create readers theater, we have included excerpts from the beginning and end of a readers theater lesson and script (Box 2.9) that was created from the bilingual book *Pepita Talks Twice/Pepita habla dos veces* (Lachtman, 1995). In this case, it is being used to build fluency in English. This particular book lends itself to the creation of a readers theater because it has multiple characters (and hence many parts for readers), has repeated phrases that lend themselves to choral reading by the class, and deals with a theme that is culturally relevant to emergent bilingual children.

**Conducting the Lesson.** Finally, readers theater used to develop oracy and fluency can be an excellent source of dialogue related to text and reader performance. Teachers should engage students in dialogues about the characters and actions in the readers theater to deepen the children's understanding of the text and text-related vocabulary and how to interpret the vocabulary and actions in the text. We suggest that readers theater can start being used in the middle of grade 1, in both Spanish and English, and that teacher and peer feedback be incorporated into the routines for readers theater. Teachers will need to model how to give feedback, and all feedback should be presented positively. This will also make those children who are viewers of the readers theater better and more positive listeners. Box 2.10 presents a checklist for assessing effective reading in readers theater presentations. We suggest that teachers use this checklist as a way of encouraging dialogue related to the performance of readers theater.

## Conclusion

In this chapter we introduced oracy, the first domain of language of the holistic biliteracy framework, considered essential to biliteracy instruction and development. We provided recommendations for generating oracy lessons that focus on the creation of sentence structures, dialogue, and vocabulary. We also provided samples of how some of our teachers have created oracy lessons as a part of larger biliteracy units. We emphasize that oracy lessons should not be created or taught in isolation; instead, they should be included as part of a holistic biliteracy framework wherein the oracy is an integral aspect of a comprehensive biliteracy program.

## Questions for Reflection and Action

- What other methods could you use to develop oracy?
- With other teachers at your school, generate a list of potential books to use for Lotta Lara and other oracy activities and create book units in Spanish and English using the three aspects of oracy (language structures, vocabulary, and dialogue).
- What books, poetry, or stories could be used to create readers theater scripts?

| BOX 2.1 | *Connecting Literacy and Oracy Objectives in Spanish Literacy* |
|---|---|
| Book | Flux, N. (2010). *Rafael Márquez*. Salem, OR: Highland Elementary School. Text created by teacher for use in Literacy Squared. |
| Grade level | 1 |
| State standard | Biography |
| Cultural relevance | Rafael Márquez is a famous contemporary Mexican soccer player |
| Literacy objective | Children will demonstrate comprehension of text by reading the short biography of Rafael Márquez and answering the following questions. <br> • *¿De quién es esta biografía?*(Who is this biography about?) <br> • *¿Dónde y cuándo nació?* (Where and when was he born?) <br> • *¿Por qué se hizo famoso?* (Why was he famous?) <br> • *Datos interesantes de Rafael Márquez son ____ y ____.* (Some interesting facts about Rafael Márquez are ____ and ____.) |
| Language structures | 1. Transformation—Question to answer and Answer to question <br> **Example** <br> • *¿Cuál es un dato interesante de Rafael Márquez?/Un dato interesante de Rafael Márquez es ____.* (What is an interesting fact about Rafael Márquez./An interesting fact about Rafael Márquez is __.) <br> • *Hágame una pregunta de la vida de Rafael Márquez./¿Dónde nació Rafael Márquez?* (Ask me a question about Rafael Márquez's life./Where was Rafael Márquez born?) <br> 2. Transformation—Question to answer reading a timeline <br> **Example** <br> • *¿Cuándo nació Rafael Márquez?/Rafael Márquez nació ____. (*When was Rafael Márquez born?/ Rafael Márquez was born on ____.) <br> • *¿Cuándo ganó su primer campeonato?/Rafael Márquez ganó su primer campeonato en ____.* (When did he win his first championship? Rafael Márquez won his first championship in ____.) <br> • *¿Qué pasó en el año 1979?/Rafael Márquez nació en el año 1979.* (What happened in 1979? Rafael Márquez was born in 1979.) |
| Vocabulary | Reading numbers on a timeline (1979, 1996, 1998, 2011) <br> • *Nació (born); Empezó (began); Ganó (won); Se hizo famoso (He became famous); Entró* (entered) |
| Dialogue | Opinion—*¿Sí o no? ¿por qué?* (Yes or no? Why?) <br> • *¿Qué opinas de esta idea?/La gente rica deberían de compartir su dinero con los pobres.* (What is your opinion about this? Wealthy people should share their money with the poor?) |

Courtesy of Noelia Flux, Highland Elementary School, Salem, OR.

| BOX 2.2 | **Connecting Literacy and Oracy Objectives in Spanish Literacy** |
|---|---|
| Book | Anaya, R. (2007). *The first tortilla/La primera tortilla*. Houston: Arte Público Press. |
| Grade level | 3 |
| State standard | Text structures in fiction |
| Cultural relevance | Bilingual story that takes place in a Mexican village and tells of how the first tortilla came to be made. |
| Spanish literacy objective | • Activating prior knowledge, predicting/anticipating, making inferences, oral and written retelling of the story<br>• Establish chronological order of events and their causal relationships<br>• Using the writing process, students will write a cohesive paragraph using description and in sequence |
| Spanish Oracy Objective | • Answer questions based on the text with the purpose of understanding the elements of fiction<br>• Retell the story with expression (via dialogue) |
| Language structures | • *¿Quién es el personaje principal?/El personaje principal es \_\_\_. ¿Quiénes son los otros personajes?/Los otros personajes son \_\_\_.*(Who is the main character? The main character is \_\_. Who are the other characters?/The other characters are \_\_\_.)<br>• *¿Qué obstáculos o problemas encontró (personaje principal)? (personaje principal) se encontró \_\_\_\_.* (What obstacles/problems did the (the main character) find?<br>• *¿Cómo (personaje principal) resolvió el/los problema(s)?/personaje principal) resolvió el problema en que \_\_\_.* (How did \_\_\_ solve the problem?/ (The main character) resolved the problem by \_\_.)<br>• *¿Quién le ayudó a resolver el(los) problema(s)?* (Who helped him/her solve the problem/s?)<br>• *¿Por cuales razones (personaje principal) tenía que ayudar a su pueblo o cuál era su motivo? Su motivo era \_\_\_\_.* (For what reasons did (the main character) help or what was the motivation?)/His/Her motivation was \_\_.<br>• *¿Qué sucedió al fin del cuento? Al fin del cuento \_\_\_.* (What happened at the end of the story?/At the end of the story\_\_.) |
| Vocabulary | • Vocabulary (for language structures): *Motivo* (motivation), *obstáculo* (obstacle), *valiente* (brave), *género* (genre)<br>• Text vocabulary: *rebozo* (shawl), *ladera* (slope), *matas* (plants), *generaciones* (generations), *vereda* (sidewalk), *angosta* (narrow), *marchitar* (to fade) |
| Dialogue | • *¿De qué piensan se tratará la historia? ¿Quién será el personaje principal? ¿Por qué piensan eso? ¿Piensan que el volcán va a explotar? ¿Qué pasaría? ¿Qué historia podríamos contar usando todo lo que vemos en la ilustración?* (What do you think the story is about? Who will be the main character? Why do you think that? Do you think the volcano will erupt? What will happen? What story could we tell using the information learned from the illustrations?) |

Courtesy of Josette Boyden, Auburn Elementary School, Salem, OR.

| BOX 2.3 | *Connecting Literacy and Oracy Objectives in Literacy-based ELD* |
|---|---|
| Book | Morales, Y. (2003). *Just a minute: A trickster tale and counting book.* San Francisco: Chronicle. |
| Grade level | 2 |
| State standard | Response to literature |
| Cultural relevance | *El día de los muertos* (The Day of the Dead) |
| Literacy objective | Children will demonstrate comprehension of text through written responses with the following comprehension questions:<br>• Why did Grandma Beetle keep saying: "Just a minute?"<br>• How do we know that Señor Calavera was getting more frustrated as the story went on?"<br>• Did Grandma Beetle really want to go with Señor Calavera? Why/why not? |
| Oracy objective | Children will learn how to change questions to answers, express different ways to be upset, and make comparisons. |
| Language structures | 1. Transformation—Verb tense changes from question to answer<br>   **Example**<br>   • What made Señor Calavera **sigh**?/He **sighed** when Grandma Beetle said ___.<br>   • What made Señor Calavera **throw** up his hands?/He **threw** up his hands when ___.<br>2. Expanding discourse—adding prepositional phrase<br>   **Example**<br>   Name one way you can show you are upset./One way you can show you are upset is by ___ (e.g., rolling up your eyes, stomping the floor).<br>3. Expressing comparison—less than, more than<br>   **Example**<br>   • If you sigh, you are **less** upset than if you stomp your feet.<br>   • If you frown you are **more** upset than if you sigh. |
| Vocabulary | Expressions to show being upset<br>• Sigh<br>• Roll your eyes<br>• Frown<br>• Tap your fingers<br>• Throw up your hands<br>• Shake your head in disbelief<br>• Stomp your feet on the floor |
| Dialogue and writing | Conditional phrases<br>What would make you ___ (e.g., sigh, frown, stomp your feet)?/_____ would make me ____.<br>If Señor Calavera came after you, what would you do to trick him?/I would say, "Just a minute, I need to ___." |

Courtesy of Literacy Squared professional development session, August 2010.

| BOX 2.4 | *Connecting Literacy and Oracy Objectives in Literacy-based ELD* |
|---|---|
| Book | Romero-Stevens, J. (1995). *Carlos and the squash plant/Carlos y la planta de calabaza*. Pittsburgh, PA: Luna Rising. |
| Grade level | 3 |
| State standard | Narrative literature |
| Cultural relevance | Carlos and his family are Latino |
| Literacy objective | Text analysis: Children will demonstrate comprehension of text through written responses to the following comprehension questions: <br> • What was the problem in the story? <br> • Who were the principal characters? <br> • How was the problem resolved? |
| Language structures | 1. Compare and contrast—Transformation question to answer <br> **Example** <br> • How are you like Carlos?/I am like Carlos because ___. <br> • How are you different than Carlos?/I am different than Carlos because ___. <br> 2. Transformation—Compare and contrast with negation <br> **Example** <br> Carlos lives on a farm, we live in a city. How are farms and cities *different*?/A farm is different from a city because a farm has ___, *but* a city does not. A city has ___, *however* a farm does not. <br> 3. Expressing comparison, connecting discourse <br> **Example** <br> • How are cities and farms *similar*?/*Both* cities and farms have____. <br> • Compare and contrast the story—what could really happen and what was fiction?/ It was real that ___. It was fiction that ___. |
| Vocabulary | • Things from the city (tall buildings, lots of people, stores) <br> • Things from the farm (animals, fields, people, crops) |
| Dialogue | Conditional phrases <br> • Would you rather live in the farm or in the city? Why? <br> • Would you rather take a bath or shower? <br> • Should everyone take a bath? Why? |

Courtesy of Veronica Sotelo, Mary Eyre Elementary School, Salem, OR.

| BOX 2.5 | *Oracy Resources* |
|---|---|
| **In Spanish Literacy** | |
| http://basica.sep.gob.mx/reformaintegral/sitio/index.php?act=buscadorlibros | |
| **In Literacy-based ELD** | |
| Dialogue | • Resource for facilitating persuasion: http://corp3.wrdsb.ca/tacs/files/2011/03/ Persuasive-Text-Read-Alouds.pdf <br> • Book: Eggleton, J. (2001). *Should this have happened?* New Zealand: Heinemann Education. |
| Language structures | English language functions and forms: <br> • www.ode.state.or.us/teachlearn/standards/elp/files/langfunc.pdf <br> • http://www.learninglive.co.uk/teachers/ema/eal/combined_language_structure.pdf |
| Vocabulary word lists | • 1,000 most frequently used words: http://www.rupert.id.au/resources/1000-words.php <br> • The 6,000 most frequently used English words: http://www.insightin.com/esl/ <br> • The First 4,000 Words program: www.thefirst4000words.com <br> • First 4,000 Word list: http://www.sewardreadingresources.com/img/fourkw/ 4KW_Source_List.pdf <br> • The Academic Word List (Coxhead, 2000): http://nottingham.ac.uk/%7Ealzsh3/ acvocab/wordlists.htm |

| BOX 2.6 | *Lotta Lara Lesson for Spanish Literacy* |
|---|---|
| Book | Ada, A. F. (2000). *No fui yo.* Doral, FL: Santillana.<br>This book is also available in English |
| Grade level | 1 |
| Literacy objective | *Fluency*—increasing automaticity, accuracy, prosody, and reading rate<br>*Inference*—using pictures and words from the text students will infer that the child in the story did some mischievous things and needed to make up for it. |
| Moral of story | *Hay que saber pedir perdón cuando nos equivocamos.* (You have to know how to say you are sorry when you make a mistake) |
| Oracy objective | *Function:* Expressing cause and effect<br>*Una vez sin querer yo ___ y ___.* (One time, by accident I ___ and ___.)<br>*Prereading:* Picture walk—with children and teacher talking about what they see in the pictures and what is happening in the story. |
| Lesson structure | 1. Prereading<br>  • Draw the children's attention in the picture walk to the fact that the child in the story is not wearing shoes; however, note that there are footprints on every page of someone with shoes.<br>  • In the picture walk, discuss every page where something is happening that might upset a grownup.<br>2. Reading: Lotta Lara repeated reading format (three fluent reads of the text)<br>  • Echo<br>  • Choral<br>  • Partner<br>3. After reading<br>  • Lead a discussion about what kind of mischief that child got into and why every page starts with, "*No fui yo*" (It wasn't me) except the last page that changes and says, "*Pero sí soy yo*" (But it was me)—why did the sentence change—what was the boy trying to do on the last page?<br>  • Discuss the fact that all children get into mischief and that mischief is not done with bad intent.<br>  • Post and discuss the sentence frames and model the asking and answering of questions.<br>  • Have students practice using the sentence frames in large groups and with partners.<br>  • Teacher and children could discuss what they would do to make amends for mischievous behavior. |
| **Examples**<br>Sentence frames with cause phrase first and effect phrase second | • *Una vez sin querer yo me comí todas las galletas en el plato y ye se enojaron mis hermanos.* (One time, by accident I ate all of the cookies and my brothers got upset.)<br>• *Una vez sin querer yo ensucié mi vestido nuevo y se enojó mi mama.* (One time, by accident I got my dress dirty and my mom got mad.) |
| **Transformations**<br>Sentence frames with effect phrase first and cause phrase second | • *Una vez, se pusieron tristes mis hermanos porque me comí todas las galletas en el plato pero lo hice sin querer.* (One time, my brothers were sad because I ate all of the cookies by accident.)<br>• *Una vez, se enojó mi mamá porque ensucié mi vestido pero lo hice sin querer.* (One time, my mom got mad because I got my dress dirty but it was an accident.) |

| BOX 2.7 | *Lotta Lara Lesson for Literacy-based ELD* |
|---|---|
| Book | Tafolla, C. (2000). *My house is your house.* Orlando, FL: Rigby. This book is also available in big book format and on DVD. |
| Grade level | 2–3 |
| Literacy objective | *Fluency*—increasing automaticity, accuracy, prosody, and reading rate |
| Oracy objective | Function: Inviting someone into your home. |

Prereading: Interactive scaffolded role play
Students are introduced to the pronouns *him*, *her*, and *them* with visual support.

1 girl = her      1 boy = him      More than 1 = them

They are then invited in small groups to come to the front of the room to participate in a whole-group scaffolded role play in which one or more students approach an imaginary door while the others invite them in. The following represents the text that would be posted to assist students:

(*Knock, Knock*)
Student 1: Who's there?
Student 2: (*Student answers with name*)
Student 1 (to group): What should I do?
Entire group advises chorally: Ask (<u>him, her, them</u>) in!
Student 1 pretends to open the door and says: Welcome! Please come in. My house is your house.

After reading: Language structures (subjunctive and additional pronoun practice)
If a _____ were at *your* door, would you ask (<u>*him, her, them, it*</u>) in?
If a _____ were at *my* door, I <u>*would/would not*</u> ask (<u>*him, her, them, it*</u>) in.

| Lesson structure | 1. Prereading |
|---|---|

1. Prereading
   - Introduce important vocabulary/phrases (grin, ask them in, my house is your house/mi casa es su casa)
   - Participate in scaffolded role-play to introduce the theme of the book and to give the students opportunities to engage in an activity with language from the text.
2. Reading: Repeated reading Lotta Lara format (three fluent reads of the text)
   - Echo
   - Choral
   - Partner
3. After reading
   - Lead a discussion expanding on the theme of the text. We love visitors, but not *all* visitors!
   - Have students brainstorm a list of potential visitors. List might include the improbable (e.g., pirates, dinosaurs, ghosts, robbers)
   - Post and discuss sentence structures. Model the asking and answering of questions using the subjunctive and the appropriate pronoun. Have students practice in whole group, collaboratively, and with partners.

## BOX 2.8 *Lotta Lara Checklist*

Lotta Lara includes both *oracy* and *repeated readings*.

| Language Environment (check one) | Observation Notes |
|---|---|
| Spanish literacy: grades 1–3 | |
| Literacy-based ELD: grades 1–5 | |
| **Book Selection** | |
| Appropriate genre (culturally and personally relevant) | |
| Appropriate to students' reading level | |
| Appropriate to students' linguistic abilities | |
| **Book Introduction (Day 1)** | |
| Brief summary is given to students | |
| Picture walk given by teacher introducing<br>• Relevant vocabulary<br>• Linguistic structures from text with opportunities for students to rehearse<br>*This should be done in the language of the book.* | |
| Opportunity for students to engage in dialogue (i.e., engagement opportunity to activate students' background knowledge) | |
| **Repeated Reading (Days 1–3)** | |
| On day 1 teacher reads entire text (**not** done on days 2 and 3) | |
| Echo reading | |
| Choral reading | |
| Partner reading (includes appropriate pairing of students) | |
| **Oracy (Days 1–3)** | |
| Day 1: Comprehension question/s with appropriate sentence structures | |
| Days 2–3: Explicit oracy instruction for students to engage in structured dialogue about text | |
| Language structures are linguistically appropriate | |
| 100% of students have *multiple opportunities* (more than once) to rehearse and use meaningfully selected language structures | |
| **Time** | |
| 20–40 minutes, including oracy and repeated readings | |

---

**BOX 2.9   *Sample Readers Theater***

---

Lachtman, O. (1995). *Pepita Talks Twice/Pepita habla dos veces*. Houston: Arte Público Press.

**Literacy objective**: Demonstrate comprehension of text by comparing and contrasting text to self, text to text, and text to world.

**Oracy objective**: Compare/contrast language:
Pepita is like me because _____.
Pepita is similar to me because _____.
Transformations: Turn positive statements into negative statements (Pepita is not like me because
_____.)

Dialogue
Knowing two languages is better/not better than knowing one.
Pepita was right/wrong to not want to speak Spanish any more.

---

***Pepita Talks Twice/Pepita habla dos veces***
Readers Theater

**Reader roles**
Storyteller
Everyone
Mr. Hobbs
Tía Rosa
Miguel
Pepita
Mamá
Papá
Juan
Mr. Jones
Miss García

---

Theater Script excerpts, adapted from the text *Pepita Talks Twice/Pepita habla dos veces*
*[Adapted from the beginning of the story]*

| | |
|---|---|
| **Pepita:** | I am never, ever going to speak Spanish any more. |
| **Juan:** | That's pretty dumb. |
| **Mamá:** | My, oh my, Pepita. Why? |
| **Pepita:** | Because I am tired of talking twice. |
| **Mamá:** | *¿Dos veces?* |
| **Pepita:** | Yes! Once in Spanish and once more in English. So, I'm never going to speak Spanish anymore. |
| **Everyone:** | She is never, ever going to speak Spanish anymore! |
| **Juan:** | How will you ask for enchiladas and tamales. . . . and tacos with salsa? They are all Spanish words you know. |
| **Pepita:** | I will find a way. |

*[Adapted from the end of the story]*

| | |
|---|---|
| **Pepita:** | Wolf! Wolf, come here! A car is coming! *¡Lobo! ¡Lobo! ¡Ven acá!* |
| **Storyteller:** | Lobo turned back just before a loud screech of the car's brakes. Pepita opened her eyes in time to see the ball roll to the other side of the street. A red faced man shouted out the window of the car, and Lobo raced back into the yard! Pepita shut the gate firmly behind Lobo and hugged him. |
| **Pepita:** | Lobo, oh Lobo you came when I called in Spanish! I'll never call you Wolf again. Your name is Lobo. Just like mine is Pepita. And, oh Lobo, I'm glad I talked twice. It's great to speak two languages! |
| **Everyone:** | **It's great to speak two languages. *¡Qué bonito ser bilingüe!*** |

---

Excerpts from *Pepita Talks Twice* by Ofelia Dumas Lachtman are reprinted with permission from the publisher. (©1995 Arte Público Press–University of Houston)

## BOX 2.10  *Checklist for Assessing Students in Readers Theater*

An effective reader does the following:
- Reads with expression, proper emphasis, and clear enunciation, using his/her voice effectively to convey meaning
- Projects to the audience
- Familiarizes himself or herself with the part and is able to read it with fluency
- Paces himself or herself effectively
- Uses props, when employed, effectively (the script is a prop)
- Demonstrates poise and self-confidence

# 3

# Reading

*Successful [Spanish-English] bilingual readers understand the relationship between the Spanish- and English-language literacy systems. Of particular importance are these students' capabilities of transferring or applying their literacy knowledge and abilities from one language to the other. They strategically implement this knowledge in a timely manner while reading.*

Robert T. Jiménez, 1997

## Key Terms

**Analytic reading approaches**

**Authentic Spanish literacy instruction**

**Biliterate reading**

**Collaborative reading**

**Gradual release of responsibility**

**Independent reading**

**Interactive read aloud**

**Literacy-based ELD**

**Paired literacy instruction**

**Shared reading**

**Synthetic reading approaches**

**Teacher-led small groups**

## Guiding Questions

■ How is paired literacy instruction different from more traditional models of bilingual and dual language reading instruction?

■ Why might paired literacy instruction better meet the needs of simultaneous bilingual learners?

■ How are the suggested grouping structures in the Holistic Biliteracy Framework different from and similar to prevailing practice?

As discussed in Chapter 1, our holistic biliteracy framework for reading instruction is a paired literacy model designed to support simultaneous bilingual children as they realize their potential as bilingual, biliterate, and bicultural learners. This framework (see Figure 1.2) encompasses the teaching of literacy in Spanish and English simultaneously and interconnectedly at different times during the day, beginning in kindergarten and continuing through grade 5. It differs from sequential literacy instruction in early-exit bilingual programs where students are initially taught to read and write in their first language, usually in grades K–2, and then in their second language. It also contrasts sharply with literacy instruction models where a strict separation of languages is enforced, as is the case in many dual language programs.

In Literacy Squared, **paired literacy instruction** in K–5 bilingual classrooms includes interactive and explicit teaching of a variety of reading skills and strategies such as the following:

- Foundational reading skills (e.g., concepts of print, decoding, fluency)
- Reading comprehension skills (e.g., describe main ideas or major events in a text and central lesson including key supporting details, distinguish elements and structure of literary and informational texts)
- Comprehension strategies (e.g., activate prior knowledge, make predictions, make personal and intertextual connections, cognate study)
- Reading of a range of text types whose complexity is appropriate to each grade level.

Children are taught how to apply these skills and strategies across languages and to see similarities as well as language-specific differences. This is completely compatible with the Common Core State Standards, and in fact moves beyond them in its emphasis on biliteracy.

This chapter describes the approaches to reading instruction recommended for each language environment—that is, within Spanish and literacy-based ELD instruction—and how these approaches are the same and different across languages. It also presents an example of a biliteracy unit to illustrate how the implementation of the reading approaches is guided by a gradual release of responsibility model.

## Authentic Spanish Literacy Instruction: What the Research Says

Paired literacy instruction challenges the view that teaching children to read and write in two languages at the same time will confuse them or impede literacy learning in English. As implemented in Literacy Squared, it includes the need for authentic reading instruction in Spanish, as well as the need to consider how learning to read in two languages differs from learning to read in English as a first language.

**Authentic Spanish literacy instruction** uses teaching approaches for reading and writing in Spanish that are grounded, to the extent possible, in the internal structure of the language, as opposed to translated instructional models designed for monolingual English speakers. Equal amounts of instructional time during Spanish literacy are devoted to oracy, reading, writing, and metalanguage. Whenever possible, it incorporates culturally and personally relevant texts that are originally written in Spanish, as well as Spanish-English bilingual texts.

In the United States, Spanish literacy instruction often mirrors English literacy instruction and commercially produced materials in Spanish are often translated or patterned after English literacy programs. Within our holistic biliteracy framework, teachers are instead encouraged to use methods to teach Spanish reading that are authentic to the Spanish language. As a starting point, both Spanish and English are alphabetic languages and share similar alphabetic principals. Approaches to literacy instruction in alphabetic languages focus on **analytic** (whole to part) and **synthetic** (part to whole) approaches. Across languages, analytic approaches are very similar, while synthetic approaches are distinct from one language to another. Researchers such as Vernon and Ferreiro (1999), Escamilla (2000), Smith, Jiménez, and Martinez-León (2003), and Beeman and Urow (2013) have helped to identify specific ways in which synthetic approaches to teaching reading in Spanish, particularly with regard to teaching decoding skills, differ from synthetic approaches to teaching reading in English. These researchers have challenged Spanish literacy instruction in the United States on the grounds that authentic literacy instruction, particularly as it relates to synthetic teaching approaches, needs to be grounded in the internal structure of the language. For example, in Spanish the five vowel sounds are consistent and do not change their sound when paired with consonants. In contrast, English vowel sounds change depending on the word pattern and their consonant pairings. Even though Spanish and English both use a Roman alphabet, their internal structures are quite different.

The approaches to teaching literacy within Literacy Squared are based on the utilization of "best practice" principles that are specific to each language. For example, it is recommended that phonological awareness in Spanish be taught through writing (see Vernon & Ferreiro, 1999), whereas the teaching of these same skills in English, according to research, is best taught through oral language (Adams, 1990). Furthermore, Literacy Squared embraces Vernon and Ferreiro's (1999) assertion that phonics, as defined in English, has no Spanish equivalent.

Thus, teachers are encouraged to use authentic methods to teach literacy in Spanish, including the utilization and adaptation of the *Programa Nacional para el Fortalecimiento de la Lectura y la Escritura Básica (PRONALEES,* 2002), which is the Mexican national literacy program. A key feature of *PRONALEES* is that Spanish literacy instruction promotes the productive language skills of oracy and writing as well as the receptive language skills of listening and reading. Teachers are also encouraged to use culturally relevant literature and literature originally written in Spanish in the Spanish literacy block.

## Literacy-based ELD: What the Research Says

In addition to a focus on authentic Spanish language literacy, the paired literacy model includes effective strategies for teaching literacy in English as a second language, which is frequently referred to as ESL or ELD (English language development). As practiced within the holistic biliteracy framework, we refer to this instruction as literacy-based ELD.

Recent research (August & Shanahan, 2006; Bernhardt, 2003; Francis et al., 2006; Grant & Wong, 2003) has established that **biliterate reading** acquisition differs from monoliterate reading acquisition in important ways, including the following:

1. Readers use their knowledge of their first language and experiences when they read in a second language.
2. Skills and knowledge transfer across languages in bidirectional ways.
3. English oral language proficiency is positively related to English literacy, particularly at higher grade levels.
4. Literacy skills in the first language facilitate the development of English reading and writing (e.g., emergent literacy skills, phonological awareness, knowledge of cognates, comprehension strategies).
5. Some aspects of reading in a second language can be more challenging for emerging bilinguals than for monolingual students learning to read in one language (e.g., unfamiliar vocabulary, cohesive signals, idiomatic expressions)

### *Literacy-based ELD Instruction*

**Literacy-based ELD** takes into account the listed characteristics of literacy development in English as an additional language. It is based on the premise that English literacy instruction for emerging bilinguals must build on the literacy skills and conceptual knowledge they have developed in Spanish (or another language) while helping them to acquire the language skills they need to successfully participate in grade-level English literacy instruction. In other words, literacy-based ELD complements Spanish literacy instruction by allowing educators to teach explicitly features and uses of the English language, including similarities between the two languages and language-specific differences, and to refine the application of literacy skills and strategies already learned in Spanish.

Literacy-based ELD should not be confused with traditional ESL/ELD instruction, which is oral language- and content-based. In contrast, literacy-based ELD instruction is text- and language-based. In other words, the foundation of both literacy and language instruction is textual rather than oral, and language development derives directly from the language needed to accomplish the literacy tasks. This is quite different than focusing language development around a content area. Further, high-quality culturally and personally relevant texts are used as a basis for oracy and literacy instruction. Early research by Elley (1991) and Elley and Mangubhai (1983) has documented the advantages of text-based English language teaching programs among primary school students in a variety of contexts. Our research updates this earlier work in that students participating in Literacy Squared classrooms with consistent literacy-based ELD are outperforming the emergent bilingual students in other program types (e.g., see Sparrow & Escamilla, 2012).

As implemented in Literacy Squared, literacy-based ELD, like Spanish literacy, has specific minimum time allocations in the daily language arts schedule and it should not be substituted with the sheltered English instruction typically done in other content areas. Table 3.1 lists the typical allocation of time in the literacy schedule suggested for each type of teaching approach within Spanish literacy and literacy-based ELD for every grade level. In practice, the use of these teaching approaches varies, depending on the language environment, grade level, and the students' language and literacy needs. For instance, we recommend that Lotta Lara be implemented only in grades 1 to 3 in Spanish literacy but used through grade 5 in literacy-based ELD.

While acknowledging the importance of using sheltered English teaching techniques in the content areas, research has concluded that it is insufficient for teaching literacy and language arts to emerging bilingual children (Gersten & Baker, 2000; Saunders, Foorman, & Carlson, 2006). Therefore, the use of direct instruction for the teaching of English literacy to emerging bilingual children is warranted.

In literacy-based ELD, metalinguistic awareness and oracy are prominently emphasized to promote reading comprehension and ensure that students make links between what they know about how to read and write in Spanish and English. Research shows that reading comprehension is a complex process and high-quality instruction in this aspect of reading is especially important for emerging bilingual children. Findings from the National Literacy Panel reveal that the performance of emerging bilingual students on word-level reading tasks (e.g., decoding, word recognition) is equal to that of native English speakers, but that they perform significantly lower when it comes to text-level skills, such as reading comprehension (Lesaux & Geva, 2006). Also, the Panel concluded that this disparity is because of students' lack of oral language proficiency in English. By contrast, high levels of oral language proficiency in English are associated with reading comprehension. Based on these findings, the Panel made the following recommendation: "Extensive oral English development must be incorporated into successful literacy instruction" (August & Shanahan, 2006, p. 4).

**TABLE 3.1**

## Reading Instruction: Time Allocations and Grade Appropriate Teaching Approaches*

| Grade | Spanish Literacy | Literacy-based ELD |
|---|---|---|
| K | **2 hours (1 hour for ½ day kindergarten)** <br> Interactive read aloud, shared reading, teacher-led small groups | **45 minutes (30 minutes for ½ day kindergarten)** <br> Interactive read aloud, shared reading |
| 1 | **2 hours** <br> Interactive read aloud, shared reading, Lotta Lara, teacher-led small groups, collaborative reading, independent reading | **60 minutes** <br> Interactive read aloud, shared reading, Lotta Lara, collaborative reading |
| 2 | **90 minutes** <br> Interactive read aloud, shared reading, Lotta Lara, teacher-led small groups, collaborative reading, independent reading | **60 minutes** <br> Interactive read aloud, shared reading, Lotta Lara, collaborative reading |
| 3 | **60 minutes** <br> Interactive read aloud, shared reading, Lotta Lara, teacher-led small groups, collaborative reading, independent reading | **90 minutes** <br> Interactive read aloud, shared reading, Lotta Lara, teacher-led small groups, collaborative reading, independent reading |
| 4 | **45 minutes** <br> Interactive read aloud, shared reading, collaborative reading (literature, genre/author studies), independent reading | **2 hours** <br> Interactive read aloud, shared reading, Lotta Lara, teacher-led small groups, collaborative reading (literature, genre/author studies), independent reading |
| 5 | **45 minutes** <br> Interactive read aloud, shared reading, collaborative reading (literature, genre/author studies), independent reading | **2 hours** <br> Interactive read aloud, shared reading, Lotta Lara, teacher-led small groups, collaborative reading (literature, genre/author studies), independent reading |

*Time allocations refer to the entire biliteracy block of which reading is a part.

## Instructional Emphasis on Whole-Group Explicit and Interactive Teaching

Most reading instruction programs include a variety of teaching approaches to ensure that the needs of all students are met, and commonly include what is referred to as reading to children, reading with children, and having children read by themselves (Cappellini, 2005; Fountas & Pinnell, 1996; Mooney, 1990; Taberski, 2000). While we agree with these basic principles, we recommend biliteracy environments place greater emphasis on explicit and interactive teaching. Additionally, our research has indicated that students benefit from increased opportunity to interact directly with the teacher. If opportunities to become biliterate are to be maximized, teachers must consider the most efficient ways to plan focused and connected lessons that are balanced in approach and in the holistic biliteracy framework. Whole group instruction increases a teacher's ability to scaffold grade appropriate learning and to teach to students' potential rather than limiting them by continual grouping and regrouping around a perceived language or literacy level.

The goal is to move students toward independent practice while ensuring that they are receiving the support they need. This is accomplished by slowly removing teacher support as students acquire targeted knowledge and skills, which is known as **gradual release of responsibility** (Dutro & Kinsella, 2010; Fisher, Rothenberg, & Frey, 2007; Pearson & Gallagher, 1983).

Gradual release of responsibility, as applied within Literacy Squared, is a model of explicit and interactive instruction where the teacher initially provides extensive scaffolding, primarily through whole groups and shared literacy and language opportunities. Gradually the teacher removes the scaffolds, providing increased opportunities for students to read and write text, develop oracy, and apply metalinguistic analyses.

At the beginning of a biliteracy unit (see Chapters 9 and 10 for examples) strong modeling with vivid examples related to students' lives is critical. We suggest that the teacher model to the whole group and that the students have the opportunity to begin to practice new skills or apply concepts in the context of meaningful reading activities while receiving appropriate guidance from the teacher (shared approach). The teacher may then structure additional opportunities for practice among peers (collaborative approach). While there is less direct modeling from the teacher, it is still important that he or she monitors students' application of skills and strategies and provide feedback. Once confident that the students have acquired the targeted language and literacy objectives, teachers may increase opportunities for focused collaborative or independent work. It is important to emphasize that teacher modeling alone is not enough; instruction must progress from modeled, to shared, to collaborative, to independent. **Teacher-led small groups** are recommended only when students indicate a need for additional guidance from the teacher to meet the identified literacy objectives

Note that in Literacy Squared, we have modified the typical mix of approaches to literacy instruction in order to ensure that they are culturally and linguistically responsive to the strengths and needs of emerging bilingual children. Table 3.2 shows how we define these different approaches. More specifically, within each instructional approach oracy, comprehension and metalinguistic awareness are placed at the center of instruction. They are not taught separately as a discrete skill; rather, they are interwoven throughout the reading lessons. In each reading approach, texts are carefully selected based on their relevance to students' interests, language and literacy proficiency, and instructional goals (content and language objectives).

### Maximizing Whole Group Instruction

In Literacy Squared, the majority of the reading instruction is dedicated to teaching in a large group setting through **interactive read aloud**, **shared reading**, and **collaborative reading**. In contrast, independent practice, which occurs during teacher-led small groups and **independent reading**, is de-emphasized. The reason for this is that whole group instruction maximizes opportunities for explicit teaching and interaction between teacher and students, which in turn improves students' biliteracy development. Our recommendation for maximizing whole group instruction is supported by data from the second

**TABLE 3.2**

## Reading Instruction: Teaching Approaches for Reading

| Spanish Literacy | Teaching/Learning Approaches | Literacy-based ELD |
|---|---|---|
| Teacher reads aloud for children modeling the enjoyment, purpose, and process. The text and/or message is one that most of the children cannot read instructionally or independently. | **Interactive Read Aloud\*** Teachers read *for* children to model fluent reading and promote enjoyment of reading. Teachers promote active student engagement in structured dialogues about the text. Teachers model metalinguistic cross-language connections. Model language structures, new vocabulary, and text-based dialogues. | Teacher chooses a text in English that can be made meaningful. The text is one the children have already read in Spanish, one in which the pictures can carry the meaning, or one for which teachers can use realia, gestures, or other types of comprehensible input to make the text understandable. Children may respond to text in Spanish. There is value in repeated text readings. Patterned text with useful language structures and vocabulary should be considered in text choice. Shorter texts may be more effective. |
| Teacher reads with children, inviting them to join in and try out strategies by themselves with teacher support. Texts should be chosen so that children will come to control them through repeated readings and written experiences. Focus on developing decoding and comprehension skills. | **Shared\*** Teachers read *for* and *with* children to scaffold literacy tasks. Teachers engage children in structured dialogues to extend understanding of texts and to enrich oral and written language repertoire. Teachers engage children in articulating cross-language connections. | In addition to the skills and strategies developed in Spanish literacy, the focus is on developing oracy and comprehension in English, with less emphasis on decoding. Focus on language structures, vocabulary expansion, and dialogue. Explicit cross-cultural dialogue in text analysis. |
| Children read with peers. Teacher creates opportunities and monitors children's interaction with text and other children. | **Collaborative\*** Teacher structures additional opportunities for reading and oracy with peers. | In addition to the structure established in Spanish literacy, the focus is on oracy and comprehension in English. Oral rehearsal and language negotiation are fundamental to the reading task. |
| Grouping can be based on students' background knowledge or area of interest. Children can read, write, speak, and listen across a range of levels related to a common theme. Teacher can provide multiple opportunities with one text rather than reading one text per day. | **Teacher-led Small Groups** Teacher addresses the specific skill needs and interests of children in small heterogeneous groups | Children's placement is based on levels of Spanish reading for the purposes of focusing on cross-language transfer and oracy development. Grouping can also be done based on background knowledge or area of interest. Children can read, write, speak, and listen across a range of levels related to a common theme. Teacher can provide multiple opportunities with one text rather than reading one text per day. |
| Children read by themselves. Teacher needs to provide opportunities to read a variety of texts and genres. | **Independent** Sustained and expanded opportunities to read and apply comprehension strategies and literacy skills. | Children read by themselves. Teachers need to provide opportunities and encouragement to read a variety of English as well as Spanish texts. |

\*The emphasis of the Literacy Squared instruction is on interactive read aloud, shared reading, and collaborative reading.

phase of the Literacy Squared research project. These data indicate that a significantly larger number of students in classrooms with high levels of implementation are reaching the grade-level benchmark biliterate reading zones across grades (see Chapter 6 for a more detailed description). Because a central aspect of fidelity implementation of the Literacy Squared instructional components requires whole group instruction, we posit that this type of instruction is critical in ensuring that students' reading achievement in both languages is within benchmark levels. Variability in students' reading levels has decreased significantly because of the emphasis on whole group work. Thus, providing differentiated instruction in a small group setting is no longer warranted for the entire student population. Only students who have not reached appropriate benchmark levels in at least one language would benefit from teacher-led small group instruction.

## Minimizing Independent Practice

One hallmark of the Literacy Squared grade-appropriate instructional approaches (see Table 1.4) is its emphasis on increasing opportunities to use and apply language. Children working in isolation have limited opportunities to engage with others to acquire language and literacy. Thus, we recommend less emphasis on independent work. This is an important paradigm shift from traditional literacy programs for emerging bilingual children. Because of the need to differentiate instruction to meet the needs of individual students, many teachers spend much of the reading instruction time meeting with students in small groups and constantly regrouping them as they gain proficiency in targeted literacy skills. During the time when the teacher meets with some students in their small groups, the rest of the children are expected to work independently. As a result, the opportunity for children to receive explicit instruction and interact with the teacher is minimized.

In short, Literacy Squared emphasizes modeled, shared, and collaborative instructional approaches to reading in both language environments across elementary grades. Teacher-led small groups are included in grades K–3 in Spanish and grades 3–5 in English. As previously noted, however, teacher-led small groups are recommended only for those students whose reading levels are not yet within the grade-level biliterate reading zones. Independent reading is incorporated from grades 1–5 in Spanish and from grades 3–5 in English. Let's now look at some of the recommended teaching approaches for reading within Spanish literacy and literacy-based ELD instruction and compare and contrast differences and similarities.

## Teaching Approaches to Develop Biliterate Reading

In Literacy Squared, Spanish literacy instruction provides the foundation for biliteracy development. The skills and knowledge that students develop in Spanish become the foundation from which literacy-based ELD instruction can be structured. Yet, because biliteracy is developed through paired literacy instruction, careful attention is given to the connection between both language environments. This interconnectedness is made explicit to students through the development of metalanguage. In other words, students are taught how to access their knowledge of Spanish when engaging in literacy activities in English and vice versa. (See Chapter 5 for an in-depth discussion of how to develop metalanguage within each language environment.)

The reading approaches suggested for Spanish literacy instruction and literacy-based ELD include the following analytic approaches: interactive read aloud, shared reading, Lotta Lara, collaborative reading, teacher-led small groups, and independent reading. While these approaches are taught similarly across the two languages, in English there is a greater need to scaffold and to pause frequently to check for comprehension. Synthetic approaches, on the other hand, are language specific and are distinct between Spanish and English. As indicated in Table 3.1, Literacy Squared recommends emphasizing interactive read aloud, shared reading, Lotta Lara, and teacher-led small groups in the early and intermediate elementary grades and that in the upper grades, literature and genre/author studies be included as part of collaborative reading. Lotta Lara and teacher-led small groups are discontinued from Spanish literacy instruction in the upper grades; however, they are maintained in literacy-based ELD.

## Interactive Read Aloud

In this reading approach, the teacher reads aloud *for* children, thus modeling the reading process and comprehension strategies while also directing students' attention to cross-language connections. Literacy Squared recommends implementing interactive read aloud in a large group setting, in both languages, from grades K–5. We use the term "interactive read aloud" rather than "modeled reading" to emphasize the importance of active student engagement in conversations about the text in order to support both literacy skills and oral language development. Without explicit attention to oracy to support comprehension and metalinguistic awareness to understand the relationships across languages, using reading aloud in English with emerging bilingual children may not have the intended benefits (O'Day, 2009).

Interactive read aloud can be used as part of Lotta Lara (see Chapter 2) before engaging the whole group in repeated readings. This helps focus on meaning making prior to fluency instruction. When used by itself, interactive read aloud is an effective method to foster children's enjoyment of reading and allows them to observe the reading processes as demonstrated by an expert reader (the teacher). Through interactive read aloud the teacher also demonstrates comprehension strategies and the language necessary to engage in conversations about the text (i.e., language structures, vocabulary, and text-based dialogue). The teacher reads aloud a text to the children that they may not be able to read on their own, thus providing an opportunity for the entire class to experience one grade-appropriate text. The teacher's careful scaffolding is essential for ensuring children's comprehension of the text.

Interactive read aloud is also a great way to share with children a variety of literature genres and topics as a way to help them build background knowledge prior to having them read a text by themselves. Texts used during read aloud should be culturally and personally relevant so that children can see themselves reflected in the themes, situations, or dilemmas presented in the book, and learn more about themselves or their peers.

It is important to emphasize that exposing children to authentic and culturally relevant literature is not enough to help them be aware of the features of different genres. Thus, it is recommended that the teacher talks explicitly to children about text features and helps distinguish them.

We now describe the steps involved in implementing interactive read aloud and compare and contrast how this procedure varies from Spanish literacy to literacy-based ELD.

**Select a Text.** Picture books (fiction) and informational texts with illustrations are wonderful for interactive read aloud. The visual representation of concepts is an excellent support for understanding the content, acquiring vocabulary, and building background knowledge. We recommend the use of books in Spanish and English that have rich and authentic language. Fiction books should have an engaging plot and lively characters. Particular modifications for text selection during literacy-based ELD include ensuring that they are meaningful and connected to the Spanish language literacy environment. Bilingual books are one way, but not the only way, to connect environments. Connections can also be made through a new text whose theme, genre, or author is the same as in the text(s) being read in the Spanish literacy environment. Shorter texts may allow for more in-depth discussion and analysis.

**Preread and Plan Oracy Objectives.** The preparation for interactive read aloud sessions includes reading the text to identify vocabulary, phrases, and concepts to teach students. Developing questions and language structures to engage students in dialogue before, during, and after the read aloud to support their comprehension of the text is also necessary. When planning the oracy objectives remember that they should correspond to the literacy objectives. Also, when appropriate, plan for the explicit teaching of metalinguistic cross-language connections (e.g., identifying cognate pairs for book parts such as *autor/* author, *título*/title/, *ilustrador*/illustrator). Oracy objectives typically differ across language environments.

**Conduct the Interactive Read Aloud**

1. *Introduce the text and activate prior knowledge.* Tell the students what the text is about and encourage them to draw on their prior knowledge and experiences to make personal connections to the topic. In literacy-based ELD, the students may need to use Spanish to demonstrate their prior knowledge. It is critically important to make explicit how what the students have learned in one environment helps them with the other.

2. *Establish a purpose for reading.* Indicate what the specific purpose for reading is that day and what they are expected to do during and after the reading.

3. *Do a picture walk.* Show students the illustrations. Ask them to share what they see and to predict what might happen. Use the pictures to teach the key concepts, vocabulary, and language structures they will need to understand the story. These should be different in Spanish and literacy-based ELD. For example, while reading about farms and farm animals one might be able to assume that young students could distinguish between *gallos* (roosters), *gallinas* (hens), and *pollitos* (chicks) without extensive scaffolding. In English, however, it is not unusual for emerging bilingual students to refer to all three as "chickens." It is incumbent upon the teacher to seize the opportunity to extend and refine vocabulary.

4. *Read the text aloud.* Read the text aloud with fluency, inflection and intonation, making the story come alive for students. This will give students the opportunity to hear the rhythm and intonation of an expert reader. The first reading of the text should be for pure enjoyment. Avoid excessive interruptions and allow students to simply enjoy the story in Spanish language literacy; however, a modification in Literacy-based ELD is to pause more frequently to discuss the content. Subsequent readings may include the use of comprehension strategies. Table 3.3 contains examples of prompts for language development to support reading comprehension.

5. *Respond to the text.* In subsequent read alouds, engage the students cognitively, linguistically, affectively, and/or physically through dialogue and, when appropriate, through writing. Encourage discussion by including not only questions whose answer can be found directly in the text, but also open-ended questions that do not have right or wrong answers (see Table 2.4 for examples of verbs to elicit dialogue and open-ended questions). Model for students how to construct questions and to respond using complete sentences. Scaffold language use by teaching key vocabulary and language structures that can help students to participate meaningfully in the dialogue. Help them use language for different functions, according to the literacy objectives (e.g., debate, clarify, interpret, respond, persuade). Ensure that all students have multiple opportunities to rehearse and use meaningfully the selected language structures and vocabulary as they participate in the dialogue. Use writing as a reading response, either in preparation for students' participation in conversations about the text or after those conversations.

## Shared Reading

In shared reading, the teacher reads *for* and *with* the children. In Literacy Squared, we suggest that this reading approach be implemented in a large group setting. In Spanish literacy and literacy-based ELD, shared reading is used in all grade levels (see Table 3.1), with oracy instruction as a core component. In contrast to interactive read aloud, shared reading calls for more direct student involvement in the actual reading of the text. It gives children the opportunity to listen to and watch the teacher read, as well as to participate in reading a text or parts of a text when they feel comfortable. Teachers engage children in guided dialogue to extend their understanding of texts and enrich their oral language repertoire while also encouraging students to articulate (not only observe) cross-language connections. With more advanced readers, shared reading can be helpful in exposing students to a new genre, directing their attention to more sophisticated language forms or literary elements (e.g., similes, metaphors, idiomatic expressions), and directly explaining and demonstrating that aspect of language or text in context. Shared reading can also be helpful when conducting book studies (literary, genre, or author studies) with advanced readers to facilitate whole group discussions about particularly challenging or complex topics.

A unique feature of shared reading within Literacy Squared is that children are encouraged to try out comprehension strategies and literacy skills with teacher support in the context of whole group instruction, instead of being expected to "absorb" these strategies and skills and later apply them independently during teacher-led small groups or independent reading. The idea of offering whole group support for the development of comprehension strategies and literacy skills contrasts with the common practice of providing

**TABLE 3.3**

## Comprehension Strategies and Prompts for Language Support

| Comprehension Strategies | Language Structures Prompts |
| --- | --- |
| Activating background knowledge | • *¿Qué sé acerca de . . . /Yo sé que . . .* /What do I know about. . . ? I know that . . .<br>• *¿Qué he visto o escuchado que me recuerda a . . . Yo he escuchado o visto que . . .* /What have I seen or heard that reminds me of . . .? I have seen . . .<br>• *¿A qué me recuerda este libro? Este libro me recuerda a. . .* /What does this book remind me of? This book reminds me of. . . |
| Making predictions | • *¿Me pregunto qué pasará cuando . . . ? Pienso que . . .va a suceder/*I wonder what is going to happen when. . .? I think that. . . will happen<br>• *Yo predigo que . . .* /I predict that. . .<br>• *Mi predicción es que. . .* /My prediction is that. . .<br>• *Yo creo que. . . porque. . .* /I think that. . . because. . . |
| Making inferences | • *¿Qué pienso que va a suceder cuando. . .? Yo pienso que . . . porque . . .* /Why do I think that . . . will happen? I think that. . .. will happen because. . .<br>• *¿Qué me hace pensar que . . . sucederá? Pienso que. . . va a suceder porque. . .* /What makes me think that . . . will happen? I think that. . .. will happen because. . . |
| Making personal connections | • *¿A qué me recuerda este evento en el libro? Este evento me recuerda cuando. . .* /What does this event in the book remind me of? This event reminds me of. . .<br>• What would I do if I were. . . ? I would. . .<br>• *¿En qué estaba pensando cuando leí sobre. . .? Cuando leí sobre. . . estaba pensando que. . .* /What was I thinking when I read about. . .? When I read about. . . I was thinking that. . .<br>• *¿Cómo me sentí cuando. . .? Cuando. . . me sentí. . . porque. . .* /What was I feeling? I was feeling. . . |
| Making connections to other books | • *¿Este libro me recuerda a otro libro que he leído? Este libro me recuerda a . . . en que . . .* /Does this book remind me of another book I have read? How? This book reminds me of (title of book) in that. . .<br>• *¿En qué se parece el personaje principal de este cuento al personaje principal en. . .? Los personajes se parecen en que ambos. . .* /How is the main character in this story similar to the one in. . .? They are similar in that they both. . . |
| Figuring out the meaning of unfamiliar words | • *¿Los dibujos me pueden ayudar a entender el significado de esta palabra?/*Can the pictures help me figure out the meaning of unfamiliar words?<br>• *¿Hay pistas en el contexto que me puedan ayudar a entender el significado de esta palabra?/*Are there context clues that can help me understand what this word means?<br>• *¿Hay alguna palabra que conozco en el otro idioma que suena como y se ve como ésta palabra? ¿Es un cognado? ¿Sé lo que esa palabra significa?/*Is there a word I know in the other language that looks like and sounds like this one/Is this a cognate? Do I know what it means in the other language?<br>• *¿Hay una palabra más pequeña dentro de esta palabra? ¿Sé lo que esa palabra más pequeña significa? /*Is there a smaller word within this word? Do I know what this smaller word means? |
| Identifying the elements of the story in fiction books (characters, magical elements, setting, problem, resolution, moral) | *Personajes/*Characters<br>• *¿Quién es el personaje principal? El personaje principal es . . .* /Who is the main character? The main character is. . .<br>• *¿Quiénes son los personajes secundarios en la historia? Los personajes secundarios son. . .* /Who are the secondary characters? The secondary characters are. . .<br>*Escenario/*Setting<br>• *¿Dónde sucedió la historia? La historia sucedió en . . .. La historia se llevó a cabo en . . .* /Where did the story take place? The story took place in. . .<br>*Elementos mágicos/*Magical elements<br>• *¿Cuáles son los elementos mágicos en la historia? Los elementos mágicos en la historia son. . .* /What are the magical elements in the story? The magical elements in the story are. . .<br>*Problema/*Problem<br>• *¿Qué obstáculos o dificultades enfrentó . . . (personaje principal)? Las dificultades que . . . (personaje principal) enfrentó fueron que . . .* /What obstacles or problem did . . . (main character) find? The problem that (main character) found was that. . .<br>*Solución/*Resolution<br>• *¿Cómo resolvió el problema (personaje principal)? . . . resolvió el problema . . ..* /How did (main character) resolve the problem? (main character) resolved the problem by . . .<br>*Final/*Ending<br>• *¿Cómo termina la historia? ¿Qué pasó al final de la historia? La historia termina en que . . .* /What happened at the end of the story? At the end. . . or The story ends when. . .<br>*Moraleja/*Moral<br>• *¿Qué fue lo más importante que aprendí de esta historia? Lo más importante que aprendí de esta historia es que . . .* /What was the most important thing you learned about_____? Why? The most important thing I learned about . . . is that. . .<br>• *¿Cuál es la moraleja de la historia? La moraleja de la historia es que . . .* /What is the moral of the story? The moral of the story is that . . . |

literacy instruction in small groups, such as guided reading (e.g., see Cappellini, 2005; Fountas & Pinnell, 1996). Literacy-based ELD includes the promotion of oral language development in English by explicitly teaching text language that students may struggle with, such as unfamiliar vocabulary, words with multiple meanings, metaphors, idiomatic expressions, cohesive signals, prepositions, or grammatical structures. Opportunities to use these aspects of language in conversations about the texts are provided to students. Greater attention is given to comprehension than to decoding. The steps for the implementation of shared reading are identical to those for interactive read aloud, except as noted in the following sections.

**Select a Text.** Big books, enlarged texts, or chapter books with multiple copies are especially recommended for shared reading. Patterned-language books are wonderful for shared reading with young readers because the repetitive patterns in the book encourage them to read along. The text chosen should be slightly above most students' reading level. The goal is that through the appropriate selection of the text, students will be able to read along.

**Picture Walk.** In addition to the procedure discussed in the interactive read aloud section, the teacher selects key passages to rehearse orally with students during the book introduction.

**Read with the Students.** Require students to join in the reading aloud of the text. Provide repeated practice so children can start to appropriate text-based language. These are different ways one might engage students:

- Students read refrains or dialogue in the story
- Act out the story while reading
- Alternate groups (boys/girls or table groups)
- Read with different tones (loudly, softly, angrily)

Comprehension strategies during this step should focus on helping students monitor their understanding of the story line as well as clarifying any unfamiliar elements. Also, engage students in articulating cross-language connections. For example, compare story elements in the texts read in Spanish literacy and literacy-based ELD or identify similarities and differences in the use of punctuation across languages.

## Collaborative Reading

In this reading approach, the teacher creates opportunities for children to read *with peers* and monitors their work. Collaborative reading complements interactive read aloud and shared reading by providing extended time for students to interact among themselves with the purpose of supporting a deeper understanding of the text. There are no specific procedures for this reading approach; however, there are a few important considerations for its implementation.

We suggest that collaborative reading be a part of Spanish literacy and literacy-based ELD in grades 1–5. In the early and intermediate grades, collaborative reading can be an extension of whole group reading and discussion and its main purpose is to provide additional opportunities for reading comprehension and oracy practice with peers. Extension activities to deepen students' understanding of the text are organized in small, collaborative groups. Some examples include retelling or rewriting the story, drawing their favorite part, acting out the story, or writing a class book that can be used later during shared reading and independent reading. In the upper grades, this reading approach can take the format of literature, genre, or author studies. In these collaborative groups, the same text can be used for discussion in small groups or each group can have a different text that is related to the topic being studied.

Modifications that are important to consider for collaborative work during literacy-based ELD are teacher-designed structures to ensure that all students have equal opportunities to participate and to rehearse targeted oracy structures (e.g., a structure that indicates how reading alternates amongst group members). Students may also need procedural language supports that teach them to interact and negotiate (e.g., May I speak please? I'm sorry I interrupted you. I disagree because. . .).

## Teacher-led Small Groups

Teacher-led small groups offer the teacher the opportunity to address specific students' needs with regard to reading skills, comprehension strategies, and interests. The implementation of teacher-led small groups is recommended only in grades K–3 in Spanish literacy and grades 3–5 in literacy-based ELD. As stated earlier, teacher-led small groups should be used only when students need additional guidance from the teacher to meet the identified literacy objectives. A fundamental modification of this reading approach for its use in literacy-based ELD is that children's placement in teacher-led small groups is based on levels of Spanish reading for the purposes of focusing on cross-language transfer and oracy development in English.

When planning teacher-led small group instruction in English, it is important to take into account the biliterate reading zones explained in Chapter 6. Because Spanish literacy provides the foundation for English literacy development, teachers should use the biliterate reading zones (see Table 6.3) as a guide for forming groups and for choosing texts in English. It is crucial that teachers select these texts based on students' Spanish reading levels rather than on their English reading levels, which do not necessarily reflect their reading levels but, instead, measure their English language proficiency. Choosing texts in this way offers instructors the possibility of teaching to the students' potential. As in Spanish literacy instruction, the purpose of having multiple engagements with a text is to expand and refine oracy and reading comprehension development as well as to reinforce the application of cross-language strategies.

## Independent Reading

Independent reading is included in grades 1–5 in Spanish literacy and grades 3–5 in literacy-based ELD. Similar to collaborative reading, there is not a systematic one-size-fits-all procedure for this reading approach, but we provide a few suggestions for its implementation.

The main purpose of independent reading is to offer children opportunities to read self-selected materials by themselves, enjoy reading, and refine the application of comprehension strategies and literacy skills. It is important to offer students a wide variety of genres to choose from for their reading. Children can also use this time to practice reading the same books from interactive read aloud, shared reading, or collaborative reading.

Independent reading should only take a small portion of the language arts schedule. Greater emphasis is given to whole group instruction where the teacher scaffolds, through interactive and explicit teaching, children's participation and learning in the reading lessons. As explained earlier in this chapter, the purpose of following a gradual release of responsibility model is to provide children with the appropriate support and guided practice before expecting them to work independently. Independent reading is not limited to students reading to themselves silently. It can be promoted by having students read to a partner, younger students, or family members at home; audio taping books; and keeping a reading log.

# Conclusion

In this chapter we presented instructional approaches to develop biliterate reading, including interactive read aloud, shared reading, collaborative reading, teacher-led small groups, and independent reading. The use of these approaches in each language environment varies depending on grade level and the students' language and literacy needs. We have modified the typical implementation of these approaches to ensure that they are culturally and linguistically responsive to the strengths and needs of emerging bilingual children. They all place oracy, reading comprehension, and metalinguistic awareness at the center of instruction.

The reading approaches outlined here are based on the use of "best practice" principles that are specific and authentic to each language. To see examples of kindergarten and grade 5 units that integrate not only all of these approaches but also all of the elements of the holistic biliteracy framework, see chapters 9 and 10. In our holistic biliteracy framework, the skills and knowledge that students develop in Spanish become the foundation for structuring literacy-based ELD instruction. In order to make biliteracy instruction more efficient and relevant to students, and to avoid redundancy, the two language environments are carefully connected. This connection is made explicit to students through the development of metalanguage.

We emphasized that reading instruction must progress from modeling in a whole group setting, to shared and collaborative practice, to independent practice. Organizing instruction according to this gradual release of responsibility model ensures that appropriate supports are in place before students are released to work independently. Also, our research findings from the past three years provide the basis for prioritizing whole group instruction over reading instruction in small groups. We believe that children's biliterate reading development can be accelerated by engaging them in whole-group explicit and interactive teaching and learning activities that connect the two language environments and integrate oracy, reading, writing, and metalanguage.

## Questions for Reflection and Action

- Are the reading approaches described in this chapter similar to ones used in your school? How are they different?
- What would your literacy block schedule look like with the integration of the reading approaches recommended by Literacy Squared for Spanish literacy instruction?
- How might you begin to modify reading instruction in English to address the strengths and needs of emerging bilingual students in your classroom?

# Writing

*Children think about writing, and their thinking demonstrates interest, coherence, value, and extraordinary educational potential. We've got to listen to them. We've got to see the child as a person who thinks and attempts to incorporate into his or her own knowledge this marvelous medium of representing and recreating language which is writing, all writing.*

Emilia Ferreiro, 2003, p. 34

## Key Terms

Approximations

Biliterate writing

Collaborative writing

Independent writing

Modeled writing

Shared writing

theDictado*

## Guiding Questions

■ Why should increased emphasis be placed on writing in the teaching of emerging bilingual learners?

■ Why should explicit and direct approaches to teaching writing be emphasized?

■ How does theDictado method enable a teacher to more efficiently teach skills within and across languages?

Unlike the research on oracy and reading with emerging bilingual students (see Chapters 2 and 3), research exploring **biliterate writing** using bilingual assessments or instruments is almost nonexistent. The need for more research in this area has been identified as one of the field's most pressing needs (August & Shanahan, 2006). Through its specific and focused attention on the development of writing in Spanish and English and the creation of a writing rubric to better understand students' trajectories toward biliteracy in writing, the Literacy Squared instructional framework and research is helping to address this gap (e.g., see Escamilla & Hopewell, 2010; Soltero-González, Escamilla, & Hopewell, 2010, 2011; Sparrow, Butvilofsky, & Escamilla, 2011; Sparrow, Butvilofsky, Wiley, & Escamilla, 2012).

The small body of existing research has found that bilingual students' writing develops in ways that are different than those of their monolingual English-speaking peers (Escamilla & Coady, 2001; Escamilla, 2006). For instance, code-switching (the alternating use of two languages) and interliteracy (the temporary application of linguistic elements from one language to the other when writing) are patterns of writing unique to bilingual individuals (Gort, 2006). Research has also shown that bilingual students' writing abilities in each language develop at different rates (Gort, 2006; Sparrow et al., 2012). This

---

*We invented the term "theDictado" to reflect the bilingual focus of this method in Literacy Squared.

variability across languages and between monolingual and bilingual students reflects a need to better understand biliterate writing development. Escamilla (2006) proposes educating teachers to understand second language writing development as typical. That is, the writing behaviors of emerging bilingual students should be seen as normal because they are inherent to the process of learning to write in two languages.

As we have described, writing instruction is a cornerstone in the Literacy Squared holistic biliteracy framework (see Fig. 1.2)—as important as attention to oracy, reading, and metalanguage for the development of biliteracy. This chapter describes the instructional approaches recommended for the development of biliterate writing. See Chapters 9 and 10 for examples of units that integrate not only all of these approaches, but also all of the elements of the holistic biliteracy framework.

Biliterate writing is an integral part of paired literacy and is closely associated with the reading and oracy objectives. Within Literacy Squared, biliterate writing instruction in K–5 bilingual classrooms includes the interactive and explicit teaching of a variety of writing skills and strategies, such as writing a variety of text types (opinion pieces, informative/ explanatory texts, narrative texts), participating in collaborative research and writing projects, and developing and publishing written products with guidance from adults and in collaboration with peers. Children are taught how to apply these skills and strategies across languages and to see similarities as well as language-specific differences. Each of these is compatible with the Common Core State Standards and in fact moves beyond the Common Core in their emphasis on biliteracy.

## Writing and Literacy Instruction for Emerging Bilinguals: What the Research Says

Because there is a dearth of research on the development of emerging bilingual learners' biliterate writing, we turn to authors whose work is centered on monolingual English speakers. In many ways, however, this work reflects what we've learned about authentic and connected literacy through our examination of the Mexican National Curriculum. One such author is Michael Schmoker who supports the integration of writing instruction with reading, oral language, and metalanguage for the literacy development of all students. Schmoker (2011) highlights the importance of connecting all four areas of instruction to maximize English literacy development. He suggests, and we agree, that all reading include a variety of genres and that writing be directly connected to reading.

With regard to writing, Schmoker suggests that starting in grade 2 students write at least nine papers a year that are directly connected with their reading. Some could be short research papers with a number of outside sources. These papers should be approximately one and a half to three handwritten pages long in the early grades and longer typewritten pages for older students. In addition, this writing should culminate in one or two oral presentations per semester. Another way to connect writing to reading is to do book studies in which students have the opportunity to summarize, argue, or respond to a question about the book.

Support for directly connecting oracy, reading, writing, and metalanguage is also replete in the Mexican national literacy program, *Programa Nacional para el Fortalecimiento de la Lectura y la Escritura Básica* (*PRONALEES*, 2002). In this program, students also read grade level materials in Spanish and there are specific writing activities connected to children's stories. Writing activities include response to literature, writing text summaries, writing around different genres and themes (e.g., biographies, poems), writing for different audiences, learning to take notes, and writing for different mediums (e.g., for newspapers, radio or television). Another key feature in *PRONALEES* is the notion that reading and writing are not only interconnected, but also that writing leads to reading development. Thus, children are taught to read by teaching them to write (Ferreiro, 2002).

An example of a teaching method used in Mexico and other Latin American countries where writing and reading go hand-in-hand is called the Dictado. This is a method used for teaching students writing conventions, reading fluency, spelling, grammar, and other features of language arts in an integrated way. TheDictado method has been adapted for use in Literacy Squared in both Spanish literacy and literacy-based ELD (Escamilla, Geisler,

Hopewell, Sparrow, & Butvilofsky, 2009) and its classroom implementation is elaborated later in this chapter.

# Instructional Emphasis on Whole-Group Explicit and Interactive Teaching

The teaching approaches in the Literacy Squared framework for writing instruction parallel those for reading (see Chapter 3), with the exception of teacher-led small groups. As with the teaching of reading, the emphasis given to each writing approach (modeled, shared, collaborative, and independent) in Spanish literacy and literacy-based ELD is different, and it changes depending on the grade levels and the time allotment for each language environment. Table 4.1 provides a comprehensive view of the distribution of teaching approaches across language environments and grade levels. Overall, a greater emphasis is given to **shared writing** and **collaborative writing** than to **independent writing**.

## Maximizing Whole Group Instruction

Dominant instructional practices favor workshop approaches in which students work independently. While very little research exists to inform writing instruction in biliteracy contexts, we do know that writing process approaches, when implemented alone, are insufficient to help emerging bilingual children develop robust biliterate writing repertoires (Genesee & Riches, 2006; Reyes, 1991, 1992). When students spend a lot of time without the aid of a more competent writer, as in a writing workshop, they may not be working in the upper range of their potential (Butvilofsky, 2010). Thus, while recognizing the value of independent writing activities, the Literacy Squared instructional framework recommends using explicit teaching and interactive strategies instead of a process approach.

Modeled, shared, and collaborative writing within Literacy Squared are whole group instructional approaches that include both explicit and interactive teaching. Thus, they

**TABLE 4.1**

**Writing Instruction: Language Time Allocations and Grade Appropriate Teaching Approaches***

| Grade | Spanish Literacy | Literacy-based ESL |
|---|---|---|
| K | **2 hours (1 hour for ½ day kindergarten)** <br> Modeled writing, shared writing, collaborative writing, independent writing <br> Spanish Dictado (Jan.) | **45 minutes (30 minutes for ½ day kindergarten)** <br> Modeled writing, shared writing |
| 1 | **2 hours** <br> Modeled writing, shared writing, collaborative writing, independent writing <br> Spanish Dictado | **60 minutes** <br> Modeled writing, shared writing, collaborative writing <br> English Dictado |
| 2 | **90 minutes** <br> Modeled writing, shared writing, collaborative writing, independent writing <br> Spanish Dictado | **60 minutes** <br> Modeled writing, shared writing, collaborative writing <br> English Dictado |
| 3 | **60 minutes** <br> Modeled writing, shared writing, collaborative writing, independent writing <br> Spanish Dictado | **90 minutes** <br> Modeled writing, shared writing, collaborative writing, independent writing <br> English Dictado |
| 4 | **45 minutes** <br> Modeled writing, shared writing, collaborative writing, independent writing <br> Spanish Dictado | **2 hours** <br> Modeled writing, shared writing, collaborative writing, independent writing <br> English Dictado |
| 5 | **45 minutes** <br> Modeled writing, shared writing, collaborative writing, independent writing <br> Spanish Dictado | **2 hours** <br> Modeled writing, shared writing, collaborative writing, independent writing <br> English Dictado |

*Time allocations refer to the entire biliteracy block of which writing is a part.

allow teachers to demonstrate explicitly the skills and knowledge about language use involved in both the writing process and the development of a written product. Interaction between the teacher and the students and scaffolded participation in the composing of various types of texts are essential aspects of shared writing and collaborative writing. These teaching approaches provide opportunities for students to write routinely for a wide range of purposes and audiences and to participate in research and writing projects while receiving guidance and feedback from the teacher and peers. In addition, reading, writing, oracy, and metalanguage come together in a fluid and natural way.

## Connection to Oracy

As in the approaches for reading instruction, oracy is a central element of writing instruction within our holistic biliteracy framework. Oracy is embedded throughout the writing lessons, rather than being added on as a mini-lesson. It is very important that any writing activity builds on and expands children's oral language skills and background knowledge. Talking about their own experiences can be the basis for authentic and purposeful writing. It can help children to organize their ideas and to expand their oral language over time. As children's oral language skills increase and become more sophisticated, their ability to write should also improve.

## Teaching Approaches to Develop Biliterate Writing

The following approaches to writing instruction are recommended for the teaching of Spanish literacy and literacy-based ELD: modeled writing, shared writing, collaborative writing, and independent writing.

## Modeled Writing

In **modeled writing**, the teacher demonstrates for students the process of writing a text as well as the multiple uses of writing as a communicative and learning tool. It is recommended in all grade levels in both language environments and is an effective whole group instructional approach to support writing development. The main purpose of modeled writing is for all children in the classroom to experience the process of creating a written text as demonstrated by an expert writer.

In modeled writing, the teacher encodes the message in large print on a board (black or SMART) or chart paper that is visible to the whole class. In the early grades, modeled writing allows the teacher to show children the different functions of writing (e.g., to remember things, to communicate with others, to label and organize things, to demonstrate our learning), to direct children's attention to concepts about print (e.g., word separation, sound-letter relationships), and to demonstrate for them emergent literacy skills (e.g., capitalization, basic punctuation, spelling of high frequency words). The explicit attention to concepts about print and emergent literacy skills developed in Spanish literacy will provide the foundation for the development of emergent English literacy skills.

Modeled writing can be used in the early and intermediate grades to show children how to write a text that requires a new set of skills and knowledge or the refinement of skills that they already possess. For example, a grade 1 teacher who wants to elevate the use of basic linking words (e.g., "and," "then") when working on the retelling of a fiction book can teach students more sophisticated vocabulary and phraseology such as "after that," "also," or "when that happened." Oracy instruction takes center stage because meaningful dialogue in which students practice vocabulary and language structures enables them to appropriate the language they need to accomplish the writing task.

As students progress, modeled writing can be useful to teach explicitly more sophisticated aspects of writing such as an author's craft, cohesive signals, or the elements and features of various types of writing genres (e.g., opinion pieces, informative texts, narrative texts). It is important that teachers explicitly explain to children the new writing techniques and language required in the writing task, and that they provide children with examples through connected discourse.

What is unique to modeled writing in literacy-based ELD is that as the teacher models how to write the text (composing), she explicitly explains aspects of writing that are specific to English (e.g., rhetorical structures, grammar, the meaning of metaphors) and points out cross-language connections with regards to conventions, mechanics, and vocabulary (e.g., cognates). Spanish can be used strategically, for example, to clarify concepts, explain the activity, or point out similarities and differences across languages.

### Steps for Implementing Modeled Writing

1. *Activate background knowledge.* Decide the topic of the text or message that you will model. Engage children in conversation about their personal experiences or background knowledge related to that topic.

2. *Negotiate the text.* Set the purpose for writing and identify the audience. Discuss what you will write.

3. *Compose the text.* Allow children to practice vocabulary and sentence structures related to the selected text orally before you begin to model how to write. Write the children's ideas in large print on chart paper or on the board, making sure that it is visible to the whole class. With young writers, model the how and why of concepts about print and emergent literacy skills by thinking aloud as you write. By doing this you will also promote the development of metalanguage. As students progress, explicitly explain the writing skills being introduced and emphasize the language required in the writing task; provide children with examples through connected discourse.

4. *Revise and edit.* After you finish writing the text, have students read it with you, ensuring first that the message makes sense. Then, model how to revise the text, making sure that the message contains all the previously discussed ideas. Depending on the instructional purpose and audience, demonstrate how to edit the text by paying attention to genre formats, general conventions, style, mechanics, and spelling.

## Shared Writing

In shared writing, the teacher and students take turns writing to construct a text *together*. It is also implemented across grade levels in Spanish literacy and literacy-based ELD. Students actively participate in the negotiation and co-construction of the text, instead of only watching the teacher do it, as in modeled writing. This can be done by "sharing the pen" with students while the text is being constructed on chart paper or on the board (McCarrier, Pinnell, & Fountas, 2000, p. xv). To ensure the involvement of all the students in the writing of the text, everybody must be writing (copying from the board or encoding along with the teacher in their notebooks). Older students can write in their notebooks; younger students can use white boards and eventually, as their visual-motor skills develop, they can begin to use notebooks. The use of notebooks (*cuadernos* in Spanish) is a common practice in the teaching of reading and writing in Latin American classrooms. We recommend using *cuadernos* because they serve as a tool for learning how to write for formative assessment, and they allow the teacher and students to see their progress over time.

The main purpose of shared writing is to provide students with the opportunity to *apply* or *try out*, with teacher support, skills and knowledge about writing and the writing process that the teacher has previously taught and modeled for them. Several aspects are involved in the writing process, including the following:

- A clear purpose or reason for writing
- A sense of audience
- An understanding of different types of texts/genres (e.g., notes, stories, book responses, letters, poems, recipes, summaries, opinion pieces)
- Knowledge about the composing, revising and editing processes

Emerging bilingual children benefit from explicit instruction on those aspects of the writing process and identifying which of them are similar or different across languages.

Shared writing activities give further assistance to children in appropriating and practicing writing skills and knowledge before they are expected to apply them collaboratively or independently. For example, a grade 4 teacher who has been teaching about persuasive writing and has modeled for the students how to write this type of text can use shared writing to move students to the next stage in the gradual release of responsibility model (detailed in Chapter 3). By doing so, the teacher invites students to jointly construct a text, prompting them to apply the knowledge about the elements and features of persuasive texts while providing them the necessary support to be successful.

Shared writing in literacy-based ELD is similar to Spanish literacy. In both environments, the teacher should emphasize which aspects of writing are the same and different across languages. When needed, use explicit instruction to help children make cross-language connections. There are specific aspects of written English that emerging bilingual students need explicit instruction to acquire. These include vocabulary, phrasing, grammatical structures, connective words, text structure, and voice. Shared writing ensures that children are provided the support they need to acquire these higher-level writing skills in English. The steps for the implementation for shared writing are identical to those of modeled writing with the exception of those in the following list.

### Additional Steps for Implementing Shared Writing

1. *Negotiate the text.* Set the purpose for writing. Discuss with the children the function that the text will serve and identify the audience. Discuss with the students the message they want to write. Guide students to think about the organization of the ideas.

2. *Co-construct the text.* Introduce or reinforce the vocabulary and sentence structures necessary for the writing of the text. Point out the difference between oral dialogue and written text. Once the ideas for the text are discussed, write the text together with the children by "sharing the pen." Have the rest of the class write the text in individual notebooks. Make sure that all children have equal opportunities to make oral and written contributions during the construction of the text. Reinforce strategies for the development of ideas, writing fluency, and voice. When appropriate, help children make cross-language connections.

3. *Revise and edit.* During the revision and editing process, reread the text with students for the purpose of having students verify that they have composed the text correctly and that it makes sense. Invite students to revise the text and ensure that it conveys the message they want it to convey. Reread the piece of writing in entirety after finishing it; again ask the students to think about the clarity of the text, organization of ideas, syntax, and word choice. When appropriate, provide sufficient guided practice for the editing of the text, promoting the application of knowledge about genre conventions, mechanics, and spelling. If editing is needed, all students should participate in their individual notebooks.

4. *Extend learning.* Use the text produced through shared writing to extend children's reading, writing, and oral language skills. For example, you can write a class book (narrative or expository) together with your students and make it available for shared reading, independent reading, or paired reading. Shared texts can be illustrated and sent home so children can read them to their family members.

## Collaborative Writing

In collaborative writing, children write *with* their *peers* and the teacher monitors their work, providing further assistance as needed. It encourages greater student involvement in the actual encoding, revising, and editing processes. There are no suggested steps for its implementation; however, a few aspects are worth highlighting. Collaborative writing in Spanish literacy is recommended for all grade levels. It is included in literacy-based ELD in grades 1–5. It provides children with extended time to continue working on their writing task, but this time is in collaboration with a partner or in teams while still receiving teacher support. Working in small groups or in pairs encourages negotiation among children and extended language practice. You may notice that students code-switch as they negotiate what they will write. Allow children to do this, but ask that the final product be in the target language.

After working in small groups or with a partner, students report their work to the whole group. This is an important aspect of collaborative writing because it holds children accountable for their work, promotes oracy development, and provides additional opportunities to learn from others and to receive their feedback. Before releasing the students to work in a collaborative writing format, the previous stages of the gradual release continuum must be in place.

In the upper grades, collaborative writing can be used as an extension of literature, genre/author studies, and for publishing projects. Again, while students work in teams or in pairs, the expectation is that they share their work with the whole group.

## Independent Writing

Independent writing is an approach to writing instruction in which children write by themselves and are offered individual feedback through writing conferences. Although students independently compose and write their own texts, they can help each other. In Spanish literacy instruction, this approach is intended to be used in grades K–5. In literacy-based ELD, it is intended to be used in grades 3–5. Independent writing is not included in the early grades because the time allotment for literacy-based ELD is reduced (maximum one hour). Thus, the use of modeled writing, shared writing, and collaborative writing in a large group setting are preferable because teacher-child interactions are maximized.

The main purpose of independent writing is to provide a space for students to try out writing techniques and craft their own texts independently across a variety of genres. Opportunities for independent practice in writing should be provided after extensive modeled, shared, and collaborative practice. Activities to promote independent writing can include writing a book, letter exchanges with students in other classes, writing an autobiography, creating a summary report of a research study, or becoming e-pals with students across the globe.

## TheDictado

TheDictado is a writing method intended for use in both Spanish literacy and literacy-based ELD. Literacy Squared uses an adaptation of the Mexican approach. The method is used to refine language arts skills in both Spanish and English, as well as to teach content, spelling, conventions, and grammar in an integrated way. More importantly, it can be used to develop students' self-correction and metalanguage skills.

TheDictado involves having the teacher dictate a series of phrases or sentences to the students. The students and teacher then collaborate to create a corrected model of the focus text. Students amend their sentences using a two-color system to draw attention to errors. The same phrases or sentences are repeated throughout the week, giving students multiple opportunities to practice and learn the targeted content, conventions, grammar, and spelling.

TheDictado method is grounded in Vygotskian theories that posit that all learning is social. Learning is enhanced for children when they have opportunities to work within their zones of proximal development and with a more capable peer or adult (Vygotsky, 1978). Working with a more capable adult (e.g., a teacher) allows children to acquire new literacy skills and knowledge that they could not have gained working alone. TheDictado is a good method for addressing the needs of children in various zones of proximal development in that it uses explicit guidance and teaching to move students to higher levels of competence in reading, writing, metalanguage, and oracy.

The explicit instruction during theDictado lesson involves not just basic writing skills within each language (using correct spelling, conventions, and grammar) but also cross-language transfer (understanding which structures are transferred in writing from one language to the other). Support for the use of theDictado in teaching spelling, grammar, and conventions comes from the work of Genesee and Riches (2006), Gersten and Baker (2000), and Slavin and Cheung (2005). These research syntheses all conclude that direct and explicit instruction is a necessary component of effective literacy instruction for emerging bilingual learners.

Because emerging bilingual children draw on all of their bilingual competencies as they become biliterate, they naturally engage in cross-language or bidirectional transfer. That is, they actively apply what they know in one language when they are learning another. TheDictado is an explicit and direct method that helps children attend to the differences and similarities across languages. By explicitly teaching what does and does not transfer across languages, and by teaching for cross-language connections, teaching can become more efficient. Ultimately, using cross-language connections can improve children's writing skills in both Spanish literacy and literacy-based ELD. The success of this strategy depends on a metalinguistic discussion about language and conventions and the opportunities students are given to read and correct their passages (Saunders & Goldenberg, 1999; Saunders, O'Brien, Lennon, & McLean, 1998).

It may be easiest to explain what happens during theDictado by showing an example. Let's look at the following sentence written by a child in first grade:

De grils layk to plei wet dols

First, note the child's strengths in writing. She is writing what she knows: "The girls like to play with dolls." Next, we see that she started the sentence with a capital letter, indicating a nascent knowledge of conventions. Further, she has drawn on her knowledge of sound-symbol correspondence in Spanish to spell words in English.

A well-chosen Dictado with explicit and direct guidance from the teacher can help this child move from her current zone to one that shows more conventional writing. In this case, teaching that sentences start with a capital letter and end with a period will help with both English and Spanish conventions. The words "the," "girls," "play," and "with" are all high frequency words, and learning them will be useful in other writing and reading tasks. Also, spelling "De" instead of "The" shows that the consonant sound *th* may still be unfamiliar to the child (understandably so because it is not present in Spanish) or that the child is pronouncing the sound *th* as he or she would in Spanish (i.e., saying "de" instead of "the"). However, this shows that the child is able to map sounds to letters in Spanish and is applying this skill when writing in English. Teaching how to pronounce and graphically represent the sound *th* in words in English while contrasting it (visually and orally) to the sound *d* in Spanish (e.g., them/dem, they/dey, Thursday/dursday) will be a useful cross-language connection that can be taught explicitly as part of theDictado lesson.

## Procedure for theDictado

TheDictado is intended for use at every grade level (K–5) in Spanish and grades 1–5 in literacy-based ELD instruction. By implementing theDictado across grade levels, teachers are using a common methodology that is culturally familiar to children and their parents. While theDictado is an important cross-language method, it is not meant to be the only writing instruction provided in the literacy environment. In fact, it is suggested that it should take no more than 15–20 minutes at a time, three to five times a week. In order not to exceed the suggested amount of time, it is important that the routine of theDictado, like all classroom practices, be made explicit to children so that it can be used to its full potential. If children do not master the routine before beginning the grade-appropriate teaching, the task will be frustrating; it will take much longer to complete; and the method will be less effective.

The following processes must be modeled and practiced until children are able to use them independently. The students will

- Listen to and repeat verbally short phrases (words at emergent level) in order to encode them on paper
- Cross-check information produced on the board to information produced on paper
- Identify **approximations**
- Use established marking code to identify and correct approximations

It is possible that some children will not always identify all of their approximations, or make standard corrections to them. It is important, however, that the expectations be made explicit and that all children be held to the highest expectations possible. The more standardized theDictado is within the school, the easier it will be for students to continue learning from this method because they will be familiar with the routine from past years.

*Suggestions for Implementing theDictado across Grades*

1. We recommend that teachers do a minimum of 15 Dictados in Spanish and 15 Dictados in English over the course of the school year. TheDictados should alternate: one week in Spanish, one week in English.
2. The development and use of a standard marking code that is the same for the entire school is recommended. (See Boxes 4.1 and 4.2 for an example in each language).
3. A notebook or composition book should be dedicated to theDictado for each student. We recommend the use of composition books for their durability.
4. Students should include the title and date of each Dictado every time it is given. Titles and dates should reflect the language of theDictado.

    Date:　9/18/13 or September 18, 2013
    Title:　The Doll (Capitalization differs by language)

    Fecha:　18/9/13 o 18 *de septiembre del* 2013
    Título: *La mariposa* (Only 1st letter capitalized)

5. Children skip lines between text to allow space for self-correction.
6. A new page should be used for each Dictado.
7. The same Dictado should be done at least three times in a week.
8. The main teaching points should be about language arts and metalanguage. The teacher should talk through these points and make the students correct these areas as necessary. Using Dictados to reinforce content teaching is fine, but content is secondary to language arts.

**Weekly Procedure for theDictado.** The weekly routine for theDictado is detailed in Table 4.2, and a checklist to guide its implementation is provided in Box 4.3. The teacher creates or selects a Dictado to be given over the course of a week. It is important to note that the Spanish and English Dictados are not the same, though they can cover a similar topic or skill, so that the teacher can point out the similarities or differences between the two languages. What students know and control in one language may or may not be different from what they know and control in the other. However, every attempt must be made to address students' developmental linguistic needs and to highlight and make explicit

| BOX 4.1  *Marcas de correccíon* | |
|---|---|
| Había<br>　había una vez . . . | Para corregir mayúsculas |
| Había<br>~~abia~~ | Para corregir palabras mal escritas |
| 　　una<br>Tenía ∧ pelota | Para agregar una palabra |
| 　　　　　parque ⊙<br>La niña está en el parque | Para agregar puntuación |
| conmigo<br>con migo | Para unir palabras |
| Había una vez<br>Había\|una\|vez | Para separar palabras |
| ¶ Había una vez una viejita que no le tenía<br>　miedo a nada . . . | Para separar párrafos |

## BOX 4.2 Standard Marking Code

| | |
|---|---|
| Once<br>  <u>once</u> upon a time . . .<br>  (double underline under "once") | To capitalize letters |
| Once<br>~~onse~~ | To correct spelling |
|          a<br>I had ∧ ball. | To insert words |
|               park ⊙<br>The girl is in the <u>park</u> | To add punctuation |
| homework<br>home‿work | To put a word together |
| Once upon a<br>Once\|upon\|a time | To separate words |
| ¶ Once upon a time there was a little old<br>   lady who wasn't afraid of . . . | To indent paragraphs |

## TABLE 4.2

## TheDictado: Weekly Procedures

| Day | Procedures |
|---|---|
| **1 TheDictado** | • The teacher reads through theDictado at a normal rate, with normal expression, so that students understand the meaning of the text to be written.<br>• The teacher repeats theDictado and, together with the children, counts the number of words (at emerging levels) or the number of sentences in theDictado (done as needed).<br>• The teacher tells the children to get ready to write, using a pencil or blue/black pen, remembering to skip lines.<br>• The teacher may begin by saying: "first word or first sentence." The teacher proceeds through the first sentence, saying it word by word for emerging writers, or phrase by phrase for transitional and fluent writers. Have students repeat the phrase/sentence before encoding. At the end of the first sentence, the teacher may say, "end of sentence," and so on (as needed).<br>• Teacher repeats phrase/sentence a minimum amount of times.<br>• When students finish writing the entire message, the teacher and students read it. At this point students can make any corrections to their writing. |
| **1 Talk-through** | • The children change their pencils for red pencils/pens.<br>• The teacher and the children *talk through* theDictado linguistically, grammatically, and metalinguistically in an *interactive and explicit manner*.<br>• *The teacher slowly constructs the standard version of theDictado on the board*, asking children to contribute to the construction of the correct model.<br>• The students *self-correct their own papers* with a red pencil, and *they do not erase*. (They *should not* check off correct words or letters either.)<br>• The teacher needs to be walking around, ensuring that the students are self-correcting and using the correct notations. |
| **2** | • Students dictate in pairs (*not* teacher directed). Then, corrections are made and compared to day 1. (This is optional.) |
| **3** | • Teacher dictates message and students encode as in day 1.<br>• Like day 1, the teacher *reconstructs* the correct model of theDictado on the board and talks through it with the children.<br>• The teacher re-emphasizes the teaching points children need the most help with, as well as any additional issues noted in the children's writing.<br>• Students self-correct their own work and compare their errors to days 1 (and 2). |
| **4** | • Repeat day 2 (This is optional.) |
| **5** | • The teacher administers the final Dictado, collects students' work, and grades it. (Talk-through is unnecessary.) |

| BOX 4.3 *TheDictado Checklist* | |
|---|---|

Teacher _____ Grade _____ Date _____

| **Teacher** | **Students** |
|---|---|
| **Procedure: Giving theDictado** | |
| | Write date and title |
| Reads message for meaning | Understand message |
| Parses Dictado text into smaller chunks (phrase/sentence level) | Repeat message |
| | Record message |
| | Skip lines |
| Rereads entire message | Read with teacher, check writing, and make necessary edits |
| **Procedure: Talk-Through** | |
| Provides standard marking code | Use standard marking code |
| | Get correction pen/pencil |
| Constructs message on board (every time) | Follow along and make necessary corrections |
| Highlights specific teaching points | |
| Engages in dialogue about metalinguistic awareness | Engage in dialogue about metalinguistic awareness |
| TheDictado is 15–20 minutes | |
| Same Dictado three times a week | |
| Rereads entire message | Reread entire message |
| **Purposeful Dictados** | |
| Creates meaningful Dictados based on students' need in both languages | Self-correct |
| Incorporates 2–4 teaching points (always includes spelling and punctuation) | Are aware of teaching points |
| Holds students accountable (grades final Dictado) | Reflect on their progress over time |
| | Transfer learning to other contexts |
| Develops metalinguistic awareness across languages | Develop metalinguistic awareness |
| Makes explicit cross-language connections | |

cross-language connections. For example, if working on questions in Spanish it might be helpful also to have the English Dictado focus on question formation, so that the differences between the use of question marks in both languages can be made explicit.

Note that there are three essential parts to theDictado; however, the most critical aspect is the talk-through. The talk-through is when the teacher provides direct and explicit instruction regarding the teaching points, which include conventions, grammar, and spelling. Additionally, metalanguage is modeled and generated and students are helped to make cross-language connections. (See theDictado samples and their teaching points in Box 4.4). It is very important that teachers reconstruct the correct version of theDictado with the children every time it is given. Children are more apt to identify and correct their errors while the teacher talks through and writes theDictado. In other words, having theDictado prewritten in any form is not considered procedural or beneficial in teaching children the art of self-correction.

**Beginning Steps for Implementing theDictado in Kindergarten.** We recommend waiting until January to begin to use theDictado with kindergarten students. In the fall, students should engage in extensive shared writing experiences so that they become familiar with writing to communicate. Young students need to understand some basic concepts about

---

### BOX 4.4 *Sample Dictados*

**Grade level: 2**
**Context:** Biography/Autobiography Unit. Students were learning about Frida Kahlo in Spanish and literacy-based ESL.
**TheDictado title:** *Frida Kahlo*
**TheDictado**

*La vida de Frida Kahlo fue muy difícil. Sufrió mucho durante su niñez y juventud. Por medio de sus pinturas y arte, pudo expresar lo que sentía en su corazón.*

**Teaching points**
- Spelling: *palabras con acentos; difícil, niñez*
- Punctuation: use of comma after prepositional phrase
- Discourse: Main idea supported with details; use of *y* to join two or more ideas
- Vocabulary: *Por medio de*

**Source:** Gladys Sarabia, CMS Elementary, Denver, CO.

---

**Grade level: 2**
**Context:** Narrative Unit
**TheDictado title:** *That's Not Fair*
**TheDictado**

After Juan untied the rope, the crocodile said, "I will eat you up." Juan answered, "That's not fair!"

**Teaching points**
- Spelling: untied, answered
- Punctuation: comma after an adverbial phrase; comma before quotation marks
- Discourse: Use of dialogue in narratives
- Cross-language connection: contrast use of quotation marks with use of the *guión* in Spanish; cognate crocodile/*cocodrilo*
- Grammar: "ed" endings; contraction: that's

**Source:** Josette Boyden, Auburn Elementary, Salem, OR.

---

**Grade level: 4**
**Context:** This dictado was taught as a part of a unit on writing about what you might be when you grow up.
**TheDictado title:** *¿Qué seré?*
**TheDictado**

*En el futuro seré un adulto, pero ¿qué haré? Tal vez estudiaré en una universidad muy conocida como Harvard, o tal vez trabajaré como médico y buscaré la manera de curar cáncer o diabetes. Puede ser que llegaré a ser gobernador de Colorado o viajaré por todo el mundo en busca de petróleo como ingeniero. Para realizar mis sueños tendré que trabajar mucho.*

**Teaching points**
- Spelling: accent marks on the first person future tense
- Punctuation: comma before the conjunction *pero*
- Discourse: rhetorical use of question in introductory sentence to draw in reader
- Culturally responsive teaching—aspiring to go to a university

**Source:** Nancy Bethencourt, Valverde Elementary, Denver, CO.

---

**Grade level: 4**
**Context:** Biography Unit
**TheDictado title:** *It's Not Fair*
**TheDictado**

In her life, Emma learned many things are unfair. For example, it is not fair for some people to be hungry and cold, while other people are throwing food and clothes away.

**Teaching points**
- Spelling: fair/unfair (prefixes)
- Punctuation: Use of commas to separate ideas; comma use after "for example"
- Discourse: Use of the phrase "for example" to add detail to writing; "while" as a word to indicate a contrast

**Source:** Yolanda Pérez-Ruíz and Sarah Quiatt, Columbine Elementary, Boulder, CO.

---

print, such as the difference between a letter, a word, and a sentence, prior to implementing theDictado method. This is critical because within Literacy Squared theDictado should always communicate a complete thought rather than a list of words.

To prepare kindergarten students to be successful with theDictado, use shared writing as a time to establish procedures. For instance, as students help you to create a morning message, have them repeat back to you the sentence that will be encoded. They could also

| BOX 4.5 | *Scaffolds for Implementing theDictado in Kindergarten* |
|---|---|
| Scaffold 1 | • Teacher reads the text aloud<br>• Students repeat after the teacher<br>• Together, count the number of words<br>• On chart paper or the board, the teacher draws lines for each word and skips lines<br>• Through shared writing, teacher repeats each word as she encodes it in standard form, inviting children to help<br>• Teacher emphasizes concepts about print and emergent literacy skills |
| Scaffold 2 | • Teacher reads the text aloud<br>• Students repeat after the teacher<br>• Together, count the number of words<br>• Teacher *and students* draw lines for each word (ensure students draw long enough lines) and skip lines<br>• Through shared writing, teacher *and students* repeat each word as they encode in standard form, inviting children to help (children can use individual white boards or white paper)<br>• Teacher reinforces concepts about print and emergent literacy skills |
| Scaffold 3 | • Teacher reads the text aloud<br>• Students repeat after the teacher<br>• Together, count the number of words<br>• *Students* draw lines for each word (ensure students draw long enough lines) and *encode the message by themselves* skipping lines (students use white paper)<br>• *Teacher encodes message in standard form* emphasizing the use of capital letter, spaces between words, and ending punctuation<br>• *Students copy the message* in standard form below their own |
| Scaffold 4 | • Continue the same procedure suggested for scaffold 3<br>• Teacher models self-correction and introduces the standard marking codes *one at a time.*<br>• Use texts produced when the previous scaffolds were introduced to model self-correction using the standard marking code |

count the words and articulate their understanding of "wordness," directionality, return sweep, and so forth. Once they are familiar with this, you can have them copy the message on small white boards. This would be a good place to reinforce proper letter formation in a meaningful context. For a more detailed understanding of how to implement theDictado in kindergarten, see Box 4.5.

**Beginning Steps for Implementating theDictado in Grades 1–5.** Assuming students experienced theDictado in kindergarten, you can implement theDictado method from the beginning of the school year. If, however, they are unfamiliar with the procedure, be sure to review the steps outlined previously and to use shared writing as a way to scaffold the skills students will need to be successful. As a reminder, the procedures for the weekly Dictado are outlined in Table 4.2 and Box 4.3.

Once you are ready to implement the formal procedure, you will need to consider carefully how to plan theDictado so that it challenges your students to move beyond what they currently know and can do in writing. TheDictado can take many forms and address multiple learning objectives. The following suggestions may be helpful as you consider how to plan, teach, and work within your students' zones of proximal development.

• Establish students' strengths and weaknesses by analyzing students' writing in both languages and connecting this to your literacy objectives. As a Spanish language example, see the first Dictado listed in Box 4.4. In this example, Ms. Sarabia and her grade 2 students were doing a biography unit and were reading a biography of Frida Kahlo. She noticed that children were not consistently using accent marks for high-frequency words in Spanish such as *difícil* (difficult) and *corazón* (heart) in their writing. She also noted that they did not use accent marks with the third person preterite and imperfect. In fact, these are quite difficult spelling rules to learn in Spanish. For this reason, Ms. Sarabia created a two-sentence Dictado incorporating words that students were using incorrectly in their writing. In addition, she noticed that the students' writing lacked sophisticated transitions. Therefore, she chose to include the phrase *por medio de* (through the creation of) to exemplify how a mature writer might expand an idea. In other words, she linked what the students were approximating in their writing to the unit of study to develop an appropriate and complex Dictado. Please note that there is a second Spanish language example in Box 4.4.

- This same process can be used by teachers in literacy-based ELD. For example, see the grade 4 English language Dictado in Box 4.4. In this example, Ms. Pérez-Ruíz and Ms. Quiatt were reading the book, *That's Not Fair*. This is a biography of Emma Temayuca, a woman who fought for the rights of migrant workers in the 1930s. During this unit, they noticed that in their students' writing the children could state an opinion, but did not offer justifications. They used this information to construct a two-sentence Dictado in which they taught students at the discourse level how to state an opinion and offer examples to justify their opinions. In this Dictado, they teach their students to use the phrase "for example" to justify their opinion of why life is not always fair. Further, they teach them that the word "while" indicates that they are going to contrast two ideas as another means of justifying their opinion. Additionally, the teachers pointed out that phrases like "not fair" can also be expressed with words such as "unfair." With this, they were able to show that there are multiple ways to express an idea and to highlight the role of prefixes. Finally, they carefully attended to the punctuation needed to express these contrasting ideas. Again, they link what the students were approximating in their writing to their unit of study.

Beyond what was highlighted in the above examples, teachers may choose to create Dictados that draw children's attention to cross-language similarities and differences. In the early grades, children frequently use their understanding of the Spanish grapheme/ phoneme relationship to encode messages in English (e.g., japi/happy or laik/like) and vice versa (e.g., awua/agua; lecktura/lectura). Knowing this, it is important for teachers to create Dictados that consistently provide explicit opportunities to help children become aware of this common practice, and to guide them to be more metalinguistically aware as they encode messages in each language. An explanation of common graphophonemic transfer from Spanish to English is provided in Table 4.3.

Remember, however, that we do not want to remain at the word level. TheDictado should also address what students need to learn in English that cannot be learned in Spanish, for example, syntactical structures such as the formation of possessives (e.g., Ana's pencil/the pencil of Ana), or concepts that cannot be understood unless examined at the phrasal level (e.g., elbow grease).

While not meant to be exhaustive, we wish to emphasize that theDictado should be used to expand and elevate students' ability to write in both Spanish literacy and literacy-based ELD. Over time, incorporate increasingly sophisticated vocabulary and grammatical structures to extend students' language. As illustrated in the examples given in Box 4.4, we can accomplish the objective of greater complexity and sophistication without creating unnecessarily long Dictados.

## Effectiveness of theDictado

After implementing theDictado for a year, Literacy Squared teachers shared their thoughts about its effectiveness. First, they reported children's enthusiasm participating in theDictado. In addition, most of the teachers found the method to be an effective way to improve students' use of structural elements such as paragraphing and punctuation. They reported improvement in students' spelling and handwriting across languages. Children's listening skills and their opportunities for language expansion were also enhanced.

Of course the effectiveness of theDictado, as with any teaching strategy, depends on its consistent and thoughtful application. Over the course of its field-testing, we developed a list of critical reminders—dos and don'ts—about how to implement this strategy so that it is of maximum benefit to the students.

**TABLE 4.3**

## Graphophonemic Transfer from Spanish to English

### VOWELS

Vowels in Spanish have only one sound. Therefore, the concepts of long vowels, short vowels, r-controlled vowels, and schwa vowels in English have no Spanish equivalent. Additionally, nearly every vowel in Spanish is pronounced, so two vowels don't "go walking" and that silent, but bossy, final "e" is conceptually foreign. However, "u" is mute when it appears after "g" and "q" and before the vowels "e" and "i," as in *Querétaro, quizá, guerra,* and *guitarra.*

| English Letter/Sound | Spanish Equivalent | Example |
|---|---|---|
| /Ā/ as in **a**ble | e; ei | trein/train |
| /Ē/ as in **e**ar | i | sin/seen |
| /Ī/ as in **i**cicle | Ai; ay; hay (the "h" is silent in Spanish) | Ay/I; bait/bite |
| /o/ as in **o**ctopus | a | cat/cought |
| /ū/ as in **u**niform | iu | ciut/cute |

### CONSONANTS—Individuals and Clusters

| English Letter(s)/Sound | Spanish Equivalent | Example |
|---|---|---|
| Cc–ck | c, k, Qu | soquer/soccer; tiket/ticket |
| D—as in foo**d** or **d**oor | d or r | fur/food |
| Soft g— as in **g**esture or **g**iraffe | y; ll | lliant/giant |
| H—as in **h**air | j | jelp/help |
| J—as in **J**ello | y; ll | yump/jump or llelo/yellow |
| Qu—as in **qu**aint or **qu**ote | cua; cuo | cuin/queen |
| Sh—as in **sh**eep. This sound only exists in Spanish words of native origin, such as U**x**mal. | X (though usually less familiar to students here); next closest approximation is *ch* | chain/shine |
| Th—as in **th**umb | d | den/then |
| V—as in **v**est | f; b/v | fine/vine |
| W—as in **W**ashington. This sound does not exist in Spanish. | gu (as in agua) | guent/went |
| Y—as in **y**arn | ll | llam/yam |
| Z—as in **z**ipper | s | sebra/zebra |

- Spanish has no S-initiated blends (sc, scr, sk, sl, sm, sn, sp, spl, st, sw. . .).
- Spanish has few contractions (del, al) and they do not use an apostrophe.
- Spanish sentences have flexible word order structures (e.g., voy corriendo; corriendo voy).
- Spanish does not require the use of pronouns, as they are indicated in the verb conjugation (e.g., hablo = yo hablo/I speak).
- Spanish rarely has double letters (hapen/happen; buk/book).

The ideas presented here were informed considerably by the work of Mónica Olguín.

### What to Do

- Create or select passages carefully. Meaning is at the core of every Dictado. Children should not be writing phrases or sentences that do not have meaning to them or that you cannot easily explain.
- Always include spelling, punctuation, and capitalization in every Dictado. Choose two to four other teaching points (e.g., plurals, past tense, cross-language connections), and use them as a part of the talk-through.
- Do the same Dictado all week long.
- Talk-through and write the corrected Dictado every time you give it.
- Include self-correction; it is critical for children to learn from their own mistakes and see their own progress.
- Use red pen/pencil to correct. During self-correction it is important that children never erase their writing. (It is fine for children to erase prior to the self-correction step.)
- Employ a standard marking code for the entire school (see Boxes 4.1 and 4.2 for examples in each language).
- Demand approximation and do not let children simply "skip" words.
- Monitor what children are producing and trying to write.

*What Not to Do*

- Do not translate from Spanish to English or vice versa.
- Do not choose unrelated Dictados.

  *Bad Example*
  I got in trouble because of you.
  What happened at recess?
  There's a TV in the living room.

- Do not mark the words spelled correctly.

In summary, theDictado is an effective cross-language method that provides emerging bilingual children with the opportunity to develop metalinguistic awareness in two languages. Because it invites a focused examination of the linguistic similarities and differences across languages, it affords children extended opportunities to expand their written knowledge in both Spanish and English. TheDictado, when integrated as part of Spanish literacy and literacy-based ELD, is effective at combining listening, speaking, reading, writing, and metalinguistic awareness.

## Conclusion

Writing instruction is as important to biliteracy development as instruction in oracy, reading, and metalanguage. The instructional approaches used within Literacy Squared are part of a holistic biliteracy framework. In addition to theDictado, they include modeled, shared, collaborative, and independent writing. As with the teaching of reading, a greater emphasis is given to shared and collaborative writing. These instructional approaches are recommended in lieu of a process approach, such as writers' workshop, because they allow teachers to demonstrate explicitly the skills and knowledge about language involved in both the writing process and product.

The importance of purposefully connecting the four core instructional elements of the Literacy Squared model (writing, reading, oracy, and metalanguage) cannot be overemphasized. When literacy activities are meaningful and authentic, writers read and talk about what they or others have written; similarly, through writing and talking they respond to what they have read. Chapters 9 and 10 have examples of integrated biliteracy units that highlight the reciprocal relationship between reading, writing, oracy, and metalanguage; these units demonstrate how that relationship is reflected in well-planned lessons.

## Questions for Reflection and Action

- What would your literacy block schedule look like with the integration of the recommended approaches to writing instruction described in this chapter?
- How might you begin to modify writing instruction to address the language and literacy strengths and needs of emerging bilingual students in your classroom?
- How does your school curriculum address the aspects of writing development promoted through the use of theDictado? How can theDictado enhance or augment your current instructional practices?
- Which beginning steps might you take to implement theDictado in your classroom? What collaboration structures are necessary for a schoolwide implementation?

# 5

# Metalanguage

*I have never known what is Arabic or English, or which one was really mine beyond any doubt. What I do know, however, is that the two have always been together in my life, one resonating in the other, sometimes ironically, sometimes nostalgically, most often each correcting, and commenting on, the other. Each can seem like my absolutely first language, but neither is.*

Edward Said, 1999, *Out of Place: A Memoir*

## Key Terms

*Así se dice*

**Anchor charts**

**Code-switching (intersententially/ intrasententially)**

**Cognates**

**Concurrent translation**

**Cross-language connections**

**Funds of knowledge**

**Literal translations**

**Metalanguage**

**Strategic use of language**

## Guiding Questions

▪ Why are metalinguistic skills important for emerging bilingual students?

▪ What does it mean to use language "strategically" in a bilingual context?

▪ How should translation and code-switching be handled in the classroom?

Becoming literate in two languages differs from becoming literate in one. An important difference is that students benefit from having two languages that interact and complement one another. As such, a critical conceptual construct of the Literacy Squared holistic biliteracy framework is attention to the development of **metalanguage**.

Briefly defined, metalanguage is thinking and talking about language, and, in the case of biliteracy, understanding the relationships between and within languages. It is the language used to talk about language, and its mastery allows students to analyze how language can be leveraged to express meaning. The development of metalanguage includes the ability to identify, analyze, and manipulate language forms, and to analyze sounds, symbols, grammar, vocabulary, and language structures between and across languages. It has been identified as one of three fundamental skills, along with the psycholinguistic abilites to decode and comprehend, required for a person to become literate (Bialystok, 2007; Koda & Zehler, 2008).

Within Literacy Squared, we emphasize consciously elevating students' abilities to detect, understand, and talk about how their languages are similar and dissimilar, so that they can use this knowledge to develop a self-extending bilingual communicative system.

We recommend that metalinguistic awareness be developed in Spanish, English, and across languages and propose that it constitute about 25% of literacy instruction.

## Importance of Metalanguage: What the Research Says

Research reveals that when learners of two languages discover similarities and differences in the two language systems, they tend to have improved phonological awareness in comparison to monolingual children (Campbell & Sais, 1995; Koda & Zehler, 2008). In a recent study, children who were read to using dual language books to help them make **cross-language connections** between French, Punjabi, Urdu, *and* English demonstrated greater gains in graphophonemic knowledge than children who were read to only in English (Naqui, Thorne, McKeough, & Pfitscher, 2010). This gain occurred specifically in the children who spoke the additional language at home. Importantly, however, the children who did not speak the additional languages showed no deficit in emergent literacy competencies; that is, the exposure to additional languages in the books they were read did not slow their literacy development in the languages they were already using. Finally, we know that the development of metalanguage results in an improved ability to compare languages in terms of words and sentence structures (Sneddon, 2008) and an enhanced ability to transfer conceptual knowledge and skills across languages (Cummins et al., 2005).

As with the other quadrants of the holistic biliteracy framework, it is evident that there is research support for the development of metalanguage and metalinguistic awareness. This chapter outlines and explains the specific strategies that teachers can use to attend deliberately and explicitly to the development of metalanguage across languages.

## Cross-Language Connections

In Literacy Squared, we refer to the development of metalanguage across languages as cross-language connections. Cross-language connections are purposefully planned opportunities to compare languages. They require students to work in groups or pairs to examine the similarities and differences in their languages. These higher-order thinking tasks are bidirectional in nature. In other words, they involve moving from Spanish to English as well as English to Spanish. This conceptual construct was added to our holistic biliteracy framework to ensure that direct and explicit attention is paid to children who are developing metalanguage regarding Spanish and English similarities and differences. The teaching of cross-language connections involves an explicit awareness of linguistic form and structure, separate from content, and is an essential element of literacy and biliteracy development.

Within Literacy Squared, we use two types of cross-language connections. The first refers to specific methods that the model has adapted from Mexico and modified for use in U.S. English/Spanish literacy programs. The second focuses on teaching children the metacognitive linguistic skills of cross-language expression in reading and writing (Escamilla & Hopewell, 2010).

As Valdés and Figueroa (1994) and others have demonstrated, cross-language adaptation and conceptualization are skills that represent the most sophisticated types of bilingualism and biliteracy. Opportunities for translation and adaptation across languages are ideal strategies for developing these cross-language metacognitive skills.

Processing and communicating across languages affords students the opportunity to strengthen their understanding of the reciprocal nature of languages. Increasingly, bilingual scholars advocate exploring practices that nurture these competencies (Cummins, 2008; García, 2009; Hopewell, 2011). In fact, a growing number of scholars currently argue that strictly separating languages is not always appropriate (Canagarajah, 2011; Creese & Blackledge, 2010; Gajo, 2007; García, 2011; Wei & Wu, 2009). Flexible pedagogical practices that expand students' abilities to analyze the similarities and differences between and within their languages deepen understanding of subject matter, strengthen language competence, and nurture powerful literacy competencies.

By definition, these comparisons require that we create spaces in which students and teachers can purposefully and deliberately use and examine their languages. Doing so is a direct challenge to programs that insist on strict language separation. While we understand the need for strong language models and the importance of practicing and using a language in order to acquire it well, we conclude that there is much to be gained in allowing for a hybrid time/space in which languages can be compared side by side. This cannot happen if we are never permitted to examine or reference both languages in a single environment.

**A Word of Caution about Concurrent Translation.** Within Literacy Squared, teachers are encouraged to plan the use of both languages strategically, so as to maximize learning and to achieve the greatest efficiency in the classroom environment: the cross-language strategies recommended in the holistic bilingual framework are described in the following sections. We *strongly* caution, however, against the use of **concurrent translation**! Concurrent translation teaches students that they need not attend to information presented in the second language (Faltis, 1996). Because they know the same information will be stated in their first language, there is a natural tendency for students to tune out when the less familiar language is used. The direct translation of every statement or instruction eliminates an authentic need to engage with and practice the newly acquired language. Creating spaces for bilingualism and the **strategic use of language** is not meant to replace the need to spend significant amounts of time focusing on only one language at a time.

## Teaching Strategies to Develop Cross-Language Connections

Related to the idea that teachers need to make connections between the literacy environments is the idea that teachers need to use explicit cross-language strategies when creating Literacy Squared lessons. Cross-language strategies are focused on teaching children the metalanguage skills of cross-language expression in reading and writing. They may be either formally planned or implemented informally when children need clarifications to ensure their understanding of lessons. The idea is to extend students' knowledge from one language to the other and to make differences explicit to children through direct instruction.

Within Literacy Squared, we suggest that effective formal strategies for teaching cross-language connections include the use of bilingual or dual language books, cognate instruction, the strategic use of language, and a unique approach we call *así se dice* (that's how you say it). All of these strategies share certain characterstics:

- Strategic integration into literacy instruction
- Purposeful planning and explicit teaching
- Explicit guidance to promote higher-order thinking
- Focus on group and collaborative projects
- Bidirectional (Spanish to English and English to Spanish)

Conversely, cross-language strategies do *not* include concurrent translation, individual assignments, or unidirectional activities.

### *Bilingual Books*

Books written in two languages (bilingual books) offer unique educational opportunities for emerging bilingual students and their teachers. In bilingual books both languages are represented in one text. Alternatively, one might use two separate interpretations of the same story or text by obtaining texts written in only one language (e.g., a Spanish language text of *La caperucita roja* and an English language text of *Little Red Riding Hood*). Because an appropriate translation should be a cultural and linguistic adaptation, the versions may vary across languages. (Note that **literal translations** should be used with caution; they are often inferior and use unnatural language that can be more problematic than helpful as children strive to comprehend.) The key feature is that the story or concept is essentially the same.

Bilingual books are commonly used around the world as a way of developing cross-language connections and metalanguage. Using bilingual or dual language books promotes children's cultural awareness in that students become attentive to the uniqueness of their own and others' cultures as well as becoming conscious of the similarities among cultures. Further, the use of bilingual books has been demonstrated to improve literacy achievement in English, even in schools where English is the sole medium of instruction. In these studies, bilingual books were used in after-school literacy programs (Ernst-Slavit, 1997; Rodríguez-Valls, 2011). Bilingual books provide opportunities for parents and students to utilize knowledge of their first language to acquire reading skills in the second language. They also assist teachers to develop a cultural biliteracy in the classroom that values and embraces the bilingualism experienced by students in their daily lives. Carefully chosen books inspire language lessons that extend emerging bilingual children's proficiencies in reading, writing, oracy, and cross-language metalinguistic awareness.

The use of bilingual books as a method to teach cross-language connections in both Spanish and English is an essential part of the Literacy Squared instructional framework. Incorporating bilingual books gives emerging bilingual children an opportunity to deepen their understanding of Spanish texts and extends their linguistic skills in English. In other words, a book that has been used to foster Spanish language literacy may also be used in the literacy-based ELD lesson, but to accomplish different tasks and learning objectives. When students are able to understand the story line and book structure with ease, they are more prepared to focus their energy on practicing and learning the oracy and literacy goals of a particular session. Bilingual books are a powerful tool for developing conceptual and strategic knowledge in one language and linguistic knowledge in the other. When using bilingual books, teachers can reduce the cognitive load of English text comprehension and instead focus on building students' English language skills. The use of bilingual books allows teachers to show students explicitly how to make use of both their languages to comprehend and create texts. These lessons are not intended to promote concurrent translation, but rather to utilize both languages in a deliberately coordinated way to deepen conceptual knowledge about literacy, to activate prior knowledge or cultural schema, and to help children make connections. We recommend beginning the use of bilingual texts in kindergarten (or sooner, if possible) to focus on developing students' knowledge of concepts about print and for co-constructing a text related to the book. Bilingual texts deepen vocabulary in both languages, create a cognitive awareness of the nuance in inter- and intracultural communication, and foster self-reflection on students' own bilingualism.

In order for these lessons to be effective, teachers need to consider carefully the book selection and their students' literacy and language needs. After selecting a book that is interesting and culturally relevant to students, the teacher should determine the skill or strategy for which the book can be used. Then the teacher proceeds to create a lesson, keeping in mind that the literacy objectives should be cognitively heavier in Spanish for this population, because what students learn in Spanish can be transferred to English. However, students will need support in developing the necessary language to communicate their understanding in English. Thus, the English objectives must be strategically and thoughtfully planned and should focus on the language that students need to learn to interact successfully with the text. To achieve this goal, oracy objectives that include targeted language structures, vocabulary, and dialogue must be identified for each lesson.

Students learning to read and write in two languages have the advantage of being able to create, interpret, and process text by accessing multiple linguistic resources. Bilingual books serve as mentor texts for capitalizing on these linguistic advantages and as anchors for connecting language and literacy environments. They provide rich models for enjoying and celebrating biliteracy. Their inclusion in literacy lessons and in classroom libraries sends a very strong message to children and families that all of their languages and cultures are valued. They provide a commendable way to keep languages in high profile and support a natural connection between home and school. Finally, and importantly, the different experiences with each text complement each other and increase access to knowledge and learning.

## Cognate Instruction

**Cognates** are words in different languages that share an etymological root resulting in similar spelling, meaning, and pronunciation. There are thousands, and perhaps tens of thousands, Spanish/English cognates. They derive from the same Latin roots and range from being identical to sharing morphological, orthographic, syntactical, and semantic characteristics. For example, *hospital* and hospital are identical in spelling and meaning. Their pronunciation varies, but only slightly. *Naturalmente* and naturally share meaning and morphology; yet, they they are spelled differently because the suffixes used to accomplish the same linguistic function vary by language. In this case, the suffixes *-mente* and *–ly* are language-specific ways to form adverbs. Then, there are simple relationships that students can be taught that will help them to recognize and utilize a greater breadth of words. For instance, most words in Spanish that end in *–dad* can be assumed to end in *–ty* in English (e.g., *elecricidad*/electricity; *universidad*/university). The importance of explicit cognate instruction is to help students understand how their two (or more) languages interact in predictable and patterned ways that can expand their ability to comprehend and create text exponentially. We must caution, however, that cognates are best taught in meaningful contexts. We do not advocate the memorization of lists of words or rules. Also, it is important to teach students that words that look and sound alike are not always cognates (e.g., *éxito*/exit or *success*/exit). Teach students to attend to the context to determine if a word that appears to be a cognate makes sense semantically given the words around it.

In a recent study of Spanish/English cognates, Lubliner and Hiebert (2011) conducted three separate analyses of Spanish/English cognates. Results revealed that both the general service list (GSL) and the academic word list (AWL) contain a substantial number of Spanish/English cognates. The GSL is a list of 2,000 frequently used base words in English identified by West (1953). The AWL contains 570 words that are not included in the GSL, but are found frequently in university textbooks across disciplines (Coxhead, 2000). In their examination, Lubliner and Hiebert concluded that carefully designed cognate instruction may provide Spanish-speaking children with a "cognate advantage" in comprehending English academic texts. However, it is important to note that despite the potential advantage that cognates offer, bilingual students often fail to notice cognate pairs even when they appear to be quite transparent (August, Carlo, Dressler, & Snow, 2005; Nagy, Garcia, Durgunoglu, & Hancin-Bhatt, 1993). For example, Nagy et. al. (1993) documented that grades 5 and 6 bilingual, biliterate Spanish-speaking students circled less than half of the known cognates that they encountered on a test of cognate identification. The authors concluded that even though cognates can be matched in orthographic, phonologic and semantic ways, this matching needs to be directly taught to students.

In Literacy Squared, we recommend that teachers use explicit instruction to teach what cognates are and how they work across languages. We also ask instructors to teach students that knowing cognates can help them become more sophisticated readers and writers in both languages. To illustrate, it is important that children understand first and foremost that true cognates share a semantic meaning across languages. That they also share similar spelling and/or morphological patterns is important, but the major understanding needs to be in the meaning of the word. If cognates are to help children make cross-language connections, then meaning must be at the center of instruction. Figure 5.1 provides an example of cognates found in the Spanish and English versions of the fable *Leonard the Lion and Raymond the Mouse*, as identified by students from a grade 3 classroom in Salem, Oregon. Figure 5.2 illustrates a cognate chart from a grade 4 classroom in Salem, Oregon, showing words commonly used in their classroom. In this chart, the teacher has helped children identify words with the same meaning in Spanish and English, and she has used a color-coding scheme to differentiate cross-language differences in spelling.

Understanding the power of cognates aids students in reading comprehension and in writing. It is a literacy strategy unique to bilingual learners. Through direct instruction and modeling, teachers help students develop their abilities to draw upon their knowledge of word-level visual and auditory relationships to expand their comprehension skills. Cognate recognition and use is a cognitive skill that helps students interpret and produce language by synthesizing what they know across languages.

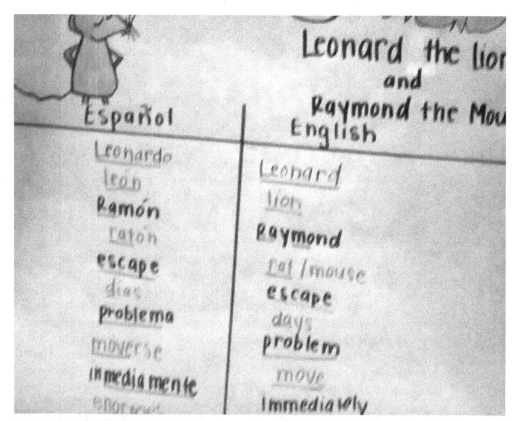

**Figure 5.1 Cross-language strategies: cognate chart.** Ms. Green had students identify the cognates used in the English and Spanish versions of the fable she was teaching, *Leonardo el león y Ramon el ratón* and *Leonard the Lion and Raymond the Mouse*. (Courtesy of Nubia Green, grade 3 teacher, Highland Elementary School, Salem, OR.)

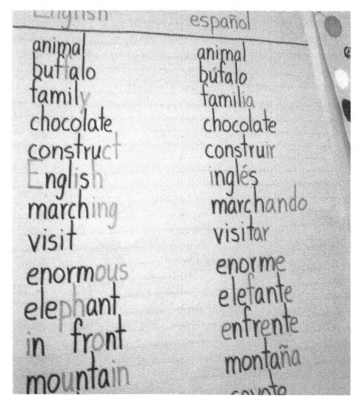

**Figure 5.2 Cognate chart: words in our classroom.** This cognate chart illustrates different spelling patterns in words in Spanish/English with the same meaning. (Courtesy of Jill Ekre, grade 3 teacher, Mary Eyre Elementary, Salem, OR.)

## *Strategic Use of Language*

When language environments are planned so that all languages are understood to be resources that can be accessed and invoked strategically, in service to language and literacy acquisition, space is created in which the deliberate and purposeful use of Spanish and/or English facilitates accelerated learning. Knowing two languages not only augments meaning-making repertoires, it expands teaching repertoires (Hopewell, 2011).

Research to support the strategic use of language is grounded in González, Moll, and Amanti's (2005) work around identifying and capitalizing on children's **funds of knowledge**. Funds of knowledge are those skills, concepts, bodies of knowledge, and ways of knowing that students acquire in their families and communities; they include language and ways of conveying meaning. Beginning in the mid- to late 1980s, Moll et al. conducted a series of studies exploring the use of a language other than English in the literacy environment (Díaz, Moll, & Mehan, 1986; Moll, 1988; Moll & Díaz, 1985). They found that successful teachers of bilingual students rejected a reductionist philosophy that valued English above Spanish and encouraged the strategic use of Spanish, so that students could demonstrate reading comprehension when in the English environment. Further, they demonstrated advanced learning gains for students when their teachers sometimes reverted to Spanish.

More recent research shows that hybrid language environments, where all languages are accessed and used strategically and systematically to maximize mutual understanding and to aid in inquiry and problem solving within the learning context, expand opportunities for collaboration and language acquisition (Creese & Blackledge, 2011; García, 2009; Gutiérrez, Baquedano-López, Alvarez, & Chiu, 1999; Martin-Beltrán, 2010). Research also confirms that hybrid literacy practices result in greater linguistic flexibility on the part of Spanish-speaking bilingual students, as demonstrated through translation skills, a tendency toward cross-language collaboration, and the development of biliteracy (Manyak, 2002).

Careful attention to how and when each language is used can enhance a student's understanding of linguistic interconnectedness. There are three formal methods used within Literacy Squared to access and use language purposefully and strategically: the preview-review strategy, the keyword method, and the incorporation of bilingual **anchor charts**.

**Preview-Review.** Preview-review is a technique in which the teacher takes a few minutes prior to teaching a lesson and a few minutes following the lesson to have a brief discussion with the students to activate prior knowledge and to summarize key concepts for the topic to be taught (Ulanoff & Pucci, 1999). Though the majority of the instructional time is spent in the targeted language, these few minutes at the beginning and end of a lesson were shown to increase student learning by allowing students to activate schema and solidify essential concepts.

**Keyword.** Another purposeful technique is the keyword method developed for language learning (Avila & Sadoski, 1996). When using this technique, the teacher asks students to create mnemonic devices in which they associate the form and meaning of a word in the target language with a word in the first language. Mnemonics are memory strategies that increase vocabulary and concept retention. Often the relationship between the associated words is acoustic and visual rather than semantic. For instance, to learn the English word "cart" a student might associate it with the Spanish word *carta* (postal letter). After selecting a word that sounds and looks similar, the student would create or be given an image that associates the divergent meanings (e.g., a cart carrying a mailbox). These visual, auditory, and semantic connections aid the student in recalling low-frequency vocabulary. Avila and Sadoski demonstrated that the keyword method is useful within and across languages, and that it aids in long-term vocabulary retention.

**Anchor Charts.** Third, we encourage teachers to create anchor charts with their bilingual students to provide explicit comparisons of language features (Buhrow & Garcia, 2006). These anchor charts are co-created by teachers and students and serve to hold a lesson firmly in place. The chart is a stable reference that students can return to when in need of clarification. Anchor charts are used to record and display student thinking, key concepts,

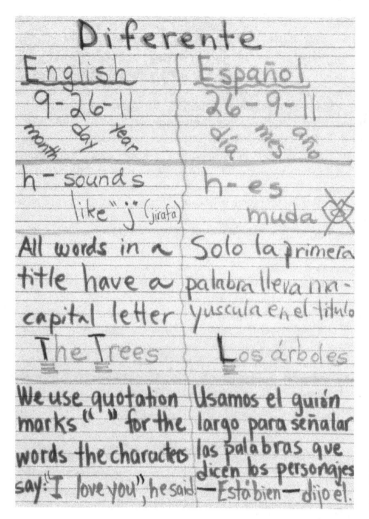

**Figure 5.3 Cross-language strategies.** This anchor chart shows different writing conventions between English and Spanish. (Courtesy of Nubia Green, grade 3 teacher, Highland Elementary School, Salem, OR.)

and essential skills. These tools for contrastive analysis help students to see the connections across literacy environments. Figure 5.3 is an example of a bilingual anchor chart created in a grade 4 classroom. This chart illustrates several important differences between Spanish and English with which students are grappling: annotation devices for writing the date in Spanish and English; differentiation between how the letter "h" works in Spanish and English, differences in how titles of books and stories are written in Spanish and English, and differences in punctuating dialogue between Spanish and English.

**Informal Strategies.** Finally, it is worth noting that some cross-linguistic strategies recommended by Literacy Squared are neither formal nor explicit; rather, they are informal and meant to be used depending on context and student need. The strategic use of both languages in a given lesson can be very effective and efficient.

As we've pointed out, concurrent translation is an ineffective method of bilingual instruction. However, during a literacy-based ELD lesson, Spanish might be used by a teacher in the following ways:

- To clarify conceptual confusions
- To activate prior knowledge or cultural schema
- To help children make personal connections to the material
- To allow children to discuss and process information heard in English (e.g., when children are talking with one another, or when a child can understand information in English but can't yet produce what he or she understands in English).

When students clearly do not understand a concept during literacy-based ELD, we suggest the teacher simply tell the children what the word is in Spanish rather than spending precious time and energy trying to teach the concept. For example, in one classroom we were observing the children were confused by the phrase "to make believe." The teacher tried to explain the phrase in various ways but the children were still clearly confused. Finally, she told them that in Spanish the phrase means *fingir*. By strategically using one Spanish word the teacher cleared up confusion, thereby enabling the children to move ahead with the purpose of the lesson ("to make believe they were a character in the story and write about it").

In another classroom, the teacher was explaining the rules for playing the game "Jeopardy" within literacy-based ELD. The purpose of the lesson was to give children opportunities to do transformations wherein they turned statements into questions. Trying to explain the rules of the game to the children was quite confusing, so the teacher decided to explain the rules in Spanish and then play the actual game in English. In this example, using Spanish strategically saved important teaching and learning time and ensured that students were able to spend the majority of their time engaged in language learning and task rehearsal, as opposed to figuring out how to participate in the activity. Again, it is important to note that this is not an example of concurrent translation. Instead, it illustrates how the teacher used one language strategically to allow for the majority of the students' time to be spent engaging in the activity in the other language, thus providing students with more time to practice and master the language objectives.

## Así se dice *(That's How You Say It)*

*Así se dice* (that's how you say it) is a cross-language strategy that we developed to validate translation as a constructive and worthwhile endeavor that engages students in a complex, sophisticated scrutiny of language and emphasizes the subtleties and nuances of communicating messages across cultures and languages. We posit that the approach of *así se dice* is an effective strategy to teach explicit cross-language connections that ultimately enhance students' cognitive and linguistic growth while providing a space in the classroom to use two languages in an interconnected way. This method is fundamentally different from using concurrent translation or repeating or emphasizing key concepts through regular rephrasing. *Así se dice* develops metalinguistic awareness because it requires students to engage in creating translations and interpretations for the express purpose of thinking and talking about the intersection of culture and language. Accurate and efficient interpretation of a text produced in one language into another through *así se dice* is a complex and sophisticated skill. It requires a deep understanding of concepts, a thorough knowledge of culture, a precise use of vocabulary and language structures, a willingness to collaborate and negotiate, and the knowledge of how and when to consult outside references. Because of its complexity and requirement of abstract thought, we recommend that the purposeful use of *así se dice* begin in grade 3.

The ability to translate effectively is indicative of higher-order thinking skills and one of the markers of bilingual/biliterate proficiency (Orellana, Martínez, & Montaño, 2013; Valdés & Figueroa, 1994). For some translation tasks, a literal translation is sufficient and requires only a simple word order change (e.g., *el carro nuevo de mi abuela es un Toyota/* my grandmother's new car is a Toyota). However, *así se dice* work should also include tasks where literal translations make no sense or are very awkward. In these cases, students will need to use conceptual translations. For example, the expression *no hay mal que por bien no venga* is much better translated as "every cloud has a silver lining" than its literal translation from Spanish to English: "there is nothing bad from which good doesn't come."

When engaging in *así se dice* tasks, student groups should articulate whether or not the translation requires literal or conceptual translations. The procedure for teaching *así se dice* is outlined in Table 5.1, and is further outlined in Escamilla, Geisler, Hopewell, Sparrow, & Butvilofsky (2009). Briefly, however, we recommend choosing short pieces of text that are conceptually rich. We have found poetry (Table 5.2) and idioms to spark rich conversation. Students are given the text to translate, asked to work with a partner or a group to construct an interpretation, and share and discuss the alternatives. The richness of *así se dice* comes from the whole group discussion and the negotiation of meaning following the small group work. We have seen children argue vehemently and eloquently over the use of

**TABLE 5.1**

Cross-Language Connections: *Así se dice* Procedure

| Procedure | Notes |
|---|---|
| Choose a text with targeted language | |
| Group students to work collaboratively to interpret and translate chosen text | Getting a "right" answer is not important—arriving at a reasonable answer with a justification is |
| Discuss the translations | Focus on why particular translations are more/less effective |
| Limit the discussion to 10–15 minutes | |
| Model | Use think-alouds to demonstrate how you read and reread text to maintain the meaning of the piece<br>Explain how you evaluate different alternatives ultimately either accepting or rejecting them |
| Illustrate that word-for-word translation is often inadequate—communicative function and context are as important as the words themselves | |
| Consult classroom resources (e.g., dictionary, thesaurus) | |
| Do shared *así se dice* exercises with shorter text | |
| Have students share their group translations | |

the word "enemy" versus "opponent." There is no doubt that every student in that classroom deepened his or her understanding of English through the debate they created. Simply asking students to translate without engaging in the conversation to clarify and expound is *not* doing *así se dice*!

It is of critical importance that teachers understand that there is not one correct way to make conceptual translations. Conceptual translations can be worded in many different ways, and the value of this strategy to metalinguistic and cross-language development is the cognitive practice of moving from one language to another and negotiating and defending one's translations within and between groups. Is the translation of *caras vemos, corazones no sabemos* "don't judge a book by its cover" or "a wolf in sheep's clothing"? The difference is subtle, but critical. One connotation is more positive while the other is negative. To understand which is more appropriate, you need to have more than vocabulary and concept knowledge. You need to reference culture and intent. Table 5.3 demonstrates student variations on *así se dice* translation tasks.

The use of the *así se dice* strategy not only gives teachers an opportunity to teach children about cross-language strategies, it also provides the opportunity to deal with false cognates and deepen students' awareness of the semantic nuances of words. Further, by undertaking this strategy, teachers can often better understand words and concepts that students are misunderstanding in Spanish. We believe that a major goal of instruction is to take students from where they are and extend their understandings to further develop their language. This particular exercise gives insights into student thinking and metalinguistic

**TABLE 5.2**

*Así se dice:* Bilingual Poetry

An example of students' translation of the poem, *Los libros,* by Francisco Alarcón

| Alarcón Spanish Original | Student Examples | Alarcón English Translation |
|---|---|---|
| *Los libros* | Books | Books |
| *Pasaportes de talla mayor* | Grand passports | Oversized passports |
| *Que nos permiten viajar* | That take us on journeys | That let us travel |
| *A dondequiera cuandoquiera* | Whenever, wherever | Anywhere, anytime |
| *Y no dejar de soñar* | And keep our dreams alive | And keep on dreaming |

From *Angels Ride Bikes and Other Fall Poems* by Francisco X. Alarcón. Copyright ©1999 by Francisco X. Alarcón. Permission arranged with Children's Book Press, an imprint of Lee & Low Books, Inc. New York, NY, 10016. All rights not specifically granted herein are reserved.

**TABLE 5.3**

*Así se dice:* Task Taken from the Legend of Popocatpetl

| Original Spanish Text | Student English Translations |
|---|---|
| *Le exige a Popo que encabece el ejército del imperio para derrotar el enemigo.* | 1. He told Popo to be the leader of the army and defeat the enemy.<br>2. He commanded Popo to take lead of the army to the empire to destroy the enemy.<br>3. He demands to be the leader of the empire's army so he could destroy all the opponent.<br>4. He tells Popo to switch the ejercit to derrotate the enemy |

Courtesy of students in Silvia Latimer's classroom, Columbine Elementary School, Boulder, CO.

awareness that is hard to discern elsewhere. As an example, one group of students was asked to translate the sentence *"le exige a Popo que encabece el ejército del imperio para derrotar el enemigo."* from Spanish to English (see Table 5.3). They wrote "he tells Popo to switch the *ejersit* to *derrotate* the enemy." When the teacher asked the students to explain their translation, she found that they made some very logical and strategic connections. They concluded that if *carro* is car, and *rancho* is ranch, then *ejército* could be ejersit. They further inferred that if *celebrar* is celebrate, and *interrogar* is interrogate, then *derrotar* could be derrotate. The students were making logical, albeit incorrect, inferences, and the example presented the teacher with an excellent teaching opportunity, another example of metalinguistic awareness!

## Code-Switching

Inevitably, when we broach the topic of developing students' metalinguistic skills through the use of cross-language strategies, we are asked about students' **code-switching**. Those who advocate strict language separation tend to view code-switching as an indication of a linguistic deficit. We see it differently.

Code-switching, defined briefly, is the alternation of languages within one linguistic context. This may take place within sentences (**intrasententially**) or in alternating sentences (**intersententially**). It is rule-governed behavior that requires a high degree of understanding of each of the languages being inserted into the communication.

Bilingual students draw on multiple resources to communicate. These resources are fundamentally based in their unique ability to process across languages. Students not only transfer skills and strategies, but also themselves, their personas, their social realities, and their knowledge of the world. Too often what bilingual children know and have to share in their writing is devalued because of the undue emphasis placed on form and convention, without regard to the ideas and voice. Historically, code-switching has been labeled a deficit behavior, used only by children who are limited in both of their languages. Code-switching has been negatively characterized as "an individual whim," "merely stylistic and largely nonfunctional," "done out of lexical need," and "a preprogrammed community routine" (Zentella, 1997). While recent research has questioned this deficit orientation, deficit views of code-switching are still pervasive in the field (Benjamin, 1996; Gort, 2006; Kenner, 2004).

We, along with others, have begun to suggest that simultaneous bilinguals—that is, children who acquire and/or are exposed to two languages from the time they are born— do not strictly separate languages. Instead they use two languages strategically in oral and written communication. Code-switching is an important aspect of their bilingual development. Bilingual children move regularly between multiple worlds. Bilingual living results in children who are able to draw on more than one set of resources when communicating. Code-switching represents a strategic use of two languages to capture and detail their lives in multiple worlds. In our professional development at Literacy Squared, we offer three recommendations regarding code-switching: teachers should understand what to ignore, what to worry about, and the instructional implications. We use evidence from a study we did of the code-switching behaviors of 327 bilingual students' writing to inform these recommendations (Escamilla & Hopewell, 2007).

## What to Ignore

Our research indicates that children often code-switch when referring to specific people and their titles. For example, one student wrote, "mi maestro se llama *Miss* Jones." They would also refer to the titles of books and television programs by their English names, even when Spanish alternatives existed and the rest of the writing sample was in Spanish. For example, "me encanta *Clifford the Big Red Dog*, se trata de un perro rojo. . ." or "mi programa favorita se llama *Sponge Bob*." Another common occurrence was a conceptual code-switch. For example, "si no se porta bien, la maestra le da un *time out*" or "over the weekend, we went to my cousin's *quinciñera*."

Contrary to being problematic, these code-switches indicate that children have a level of cognitive flexibility with regard to the use of two languages. For example, they know that one should not change proper names, that book titles and TV shows are named in the language that they are read or watched, and that some concepts cannot be translated across languages (e.g., you cannot translate the word *enchiladas* into English). Similarly, classroom concepts such as "time out" are culturally bound to U.S. classrooms and quite frequently are taught and learned only in English. Teachers need to understand that students make a series of linguistic decisions as they communicate, some of which indicate that students are making logical, often sophisticated choices.

## What to Fix

Our research indicates that the vast majority of code-switches were related to cross application of phonetic principles. They were literally code (convention) switches. Often students would attempt to encode words they knew orally in one language using the phonetic principles from the other ("guan a si" for "want to see"). In most cases, as in this example, the words are high-frequency or high-utility words that students have had insufficient exposure to in written form.

Individually, these words do not pose problems to a person who is trying to read a child's writing. However, in the study, many of the children's writing samples demonstrated that children frequently use Spanish phonetics and invented phrasing to express themselves in writing, thus making it difficult to read an entire story. The following example illustrates this issue.

### THE DAY A GO TO MEXICO

The day a go to Mexico was a day very Happy Y was to nerves dicos y was can a si my grama y neve si her a log time ago then wiget into the hause end a si may grama the was very espechol.

*The day I went to Mexico was a very happy day. I was very nervous because I was going to see my Grandma and I haven't seen her for a long time. We get to her house and I saw my Grandma. This was very special.*

The child who wrote the above story is code-switching in multiple ways (e.g., Spanish phonics in English—y for I; invented phrasing—wiget for we get; cross-language homophones—si for see). Collectively, she is using many strategies to express herself in writing. However, her strategies make it difficult to read her work. It is important that teachers directly and explicitly teach children to maintain their voices in writing and express themselves in a standard way in both of their languages.

## Instructional Implications

Given that the majority of code-switching entailed applying Spanish phonetics to English (or vice versa) or that children did not know appropriate English phrasing, one effective strategy for moving children toward more standard ways of writing is the use of theDictado (see Chapter 4).

Further, at the word level, we recommend that students be taught to indicate that they are consciously choosing to code-switch by encasing the word or phrase in quotation marks, using italics, or using words to signal that the alternate language text is appropriate. For example, "my favorite book *in Spanish* is *Caperucita roja*" or "fuimos al acuario y vimos "jellyfish." These indicators alert the reader that the writer is cognitively aware of code-switching, a sign of developing metacognition about bilingualism.

Children should learn when and with whom to code-switch. A knowledge of the whens, whys, and hows of code-switching is an important metacognitive skill associated with bilingualism. Some strategies for developing metalinguistic awareness of sophisticated code-switching are the following:

- *Bilingual word walls.* In addition to having individual Spanish and English word walls, it may be beneficial to have a bilingual word wall highlighting differences between English and Spanish.
- *Adivinanzas.* As a way of helping children learn the whys, whens, and hows of code-switching, teachers could ask children to translate jokes or riddles from one language to another and then discuss whether or not these sayings make sense when translated.
- *Author studies.* Analyze the writing of published bilingual writers to understand how, when, and for what purpose they code-switch.
- *Bilingual poetry:* Have students write poetry in which they deliberately use two languages. Discuss their linguistic choices with the whole group.

In short, the research on code-switching is telling us not to censor or eradicate this skill if we want to make space in our classroom for bilingualism. We should explicitly teach children about code-switching and about when and how to be strategic and effective code-switchers.

## Conclusion

Cross-language strategies are used formally and explicitly to teach specific similarities and differences between Spanish and English (e.g., writing patterns typical to English but not to Spanish, grammatical rules that are the same or different). This assists students in creating metalinguistic awareness, which allows them to develop the ability to talk about and reflect on language. Within the holistic biliteracy framework created at Literacy Squared, metalanguage is developed in Spanish, in English, and across languages and children are taught explicitly how to make cross-language connections. Talking about language helps children to develop cross-linguistic grammatical, morphological, and orthographic awareness; use of punctuation; rhetorical structures; and so forth.

Given our emphasis on the holistic nature of bilingual and biliterate development, we encourage teachers to note and list the formal cross-language strategies they will be teaching or using. The Literacy Squared framework emphasizes that teachers need to be thinking about how students' two languages can be used strategically to enhance their intellectual and linguistic growth. Further, we reiterate that cross-language strategies must be carefully and thoughtfully taught and employed. Creating a space for students to be deliberately and strategically bilingual is fundamentally different than randomly switching back and forth between languages or the persistent or consistent use of concurrent translation. Concurrent translation is ineffective for any type of biliterate development. Informal cross-language strategies, however, including the occasional use of Spanish within literacy-based ELD, are encouraged to help clarify concepts for children, for efficiency in instruction, and to help children see their two languages working together in the process of becoming biliterate.

## Questions for Reflection and Action

- Analyze the language policy in your school or school district. How does it foster or deter the development of metalanguage for your emerging bilingual students? What recommendations might you make given the information presented in this chapter?

- Create an action plan for using language strategically. What specific parameters will you use to determine how and when to alternate languages? How will these boundaries ensure that you do not defer to concurrent translation?

- Choose a cross-language strategy (e.g., bilingual books, *así se dice*). Develop a plan for how the strategy could be implemented at your grade level within your biliteracy program. What will your teaching and learning objectives be? How do these reflect the goal of direct and explicit instruction to raise students' metalinguistic awareness?

# ASSESSMENT

# Monitoring Trajectories for Biliteracy in Reading and Writing

Assessment provides us with a small window in which to observe and garner information about what a student knows. During this time we want to see not only what students know about biliteracy but how they process this information. When assessing emerging bilingual students, it is important to take the time to observe this processing and to gather as much information as possible about what they know in Spanish and English literacy to inform paired literacy instruction.

Literacy Squared promotes and supports the premise that students' languages are cultural and societal resources that should be embraced and nurtured by our educational institutions. The co-existence of two or more languages in young children contributes to a uniquely endowed human being whose experiences and knowledge can never be measured or understood as independently constrained by each language separately. There is no reason to believe that emerging bilingual children can, or should, demonstrate the totality of their literacy capabilities solely in one language. As Grosjean (2006) reminds us, ". . .bilinguals are speakers-hearers in their own right who will often not give the same kinds of results as monolinguals" (p. 36).

In Chapters 6 and 7, we demonstrate a paradigm shift from a *parallel monolingual* to a *holistic bilingual* view of assessment—from looking at biliterate development as a set of independent cognitive and linguistic processes that are traditionally assessed and interpreted separately—to looking at the development of biliteracy of Spanish-English emerging bilingual children through a holistic lens (see table on next page). In this part, while we continue to assess children's biliteracy development separately, we propose that a holistic interpretation of outcomes is a more authentic way to observe, evaluate, and monitor students' biliteracy trajectories.

## Comparing Paradigms

| Holistic Bilingualism | Parallel Monolingualism |
| --- | --- |
| Languages are viewed as mutually reinforcing; children are acknowledged to be capable of bidirectional transfer. | Languages must be strictly separated. They are thought to develop independently. |
| Literacy assessment is administered separately, but analyzed in both languages concurrently, for cross-language comparison and to document students' biliteracy trajectories. | Literacy assessment in both languages is administered and analyzed separately, denying teachers opportunities to see how children work across languages. |
| Literacy assessment instruments are authentic, taking into consideration features of language, organization, and discourse styles that are unique to each language. | Literacy assessment instruments are a translation of English literacy skills and strategies, rather than authentic to the language assessed. |
| Students are expected to show different strengths in performance of tasks in different languages. | Bilingual students are expected to perform all linguistic tasks equally well in both languages. |
| Bilingual strategies are seen as part of the process of learning to read and write in two languages. | Bilingual strategies such as code-switching, lexical borrowing, and bidirectional transfer (phonetic, syntactic, semantic, and rhetorical structure) are viewed as markers of low language proficiency in both languages. |
| Biliteracy development is measured against development standards created for emerging bilinguals. | Bilingual students are compared to the performance expectations established for monolingual speakers of each language. |

# 6 Reading Assessment

*No expert in track and field would ever compare a high hurdler to a sprinter or to a high jumper, even though the former blends certain characteristics of the latter two. A high hurdler is an integrated whole, a unique and specific athlete; he or she can attain the highest levels of world competition in the same way that the sprinter and the high jumper can.*

François Grosjean, 1989, p. 6

## Key Terms

Biliterate benchmarks

Biliterate reading zones

Holistic bilingualism

Teaching to the potential

Trajectory toward biliteracy

## Guiding Questions

- How does the theory of holistic bilingualism differ from theories of parallel monolingualism?
- Why is it important to know what emerging bilingual students can do in both languages?
- How do holistic bilingual reading assessments inform instruction?

Within Literacy Squared, we use the concept of **holistic bilingualism** to examine the biliteracy development of Spanish-English emerging bilingual children in the elementary grades. A holistic view of bilingualism (Grosjean, 1989; Valdés & Figueroa, 1994) provides a premise to observe a student's language processing and learning in Spanish and English as a whole, rather than as separate, parallel processes in two languages—much as the performance of the high hurdler in the opening quote would be viewed by a track and field judge as an "integrated whole," rather than as possessing two separate athletic skills, jumping and sprinting. This holistic stance toward literacy development allows us to take into consideration what a student knows in each language and its impact across languages and cultures. (The table on the preceding page contrasts descriptions of holistic bilingualism and parallel monolingualism, as applied to literacy assessment for emerging bilingual children.)

A simple example can be seen in the assessment of an emerging bilingual student who was doing a picture walk (pretelling) in English. She came across a picture of a newspaper and she couldn't recall the word in English. The teacher asked if the child knew what the object was in Spanish. She said yes. She was then told to say it in Spanish (*periódicos*) and continued the picture walk in English. By allowing the child to express what she knew in

Spanish, the teacher could ascertain that the child, in fact, had a concept for newspaper. When completed, the student read the text and the teacher kept a running record. When the student came to the word, "newspaper" in the text, she decoded it correctly in English. More importantly, in the retelling, she used the word "newspaper" correctly in her description of the event. By allowing the student to use what she knew in Spanish in the initial picture walk, the teacher activated background knowledge and demonstrated to the student that what she knew in Spanish could be used when learning to read in English. As a result, the child likely demonstrated a greater level of comprehension of text than she might have done had she been limited to strict monolingual assessment.

Research on authentic literacy assessment for bilingual students confirms the concept that emerging bilingual children use their knowledge of both languages and cultures to develop literacy in both languages (Escamilla, 2000; Garcia, Bravo, Dickey, Chun, & Sun-Irminger, 2002; Gort, 2006; Martínez-Roldán & Sayer, 2006; Valdés & Anloff Sanders, 1999). We have used this research to develop a **trajectory toward biliteracy**, which allows us to better capture and assess the blossoming biliteracy abilities and knowledge of emerging bilingual children.

## Biliterate Reading Trajectory

It has been axiomatic in the field of U.S. bilingual/dual language education that what one knows in one language can be positively transferred to learning to read in another language. This theory, commonly referred to as transfer theory, has been the theoretical, legal, and foundational rationale for bilingual education for more than 40 years. There is a plethora of research to support transfer, and more recently research to support bidirectional transfer. Sadly, over the years, teachers and students have been given very little practical guidance in how to maximize the potential of transfer theory either in instruction or assessment. As a result, educators have assumed that transfer occurs automatically; that gaps between what students can do in one language when compared to the other will be large; or that literacy instruction must begin anew in the second language. As we developed Literacy Squared, we embraced transfer theory, including bidirectional transfer. However, we questioned the assumption that transfer happens automatically; large gaps in literacy outcome data are to be expected; and literacy instruction should begin anew or be duplicative.

We hypothesized that if we used paired literacy instruction in purposeful ways, we could provide more concrete direction to teachers in how to maximize cross-language transfer. The creation of the biliterate reading trajectory represents one tool to help teachers better understand and use what children know about reading as they plan instruction across languages. We believed that if literacy were planned in a holistic manner that capitalized on students' abilities, regardless of the language in which they demonstrated them, that we would see greater achievement in outcomes in both languages. Our research has since confirmed these hypotheses.

The biliterate reading trajectory reflects the results of our research: emerging bilingual students from Spanish-speaking homes receiving paired literacy instruction positively develop Spanish and English reading competencies in a coordinated manner. In other words, students progress along a trajectory toward biliteracy, with their Spanish language literacy slightly more advanced than their English language literacy. Our trajectory has demonstrated that while students' reading scores in Spanish and English are not absolutely equivalent, there need not be a large discrepancy between the two. Using the *evaluación del desarrollo de la lectura* (EDL2; Celebration Press, 2007a) and the developmental reading assessment (DRA2; Celebration Press, 2007b), the trajectory reflects realistic, logical, and empirically based goals for achievement of biliteracy development in both languages. Figure 6.1 depicts this idea for a K–6 biliterate reading trajectory.

Note that the black bar represents a Spanish-language reading level and the gray bar represents an English-language reading level, as determined through the use of a diagnostic reading assessment. (There is more information about the EDL2 and DRA2 measures in the following sections.) While the Spanish-language reading level is greater than the English-language reading level, it is only slightly more advanced. Holding this expectation for biliteracy growth changes how we teach. When teachers understand what students know

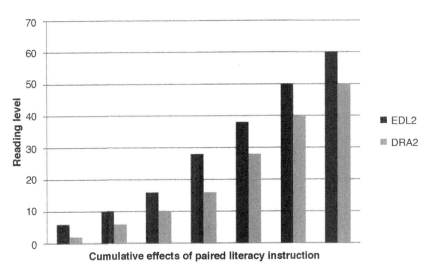

**Figure 6.1**  Biliterate reading trajectory.

and can do in each language, and they teach to students' biliterate potential, they contribute effectively to a more robust overall biliteracy development.

## Rationale and Development: The Literacy Squared Study

Initially, in 2004, we created a hypothesized trajectory about the expected relationship between Spanish and English literacy achievement with the hope that the attention to these relationships would result in the maintenance of Spanish literacy and an acceleration of English literacy. Further, we hoped teachers would use the trajectory to establish biliteracy goals and to develop lesson plans that built on these biliteracy expectations. Because of the iterative process of the Literacy Squared design, we were able to conduct research while modifying the trajectory based on our findings. We used student reading outcome data to create a trajectory that was realistic and theoretically defensible. We have observed that by combining paired literacy with increased attention to the biliteracy trajectory, each year, the achievement of more and more students reflects this rather rigorous trajectory, especially children who have participated in Literacy Squared since kindergarten and grade 1.

Only through assessing their writing and reading in both Spanish and English can we approximate a better understanding of students' trajectories toward biliteracy. Holistic assessment allows students to demonstrate their abilities across languages, provides teachers with instructional goals, and sets high expectations for biliteracy development.

**Diagnostic Measures: EDL2 and DRA2.** The creation of a trajectory requires us to assess students with parallel instruments in Spanish and English. While any measures could be used to create a comparable trajectory, in Literacy Squared reading achievement has been assessed each spring for grades K–5 using EDL2 and DRA2. The EDL2 was created as a reconstruction of the DRA2, making sure that it reflected the development of Spanish language skills and strategies. It is grounded in the Observation Survey (Clay, 1993) and *Instrumento de Observación* (Escamilla, Andrade, Basurto, & Ruíz, 1996). EDL2 measures comparable reading behaviors in the areas of reading engagement, oral reading fluency, accuracy, and comprehension. The DRA2 measures these same behaviors in English.

These assessments, using numeric leveling to break down skills and strategies in early grades, were created to help focus on instruction areas. These levels correlate to publisher suggested grade-level criteria (Table 6.1). The Literacy Squared biliteracy zones use the EDL2/DRA2 numeric leveling to inform instruction in paired literacy and to document and interpret outcomes. This is explained in detail later.

For the most part, the EDL2 and DRA2 are given one on one, with the teacher making observations of students in the act of reading and responding to text. Before reading, students are asked to preview or predict. Running records are taken to observe problem solving on text, accuracy, and fluency rates and expression and phrasing. Once the text reading is completed students are asked to retell, make connections, respond to a reflection question,

TABLE 6.1

## EDL2/DRA2 Levels by Grade Level

| Grade | EDL2/DRA2 Levels |
|---|---|
| K | A, 1, 2, 3 |
| 1 | 4, 6, 8, 10, 12,14, 16 |
| 2 | 18, 20, 24, 28 |
| 3 | 30, 34, 38 |
| 4 | 40 |
| 5 | 50 |

or use text features. With regard to text response, from levels A–24, the student responds orally while the teacher scripts the responses. From levels 28 and up, the student responds in writing. At the written level, students complete a summary, respond to literal comprehension questions, and use personal or textual information to support their responses. The teacher then uses a rubric to analyze the information to determine the student's independent reading level and areas of strength and the need to set an instructional focus.

**Choosing Texts for Assessment.** Because the titles and stories are essentially the same in the EDL2 and DRA2, and to ensure that a child does not read the same text in Spanish and English, the chart in Table 6.2 identifies which text to use in each language at every level. This is to make certain that an equal number of texts are available at each level in each language, and that the genre (e.g., nonfiction vs. fiction) is balanced. The list provided

TABLE 6.2

## Literacy Squared Recommended Assessment Texts: DRA2/EDL2

| Level | EDL2 (Spanish) | DRA2 (English) |
|---|---|---|
| A | ¿Sabes cantar? | If a child is reading independently at |
| 1 | Mira lo que se va | EDL2 levels A–2, do not assess on |
| 2 | Yo veo | the DRA2. |
| 3 | ¿Qué te gusta? | Look at Me |
| 4 | ¿Dónde está mi gorra? | Get Your Umbrella |
| 6 | ¿Por qué paramos? | Time to Play |
| 8 | Duque | The Lost Book |
| 10 | Las cajas de zapatos | Grandma's Surprise |
| 12 | La amiga nueva de Roberto | Allie's Wish |
| 14 | El cochecito | A New School |
| 16 | Rigo el rascate<br>Los pajaritos* | Monkey's Stepping Stones<br>Animal Homes* |
| 18 | Un gigante en el bosque | Game Day |
| 20 | Reni la rana | Turtle's Big Race |
| 24 | El día más maravilloso | Thin as a Stick |
| 28 | Yo no te veo hermosa<br>Los animales pueden ayudar* | Missing Sneakers<br>From Peanuts to Peanut Butter* |
| 30 | Los ayudantes ocupados | Tiger's Whirlwind Day |
| 34 | El misterio en la casa de los Kuan | Summer Discovery |
| 38 | Temor en la laguna de los castores<br>La manera de los Navajo* | A Trip Through Time<br>Mae Jemison: Shooting for the Stars* |
| 40 | Hasta abajo<br>Una manada de lobos* | A Journey to Freedom<br>The Amazing Octopus* |
| 50 | Reclamar la falta<br>Los cazatormentas* | Friends in America<br>Lights! Camera! Action!* |
| 60 | Ranita y princesa<br>Un corazón valiente | Mike Fink, King of the Keelboatmen<br>One Brave Heart* |

*Nonfiction text.

**TABLE 6.3**

Biliterate Reading Zones

| EDL2 Level (Spanish) | DRA2 Level (English) |
|---|---|
| A–3 | A–3 (exposure) |
| 4–6 | A–3 |
| 8–10 | 4–6 |
| 12–16 | 8–10 |
| 18–28 | 12–16 |
| 30–38 | 18–28 |
| 40 | 30–38 |
| 50–60 | 40+ |

gives the texts used for summative purposes each spring. Interim assessment is recommended, but it is important that alternative texts be used for formative purposes.

## Biliterate Reading Zones: Teaching to the Potential

The conceptualization of a trajectory toward biliteracy required us to think about how the measurement tools used could aid us in understanding more precisely the relationship between Spanish and English literacy. We created ranges of levels for EDL2 Spanish reading reflecting the knowledge of how reading behaviors and challenges vary from level to level. For example, levels A–3 reflect skills and strategies that are emergent behaviors, such as directionality, one-to-one matching, and the concept of beginning/end. These ranges were then projected to DRA2 English reading levels to create expected learning zones for students in English reading (Table 6.3).

A student who has mastered reading behaviors associated with an EDL2 level 10 is expected to be learning to read concurrently in English between DRA2 levels 4 and 6. Even if that child's DRA2 score does not indicate these levels as instructional, we use the Spanish score to support the idea that the student reaching level 10 has the reading strategies to support working at levels 4–6 in English. Teachers should choose books in this range for literacy-based ELD instruction. In other words, the teacher would be focusing instruction in English literacy to the related zone, or **teaching to the potential**.

The implication of knowing what students can do in both Spanish and English reading is important for planning paired literacy instruction. Students' Spanish reading scores provide the teacher with data to inform instructional decisions for both Spanish literacy and literacy-based ELD. The premise is that if a student has a higher score in Spanish reading than in English reading, the difficulty is not about "reading," but rather a language issue. Thus, the **biliterate reading zones** allow for the teacher to plan literacy-based ELD instruction around what the child already knows about reading in Spanish, and focuses on developing oracy skills while using developmentally appropriate texts in English.

We now have empirical evidence to support the validity of these ranges for students from Spanish-speaking homes. Students who participated in the Literacy Squared research project were able to attain the reading trajectories projected by the biliterate reading zones. The trajectory toward biliteracy, then, provides a foundation for changes in pedagogy, as well as a tool to guide teachers as they plan appropriate instruction with research-based and research-tested expectations for biliteracy development.

None of the participating students in our research were from monolingual English-speaking homes. Research is needed to determine the actual biliterate reading trajectories of these students in dual language programs.

## Biliterate Benchmarks

As we have suggested, Spanish and English reading achievement should closely parallel one another, and the creation of the biliterate reading zones enables us to see this relationship more concretely. In addition, we have identified **biliterate benchmarks**, to help teachers plan end-of-year projections in a paired literacy environment, and to determine

**TABLE 6.4**

Biliterate Benchmarks by Grade Level

| Grade | EDL2 Level (Spanish) | DRA2 Level (English) |
|---|---|---|
| K | 3–4 | A–2 |
| 1 | 12–16 | 8–10 |
| 2 | 24–28 | 12–16 |
| 3 | 34–38 | 24–28 |
| 4 | 40 | 34–38 |
| 5 | 50+ | 40+ |

whether students are on a grade-appropriate biliterate trajectory. Because EDL2/DRA2 is a diagnostic assessment that requires teachers to listen, observe, and analyze a student's use of strategies as they read and respond to authentic text, many of the strategies required of Common Core State Standards can be captured. For example, there are Common Core requirements in the areas of speaking, listening, reading, and writing. There are comprehension standards for reading a range of literature and informational texts across grade levels. Foundational skills such as print concepts, phonological awareness, phonics, word recognition and fluency are addressed as well. EDL2/DRA2 provide opportunities for teachers to assess students in all these areas in both languages and help teachers set a high-expectation literacy goal in both languages.

In monolingual instructional contexts where monolingual frameworks are used, students are assigned a fixed benchmark score to indicate proficiency in each grade level. In Literacy Squared, we recognize that literacy acquisition in two languages may result in pacing that differs from expected pacing in monolingual settings. Therefore, we acknowledge through our framework that students on a normal trajectory may fall within a range of levels in either language. One way to measure and document this trajectory is to assess each student in each language and to interpret these assessments side by side. The resulting trajectory considers Spanish language literacy achievement plus English language literacy achievement, allowing for a broader range of levels to represent adequate progress toward biliteracy proficiency. Based on our longitudinal research with emerging bilinguals from Spanish-speaking homes, we have designated biliterate benchmarks by grade level (Table 6.4). It is important to recognize that these ranges represent high expectations, and only through consistent and coherent paired literacy instruction can we expect such reading development for emerging bilingual students.

## Holistic Bilingual Reading Assessment in Action

In Literacy Squared, Spanish and English reading assessments are done a minimum of once a year for summative purposes and to provide teachers with information on how students are progressing on the biliterate reading trajectory. The assessment also allows us to observe the relationship of skills and strategies across languages. The previous spring's scores can be used by the current teacher to make instruction decisions beginning in the fall. If, however, there are no scores from the previous spring, it is important that teachers collect baseline EDL2/DRA2 data for formative assessment purposes.

Assessing students in both Spanish and English reading allows teachers to begin to determine what skills and strategies have been taught and learned in Spanish and what has been transferred or learned in English. The Spanish assessment provides information on the student's reading level and can inform reading instruction for learning in both languages. Information gleaned from the English assessment also provides important information that is likely more related to a student's language level than a reading level. However, the Spanish reading scores are the best indicator about what needs to occur instructionally, in both Spanish and English, because most reading skills transfer across languages. Using the biliterate reading zones listed in Table 6.3, teachers can begin to understand their students' ranges of levels. This will allow them to facilitate cross-language

---

**TABLE 6.5**

## Sofia's Written Summary for Assessment

EDL2 Spanish level 38, *Temor en la laguna de los castores*
DRA2 English level 28, *Missing Sneakers*

| Spanish Level 38 | English Level 28 |
|---|---|
| **Al principio**, la mama estada construiendo su casa y estada cuidando a sus castorsitos. **Entonces,** los castorsitos se fueron a la oria del lago. **Luego,** un oso aparesio. El oso se queria comer a los castorsitos. **Después de eso,** la mama castor se metio a la agua para llamar atension del oso. **Al final**, la mama se debolvia a la casa y ay estaban los castorsitos. | **In the beginning,** Sara Was Packing to move. **Next**, her mother told her to put Sneakers in the crate. **Then,** Sneakers got lost. **After that,** Sara loked por Sneakers. **In the end,** sara faund Sneakres. |

---

connections and to teach explicitly those skills and strategies in both languages needed to progress on the trajectory toward biliteracy.

## Using Assessment Outcomes to Plan Reading Instruction for Individual Students

Using student examples, we can clearly see the relationship between Spanish and English literacy development and how we need to have students working toward their potential based on what they can do in both Spanish and English. These student assessment samples in Tables 6.5 and 6.6 are written summaries of texts the two students read, which were chosen to match each student's independent levels for Spanish and English. This means that the student was able to read texts at these difficulty levels with both adequate accuracy and fluency. The written summaries show the students' comprehension of what was read and their ability to demonstrate aspects of a summary. Putting the Spanish and English summaries side by side gives us a more complete understanding of the student's literacy competencies. The Spanish text was titled *Temor en la laguna de los castores* (*Trouble at the Beaver Pond*). Briefly, it is a story about a mother beaver who had to lure a bear away from her young in order to save them. The English text was *Missing Sneakers*. It is about a little girl named Sara who loses her cat named Sneakers while packing to move. She eventually finds him in one of the boxes playing with his toys.

The summaries in the tables were typed up exactly as the students wrote them on the student assessment form. Any words that are bolded were already written for the student, to provide the structure for the paragraph.

**Analysis of Sofia's Reading Summary.** To begin, Sofia has demonstrated understanding of both stories. In this retelling, we see that across languages, she understands that a written

---

**TABLE 6.6**

## Martín's Written Summary for Assessment

EDL2 Spanish level 38, *Temor en la laguna de los castores*
DRA2 English level 28, *Missing Sneakers*

| Spanish Level 38 | English Level 28 |
|---|---|
| **Al principio**, la mama estaba aciendo la madrigera y al mismo tiempo estaba biendo a sus hijos. **Entonces**, vino un oso Viejo que se queria comer a sus hijos. **Luego,** la mama se metio al agua para distraer el oso de sus hijos. **Después de eso,** el oso no regreso a la selva nunca jamas. **Al final**, la mama estaba con sus hijos otra ves. | **In the beginning,** Sara was moving to onthore hous. **Next,** she whas paking snekars toys and stuf of her. **Then,** the mom of sara thal he kep an ai on snekers. Or he get lost. **After that**, Snekars was lost then a men had a box from the box caim a nois laik a cat. **In the end**, sara faind Snekers in his toys then Sara thal Snekers com her to pot you an your crate first thing. |

summary involves a sequence of events, the inclusion of character names, and stating the problem and solution. However, in Spanish more details are included in the summary.

Information learned from this analysis indicates the teacher might take the following steps in Spanish literacy instruction:

- Work at a Spanish level 40, introducing Sofia to new vocabulary and genres
- Continue to reinforce how to write a summary, and provide opportunities to expand on more precise language in the description and elaboration
- Provide models for conventional spelling of high-frequency words such as *mamá* (mom), *estaba* (was), and *allí* (there).
- Provide direct instruction on the use of accent marks in preterite and imperfect tenses such as *apareció* (appeared), *quería* (wanted), *se metió* (jumped in), *devolvía* (returned)

To teach to the potential in literacy-based ELD, the instructor might

- Work at levels 28–30 in English and provide explicit support in developing language through oracy instruction. Using this range of leveled texts, the teacher can build the language needed in English to read with the same level of Spanish comprehension.
- Provide opportunities to practice writing more summaries, guiding the expansion of details
- Provide language structures that will increase the use of details and the length of sentences (e.g., compound and complex sentences; increased use of prepositional phrases)

**Analysis of Martín's Reading Summary.** In this example, Martín demonstrated similar skills across languages. He understands that a written summary involves a sequence of events, using character names, and stating the problem and solution. In addition, both summaries include events and details using descriptive language. In English, we find many cross-language connections at the sentence/phrase and phonetic level.

In Spanish instruction, the teacher might

- Work at a Spanish reading level 40, introducing Martín to new vocabulary and genres
- Continue working at summaries and expanding on details, providing more information at the middle and end of the summary.
- Model and support spelling patterns with silent h; s/z/c; b/v; past-tense written accent marks.

To teach to the potential in literacy-based ELD, the teacher might

- Have the student read at levels 34–38 with teacher support
- Provide opportunities to model similarities and differences in language structures (e.g., the mom of Sara vs. Sara's mom; stuff of her vs. her stuff)
- Provide opportunities to model conventional spelling in English (e.g., another, like, came)
- Provide opportunities to practice pronoun agreement

These are just teaching points from observing the summaries side by side. However, if we had looked at other comprehension responses, such as interpretation, question response (how to interpret), or a reflection question response (how to determine importance), we could glean more information to guide what language, structures, and concepts might be needed to inform instruction in both Spanish and English.

## Using Biliterate Reading Zones to Plan Instruction for a Class

In the example that follows, a set of scores has been created to demonstrate how Spanish and English language assessments each contribute critical pieces of information that guide instructional decisions at the start of a school year. The spring Spanish and English reading scores for a group of grade 1 students are listed in Table 6.7. Their grade 2 teacher will

**TABLE 6.7**

Spring Reading Scores for a Grade 1 Class

| Student | EDL2 Spanish | DRA2 English |
|---------|--------------|--------------|
| Susie | 8 | 4 |
| Tomás | 16 | 8 |
| Felicia | 16 | 4 |
| Andrina | 28 | 16 |
| Sabrina | 24 | 14 |
| Leticia | 18 | 12 |
| Juan | 28 | 6 |
| Martín | 16 | 6 |
| Sandra | 18 | 12 |
| Ricardo | 20 | 6 |
| Daniel | 14 | 8 |
| Michael | 20 | 14 |
| María | 24 | 4 |
| Victoria | 18 | 8 |
| Mayte | 4 | 4 |
| Rudy | 24 | 10 |

use these scores to plan for Spanish literacy and literacy-based ELD instruction in the fall. In order to do so, the teacher needs to

- Analyze the scores to understand which students meet or exceed biliterate benchmark expectations in Spanish.
- Examine students' Spanish reading levels in relation to their English reading levels.

A first level of examination will involve determining which students are or are not in the expected targeted biliterate reading zones (see Table 6.3). This will affect what the students are taught in whole group instruction and how to group for instruction in Spanish literacy. Furthermore, if we expect students to be on a trajectory toward biliteracy within the targeted biliterate reading zones, they must be at or near the biliterate benchmark in Spanish at the end of the year.

What we have found at the grade 1 level is that many students may have reached their end-of-year benchmark in Spanish, but may not fall within the biliterate reading zone because their English levels are lower. As they continue through the grades, the distance between Spanish and English decreases significantly. Using Table 6.3, we then compare the Spanish EDL2 results to the English DRA2 results. Children whose EDL2 and DRA2 outcomes align within the zones on the table are on a positive trajectory toward biliteracy.

**Analysis of EDL2 and DRA2 Results.** In conducting this analysis, both the biliterate reading zones (see Table 6.3) and the biliterate benchmark (see Table 6.4) charts need to be used. To begin analyzing the results we first need to determine the following:

- How many students meet the end-of-first-grade biliterate benchmark in Spanish (EDL2 levels 12–16)? (Table 6.8)
  - Fourteen out of 16 students meet the benchmark.
  - Two students (Susie and Mayte) did not meet the Spanish biliterate benchmark because they scored at EDL2 levels 8 and 4, respectively.
  - Fourteen students met or exceeded the Spanish biliterate benchmark, with their scores ranging from EDL2 levels 14–28. This is 88% of the class.

| TABLE 6.8 | | | |
|---|---|---|---|
| **Spring Reading Scores for Same Grade 1 Class in Relation to the Spanish Biliterate Benchmark** | | | |
| **Student** | **EDL2** | **DRA2** | |
| **At or above Benchmark in Spanish** | | | |
| Felicia | 16 | 4 | |
| Daniel | 14 | 8 | |
| Tomás | 16 | 8 | |
| Martín | 16 | 6 | |
| Victoria | 18 | 8 | |
| Sandra | 18 | 12 | |
| Leticia | 18 | 12 | |
| Ricardo | 20 | 10 | |
| Michael | 20 | 14 | |
| María | 24 | 4 | |
| Rudy | 24 | 10 | |
| Andrina | 28 | 16 | |
| Sabrina | 24 | 14 | |
| Juan | 28 | 6 | |
| **Below Benchmark in Spanish** | | | |
| Susie | 8 | 4 | |
| Mayte | 4 | 4 | |

| TABLE 6.9 | | |
|---|---|---|
| **Spring Reading Scores for Same Grade 1 Class in Relation to the Biliterate Zone** | | |
| **Student** | **EDL2** | **DRA2** |
| **At or above Spanish Benchmark** | | |
| Felicia | 16 | 4 |
| **Daniel** | 14 | 8 |
| **Tomás** | 16 | 8 |
| Martín | 16 | 6 |
| Victoria | 18 | 8 |
| **Sandra** | 18 | 12 |
| **Leticia** | 18 | 12 |
| Ricardo | 20 | 10 |
| **Michael** | 20 | 14 |
| María | 24 | 4 |
| Rudy | 24 | 10 |
| **Andrina** | 28 | 16 |
| **Sabrina** | 24 | 14 |
| Juan | 28 | 6 |
| **Below Spanish Benchmark** | | |
| **Susie** | 8 | 4 |
| **Mayte** | 4 | 4 |

Names in **bold** indicate students who are within the biliterate zone.

- How many students are within a biliterate reading zone?
  - Nine out of 16 students, or 56%, are within a targeted zone at the end of grade 1 (Table 6.9). This means that their Spanish and English reading levels reflect the corresponding Spanish and English levels of proficiency on the targeted biliterate reading zones shown in Table 6.3. (E.g., Daniel is 14 in Spanish and 8 in English, which reflects EDL2 levels 12–16 and DRA2 levels 8–10 in the biliterate reading zone.)
- How many students are not in a biliterate reading zone?
  - The remaining 7 out of 16 students are not within a targeted biliterate reading zone.
  - However, 6 of the 7 students had met or exceeded the Spanish biliterate benchmark. This indicates the need to focus on teaching to students' biliterate potential during literacy-based ELD.

Table 6.10 is a blank chart to guide teachers in recording their student assessments for planning paired literacy instruction in their classrooms.

## Using Information from the Biliterate Reading Zones and Benchmarks

A holistic approach to biliterate reading assessment is useful on two levels. First, teachers can use the results to celebrate and measure students' progress toward biliterate reading acquisition. In fact, we would hope that these outcomes would be published and celebrated as widely as the current monolingual frameworks. Rather than the predominant deficit view that emerging bilingual children are below grade level, sometimes in both Spanish and English, we can reframe the discussion around what children are accomplishing and becoming. This even presents an opportunity to change the discourse at a school to biliteracy being a superior literacy form compared to monoliteracy.

Secondly, and equally as important, these zones can serve to guide instruction. The ranges expand teachers' options for text selection, genre, themes, teaching focus, and cultural and linguistic relevance. We reiterate our recommendations that, to the extent pos-

**TABLE 6.10**

Blank Chart to Record Reading Results

Grade _____

| Student | EDL2 Score | DRA2 Score | Meets Spanish Benchmark | In Biliterate Zone |
|---|---|---|---|---|
| | | | | |
| | | | | |
| | | | | |
| | | | | |
| | | | | |
| | | | | |
| | | | | |
| | | | | |
| | | | | |
| | | | | |
| | | | | |
| | | | | |
| | | | | |
| | | | | |
| | | | | |
| | | | | |

Using the data
- How many students are not in a biliterate reading zone?
- How will you group students for Spanish literacy?
- In grades K–2: what range of text should be used for whole-group English literacy?
- In grades 3 and higher: how will you group students for English literacy?

sible, children be taught in whole groups. However, we recognize that individual schools and individual teachers have preferences for how they structure literacy environments. These zones can help teachers make decisions regarding the organization of literacy blocks. Finally, utilizing what children know in Spanish to make instructional decisions related to literacy-based ELD increases the likelihood that students will be challenged in appropriate ways to meet high standards.

## Conclusion

The concept of holistic assessment provides teachers with a new way of thinking and a new way of analyzing and using information to enhance our knowledge about teaching emerging bilinguals. Using measures of Spanish and English reading—EDL2 and DRA2—side by side, allows us to see students' strengths and needs, what they know in both languages, and gives us guidance to teach to a students' potential.

## Questions for Reflection and Action

- How might you use reading assessments in two languages as tools to look at the biliterate reading development of students at your school? What factors might you consider in choosing assessments?
- Gather reading assessment data in Spanish and English for the students in your classroom. How can you use this empirical evidence to strengthen your biliteracy instruction?

# 7

# Writing Assessment

*[T]he bilingual student brings to learning a linguistic repertoire that cannot be measured in a single language. Regardless of the language they are using and their particular proficiency level, bilinguals are influenced by their knowledge of another language and their cross-cultural experience.*

Mileidis Gort, 2006, p. 326

## Key Terms

**Bilingual strategies**

**Biliterate writing potential**

**Biliterate writing trajectory**

**Language-specific approximations**

**Literacy Squared writing rubric**

## Guiding Questions

■ What are the advantages of recording an emerging bilingual child's writing scores in Spanish and English on a single assessment rubric?

■ How does analyzing children's biliterate writing enable us to observe cross-language transfer, including Spanish to English and English to Spanish?

■ How do holistic bilingual writing assessments inform instruction?

As we saw in Chapter 6 with regard to reading, using a holistic bilingual lens emphasizes the importance of assessing children's Spanish and English literacy development simultaneously. Working within a holistic bilingual framework, teachers are able to understand and document how each language can mediate the development of the other, and to make informed instructional decisions to accelerate biliterate development. This holistic stance toward biliteracy development requires an assessment approach that connects the examination of students' writing in Spanish and in English because we know that emerging bilingual children use all of their linguistic resources when communicating in either language. Thus, one of the hallmarks of the Literacy Squared approach to assessment—an essential and unique component of our holistic approach to bilingualism—is a side by side examination of children's Spanish and English writing skills and abilities.

In order to put this holistic biliterate writing assessment into practice, it became necessary to develop a new and different assessment tool: the **Literacy Squared writing rubric**. In this chapter, we describe the rubric and its development, demonstrate how to use it to evaluate actual students' Spanish and English writing samples, and show how this assessment data can inform biliterate writing instruction within paired literacy.

## Shifting the Lens: Parallel Monolingual to Holistic Bilingual

Let's begin with a simple example of how a student's writing might be perceived, first from a parallel monolingual perspective and then from a holistic bilingual one.

The writing sample in Box 7.1, if read from a parallel monolingual framework, would be considered unreadable.* The second grader who wrote it, Elias, might be described as confused or semilingual because of his use of Spanish syntax, unusual English phrasing, code-switching, and application of Spanish phonetic principles: The *lob* (wolf) *tiro* (blew) down the house of *paja* (straw) within the English composition. In other words, it may be said that Spanish is interfering with his English literacy and language development. He may even be referred to special services to receive more phonics-based instruction because of his unconventional spelling (roning/running, japen/happen). Reading this child's composition using a holistic bilingual lens, however, we would find that he not only communicated a meaningful message related to his favorite book, the *Three Little Pigs*, but also that he utilized a variety of linguistic, cultural, and written strategies to encode his message. (See Table 7.1 for an interpretation of the **bilingual strategies** employed in this writing sample.)

---

**BOX 7.1    *The Tree Little Piks***

Translation

The Three Little Pigs

My story is about of three little pigs and 1 *lob* (*lobo*/wolf) *feroz* (ferocious). The *lob tiro* (blew) down the house of *paja* (straw). Then the little pig go running to the house of his brother and say what happen to the house. And his brother say *o que feroz lobo* (Oh what a <u>wolf ferocious</u>). Then the *lob* (wolf) go to the house of the other pig and the house go down. Then the 2 little pigs go with his brother and he say what happen to the house of the 1 pig and the house of the 2 pig. Then the *lob* go to the other house and the other house is of *ladrillos* (bricks) and he can (can't) *deribarla* (*derribarla*/blow it down)

---

*In translating emerging bilingual students' writing samples, we interpreted to the best of our ability the message communicated using standard spelling. We did not insert standard punctuation. Further, to illustrate emerging bilingual students' developing understanding of language, we attempted to translate linguistic approximations literally, and underlined them as a signal to the reader.

**TABLE 7.1**

## Holistic Bilingual Interpretation of "The Tree Little Piks"

| Strategic Behavior | Teacher-Identified Resources* |
|---|---|
| Communicative competence | • Retelling of the story of the *Three Little Pigs* in sequence, with all essential parts, an introduction, and a conclusion. |
| Spanish syntax | • The house of *paja/casa de paja* → straw house |
| English syntax (in Spanish code-switch) | • The student may have been drawing on English syntax, adjective/noun placement, *feroz lobo* (ferocious wolf) |
| Lexical code-switches | • *Feroz* for ferocious<br>• *Paja* for straw<br>• *Ladrillos* for bricks |
| Rule-governed hypotheses | • *Lob*/lobo: Many cognates in English drop the final vowel, for example *carro* becomes car. The child is overgeneralizing this rule |
| Spanish phonetics to encode | • J for H in English—*jis* for his, *japen* for happen, *ji* for he<br>• *Gua* for wha—*Guat* for what<br>• D for th—da, den |

*Using a bilingual lens, the teacher identifies the resources the student is utilizing.

Within a holistic bilingual framework, we would also need to recognize and understand this same child's capabilities when writing in Spanish. The English writing sample gives us only one part of the picture. Thus, we need to examine his Spanish and English writing side by side, to determine what he can do in both languages (Box 7.2). In many cases, students will transfer certain skills from one language to the other, while other writing skills and behaviors may only be observed in one language. If we do not look holistically at a student's biliterate writing, we will not see all that the child can do, which can have detrimental effects for the child and lead to ineffective instruction. In other words, we need to assess what emerging bilingual children know in their entirety across languages so that we can teach to their potential.

In this case, it is clear that Elias can relate the plot of a television program, in Spanish, in a similar manner to what he has done for the *Three Little Pigs* story in English—sequentially, with an introduction and conclusion. Seeing what he can do in Spanish alongside the English sample provides a better understanding of all the student can do in writing.

**BOX 7.2 *"The Tree Little Piks" Student's Spanish and English Writing Samples***

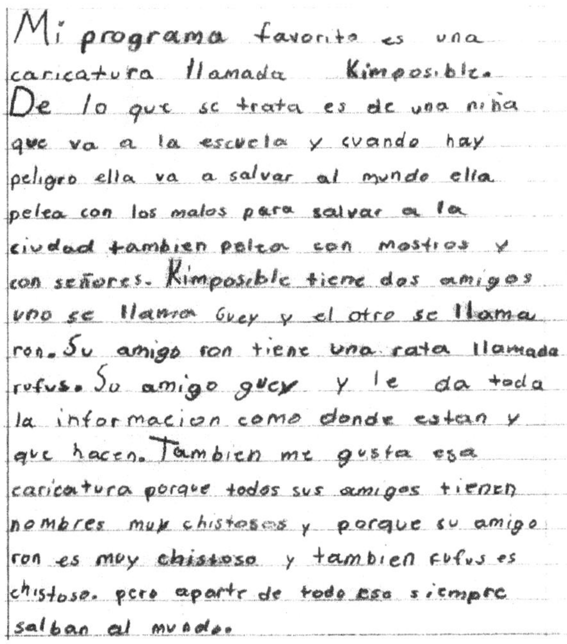
Mi programa favorito es una
caricatura llamada Kimposible.
De lo que se trata es de una niña
que va a la escuela y cuando hay
peligro ella va a salvar al mundo ella
pelea con los malos para salvar a la
ciudad tambien pelea con mostros y
con señores. Kimposible tiene dos amigos
uno se llama Guey y el otro se llama
ron. Su amigo ron tiene una rata llamada
rufus. Su amigo guey y le da toda
la informacion como donde estan y
que hacen. Tambien me gusta esa
caricatura porque todos sus amigos tienen
nombres muy chistosos y porque su amigo
ron es muy chistoso y tambien rufus es
chistoso. pero apartr de todo eso siempre
salban al mundo.

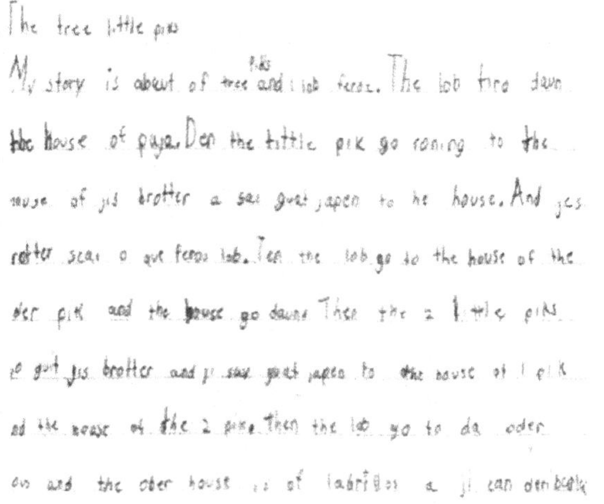
The tree little piks
My story is about of tree and 1 lob feroz. The lob tiro daun
the house of paja. Den the tittle pik go roning to the
house of jis brotter a sae guat japen to he house. And jes
brotter scar o que feroz lob. Ten the lob go to the house of the
der pik and the house go daun. Then the 2 little piks
go jis brotter and ji sae guat japen to the house of 1 pik
ad the house of the 2 piks. Then the lob go to da oder
and the oder house of labrillos a ji can denbeak

**Translation of Spanish sample:** My favorite program is a cartoon called Kimpossible (Kim Possible). What it is about is a girl that goes to school and when there is danger she goes to save the world she fights with the bad guys to save the city she also fights with monsters and other men. Kimpossible has two friends one is named Guey (Wade) and the other is named ron. Her friend ron has a rat named rufus. Her friend guey and gives her all the information such as where they are and what they do. I also like this cartoon because all her friends have funny names and because her friend ron is very funny and rufus also is funny. Aside from all of that they always save the world.

## Biliterate Writing Trajectory

The underlying principles of the **biliterate writing trajectory** in Literacy Squared are similar to those in the biliterate reading trajectory discussed in Chapter 6: emerging bilingual students receiving paired literacy instruction will positively develop Spanish and English writing competencies in a coordinated manner. That is, as students develop Spanish writing competency, most of the abilities and skills transfer to English writing and vice versa. Using measures of biliterate development rather than grade levels or other monolingual norms, we have observed and documented these relationships in students' abilities to express and organize content and through their use of punctuation. The main difference between the biliterate reading and writing trajectories is that we have only hypothesized students' biliterate writing trajectory using the Literacy Squared writing rubric. In reading, the trajectory has been tested and confirmed with diagnostic measures (see Chapter 6 for details). Similar to the development of the biliterate reading trajectory, we are beginning with a hypothesis that emerging bilingual students can develop biliterate writing competencies in paired literacy contexts.

The biliterate writing trajectory is based on notions of holistic bilingualism where the totality of an emerging bilingual student's writing accomplishments is only understood when writing in both languages is assessed. The information gleaned from such understanding and analysis is used to inform writing instruction that taps into students' biliterate potential within Spanish literacy and literacy-based ELD. Finally, it helps illustrate that, in a paired literacy situation, emerging bilingual students can develop writing skills in both Spanish and English.

# Literacy Squared Writing Rubric

When we began our research in Literacy Squared, it was common for us to see many of our emerging bilingual students produce English writing samples very similar to Elias' *Three Little Pigs* narrative (see Box 7.1). That sample was produced in the pilot year of the project, when our research sites were just beginning to implement paired literacy instruction. At that time, because bilingual programs had traditionally withheld any English reading or writing instruction until grade 3, many students' Spanish and English writing was very different. In general, students' English writing was more limited because they produced less text, included fewer complex ideas, and relied more heavily on Spanish phonetics to encode words. Over time, with the introduction of paired literacy instruction, we have observed our emerging bilingual students' writing skills improve across languages. Our students are not confused when they learn to write and read in two languages. Most importantly, we have learned that as students receive consistent and comprehensive paired literacy instruction from grades K–5, differences in abilities between both languages diminish and, much like in reading, students are on a positive trajectory toward biliterate writing development. Later in this chapter we share these observations through student samples that use the Literacy Squared writing rubric to demonstrate **biliterate writing potential**. Let's turn to the rubric itself.

## *Development of the Rubric*

The Literacy Squared writing rubric (Box 7.3) is designed to assess the Spanish and English writing of emerging bilingual children in the elementary grades. It has the potential for use with various genres and can be used as either a formative or summative measure. The students who have used it thus far have been part of Literacy Squared. They have received paired literacy instruction beginning in kindergarten, with an emphasis on direct and explicit instruction linked to shared and collaborative learning structures. Writing development is monitored and analyzed through the collection of Spanish and English writing samples at least once a year.

For the research project, these samples were collected midyear for summative purposes, and we encouraged teachers to collect additional Spanish and English writing samples throughout the year to inform their instruction. Over the course of eight years and different phases of the Literacy Squared research project, we have collected biliterate writing samples from over 5,000 emerging bilingual students in grades K–5 in three states, eight school districts, and 33 schools. We began piloting the development of the model in 2004 in grades 1–3; implemented and researched the model more formally in phase I of the study (beginning in 2006) in grades 1–5; and in phase II (beginning in 2009) replicated phase I, studied specific case study schools, and started paired literacy kindergarten instruction for the first time.

Knowing that emerging bilingual children are likely to distribute their knowledge and competencies across two languages, a chief concern was to design an instrument that would allow us to evaluate and record a child's Spanish and English writing scores using a single rubric. The writing rubric presented in this book is our second iteration, revised to capture the more refined distinctions we have observed while assessing the Spanish and English writing of thousands of emerging bilingual children over the course of our research.

A strength of our data is that we can look longitudinally at individual emerging bilingual children's writing, to try to understand patterns of development over time. An evaluation of our data revealed that students' writing improved in ways not previously captured by the rubric's descriptors. That is, a student's writing ability could improve in perceptible and tangible ways without a concurrent numeric increase on the rubric. Further, we noted that the guidance and structure we gave teachers to observe and report qualitative annotations were limiting and narrow. Before revising the rubric, we re-examined the writing of some of the students previously in the study, took into consideration the teacher feedback we have received over the years, consulted the scant literature that addresses bilingual writing, and kept in mind that phase II would include kindergartners. The result is a rubric that both mirrors, and diverges from, previous iterations.

## BOX 7.3  *Literacy Squared Writing Rubric*

| Rater ID: | | Not to prompt (circle) |
|---|---|---|
| Student ID: | | Span ǀ Eng |

Grades: K, 1, 2, 3, 4, and 5 *(circle grade)*

| SPANISH SCORE | CONTENT | ENGLISH SCORE |
|---|---|---|
| 10 | Focused composition, conveys emotion or uses figurative language, is engaging to the reader; clearly addresses the prompt; book language | 10 |
| 9 | Organization of composition includes effective transitions and vivid examples | 9 |
| 8 | Writing includes complex *sentence* structures and has a discernable, consistent structure | 8 |
| 7 | Sense of completeness—Clear introduction and clear conclusion | 7 |
| 6 | Includes descriptive language (use of adjectives, adverbs at the word level) or varied sentence structures | 6 |
| 5 | Main idea discernable with supporting details, or main idea can be inferred or stated explicitly, or repetitive vocabulary: may include unrelated ideas | 5 |
| 4 | Two ideas—*I like my bike **and/because** it is blue* | 4 |
| 3 | One idea expressed through a subject and predicate, subject may be implied (*I like my bike, amo,* or *run*) | 3 |
| 2 | Label(s), list of words; may communicate an idea without subject and predicate | 2 |
| 1 | Prewriting: Picture only, not readable, or written in a language other than the prompt | 1 |
| 0 | The student did not prepare a sample | 0 |
| | **STRUCTURAL ELEMENTS** | |
| 5 | Multiparagraph composition with accurate punctuation and capitalization | 5 |
| 4 | Controls most structural elements and includes paragraphing | 4 |
| 3 | Controls beginning and ending punctuation in ways that make sense and is attempting additional structural elements (commas, question marks, guiones, apostrophes, ellipses, parentheses, hyphens, and indentation) | 3 |
| 2 | Uses one or more of the structural elements *correctly* | 2 |
| 1 | Uses one or more of the structural elements *incorrectly* | 1 |
| 0 | Structural elements not evident | 0 |
| | **SPELLING** | |
| 6 | Accurate spelling | 6 |
| 5 | Most words are spelled conventionally | 5 |
| 4 | Majority of high-frequency words are correct and child is approximating standardization in errors | 4 |
| 3 | Most words are not spelled conventionally but demonstrates an emerging knowledge of common spelling patterns | 3 |
| 2 | Represents most sounds in words and most high-frequency words are spelled incorrectly | 2 |
| 1 | Represents some sounds in words | 1 |
| 0 | Message is not discernable | 0 |

*Continues*

| BOX 7.3 | *Literacy Squared Writing Rubric* (Cont.) |

**Qualitative Analysis of Student Writing**

**Bilingual Strategies**

| | (Spanish → English) | (English → Spanish) | Spanish ←→ English (bidirectional) |
|---|---|---|---|
| DISCOURSE<br>• *Rhetorical structures* (first, next, last)<br>• *Punctuation* (signals awareness of code-switches—*me gusta* "basketball," or ¡Run fast!) | | | |
| SENTENCE/PHRASE<br>• *Syntax* (subject omission, word order—the bike of my sister)<br>• *Literal translations* (*agarré todas bien*/I got them all right)<br>• *Code-switching* (*no puedo hablar in just one language*) | | | |
| WORD LEVEL<br>• *Code-switching*<br>• *Loan words* (soccer, mall)<br>• *Nativized words* (*spláchate*/ splashed) | | | |
| PHONICS<br>Spanish → English (japi/happy)<br><br>English → Spanish (awua/*agua*)<br><br>Spanish ←→ English (bihave/behave, lecktura/*lectura*) | | | |

**Developmental Language-Specific Approximations**

| SPANISH | ENGLISH |
|---|---|
| Structural elements, syntax, spelling, hypo/hypersegmentation | Structural elements, syntax, spelling, hypo/hypersegmentation |
| | |

## What the New Rubric Captures

The rubric asks evaluators to assess emerging bilingual student writing both quantitatively and qualitatively. While writing assessment systems in many states, districts, and schools use holistic rubrics to quantitatively score students' constructed compositions in response to a prompt, they neither assess emerging bilingual students' writing development in two languages nor do they use a rubric designed using a holistic theory of bilingualism. The Literacy Squared writing rubric provides numeric scores for students' compositions written in Spanish and English, so that their biliterate writing development can be quantified side by side, using a uniquely designed instrument. Another novel aspect of the rubric is the inclusion of an area in which specific linguistic aspects of emerging bilingual students' biliterate writing development can be noted qualitatively. Thus, the rubric quantitatively tracks emerging bilingual students' biliterate writing development in a summative manner to track growth across time and provides a space to analyze students' writing qualitatively. Teachers can then use the information formatively to plan for paired writing instruction. Each side of the rubric allows us to focus on different aspects of students' biliterate writing development.

**Quantitative Data.** The quantitative portion consists of three areas for consideration: content, structural elements, and spelling. A unique aspect of this writing rubric is that it does not assign equal weight to each of the three areas. The ability to communicate a message effectively carries more weight than spelling individual words correctly. In other words, it distributes the scores in ways that do not penalize students for errors or approximations that are due to the acquisition of two writing systems. The new scale is based on an overall ceiling of 21 points: 10 points for content, 5 points for structural elements, and 6 points for spelling. We believe that weighting each area differently helps to capture the writing traits students include and control in their writing.

**Qualitative Data.** The qualitative portion of the rubric merits its own page and is printed on the reverse of the numeric scales. It consists of two tables, each structured to help teachers identify and categorize students' organizational, linguistic, and encoding strategies and approximations. The tables are separated to help teachers plan appropriate instruction to address the linguistic hypotheses children are utilizing as they gain biliterate writing competencies. The ultimate purpose is to provide a visual scaffold for identifying patterns within and across languages to inform planning and instruction. The upper table, bilingual strategies, lists the most frequently employed writing strategies that can be clearly associated with learning two languages. The lower table, developmental **language-specific approximations**, provides space for language-specific approximations that require attention but are not always attributable to the simultaneous development of Spanish and English writing students experience during paired literacy instruction.

In the following sections, we provide examples to discuss how to score and understand children's Spanish and English writing using the quantitative and qualitative sides of the Literacy Squared writing rubric. Then we conclude with the scoring of five students' illustrative samples from grades K–5, to give a sense of the biliterate writing trajectory across the elementary grades.

## Using the Rubric to Score Student Writing

All teachers in the Literacy Squared research projects attend professional development sessions where in-depth training about how to use the Literacy Squared writing rubric is provided by our research team and inter-rater reliability is established. The guidelines that follow here are not intended to replace that comprehensive training, but to provide teachers with an overview of the scoring process so that they can use the rubric for instructional support throughout the school year.

As we have discussed, using a holistic bilingual framework requires that emerging bilingual children's Spanish and English writing samples be scored side by side using one rubric. Therefore, when scoring, begin by physically placing a student's Spanish and English writing samples next to each other, to notice similarities and differences between the samples. (E.g., see Mateo's Spanish and English writing samples placed side by side in Box 7.4.) General observations to make across languages include the amount of text written in each language, physical organization and layout of text, and use of structural elements.

**BOX 7.4  Mateo's Writing Samples: Placed Side by Side**

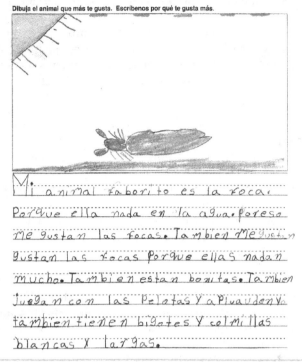

Dibuja el animal que más te gusta.  Escríbenos por qué te gusta más.

Mi animal faborito es la foca.
Porque ella nada en la agua. poreso
me gustan las focas. Tambien me gustan
gustan las focas porque ellas nadan
mucho. Tambien estan bonitas. Tambien
juegan con las pelotas y aplaudenyo
tambien tienen bigotes y colmillas
blancas y largas.

Draw a picture of your favorite toy. Write about why it is your favorite.

My friboret toy it tha nintendo ds.
Bcas you cant yamp. End fit end you
cam rit. I like my toy becas ets redend
blak. End a play ved ger o the time
end a gat 2 games end a gene
ge more games. My dad ets gene
bra me more gemes bata romo
guen. I lave my toy.

**Translation of Spanish Sample**: My favorite animal is the seal. Because she can swim in water. That is why I like seals. I also like seals because they swim a lot. Also they are pretty. Also they play with balls and they applaud and they also have whiskers and white and long tusks.

**Translation of English Sample**: My favorite toy it the nintendo ds. Because you can't jump. And fight and you can ride. I like my toy because its red and black. And I play with her (it) all the time and I have 2 games and I gonna get more games. My dad its (is) gonna buy me more games but I don't know when. I love my toy.

Examining students' Spanish and English writing using a holistic bilingual lens requires a side-by-side analysis. When examining Mateo's samples without paying too much attention to the content, we can observe many writing skills that are present in both languages. Mateo, a first-grader,

- Wrote about the same amount of text in both samples
- Has developed the concept of word
- Used beginning and ending punctuation

On closer examination, we can note in both samples that Mateo

- Uses similar structure, in that he responded to the prompts with introductory sentence and provides relevant details to the main idea using Spanish adjectives and adverbs
- Links ideas together using *también* in Spanish and "and" in English
- Uses improper ending punctuation: segmented complete sentences, making them incomplete, before the word *porque* and "because" in both samples

Differences between Spanish and English

- Included a conclusion in English
- Used standard spelling for most high-frequency words in Spanish
- Has many spelling approximations in English, of which many are influenced by the student's knowledge of Spanish phonetics (yamp/jump, ets/it's, guen/when)

Ultimately, this kind of analysis informs writing instruction within paired literacy. Recognizing that Mateo included a conclusion in his English sample simply means the teacher recognizes this and will hold him accountable for including conclusions in Spanish as well. The teacher may want to have Mateo write more complex sentences. The instruction of how to do this could occur in Spanish literacy. In English, the same skill is reinforced, but the focus would be on providing different "connector" words to join ideas together.

# Quantitative Scoring

Begin evaluating the writing by reading each sample three times: first, to evaluate the content; second, to identify the presence or absence of structural elements; and, third, to focus on spelling.

All samples get scored because we want to know how well the student is able to communicate in writing. However, if the student has not addressed the prompt, note this in the box in the upper righthand corner of the rubric. We find it helpful to use highlighters to mark the text: one color for structural elements, a second color for spelling.

**Content.** Read each descriptor in the content area of the rubric carefully. For scoring purposes, the descriptors are cumulative; therefore, a student cannot advance if any of the previous benchmarks are absent. On reaching a final decision, circle the earned score on the left for the Spanish language sample and the right for the English language sample. One note of caution: the cumulative nature of the rubric is tentative and, as with all holistic writing rubrics, we should not presume equal intervals between the various numeric levels.

### Key Scoring Points

- A sample that is unreadable or in a language other than the prompt gets a 1.
- The lower end of the rubric (scores from 2–4) is used when the writing produced is limited to the simple presence of ideas and the ability to communicate them in the appropriate language. (See Box 7.5 for some examples at the earlier levels of writing development.).

---

**BOX 7.5  *Scoring Content at the Earlier Levels of Writing Development***

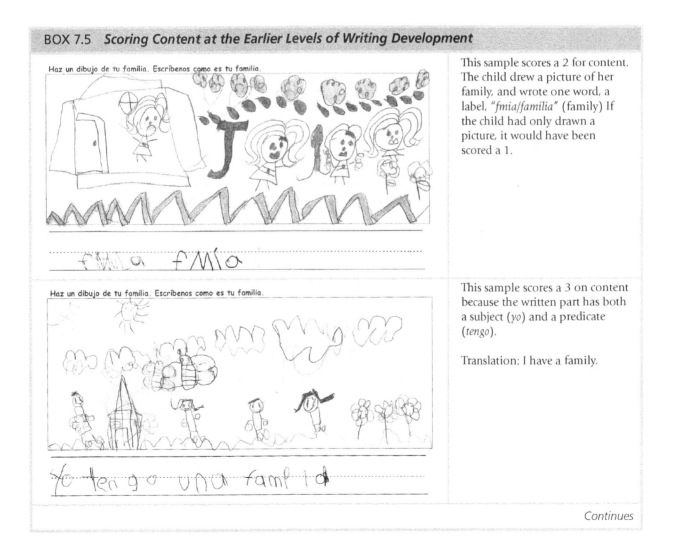

This sample scores a 2 for content. The child drew a picture of her family, and wrote one word, a label, *"fmia/familia"* (family) If the child had only drawn a picture, it would have been scored a 1.

This sample scores a 3 on content because the written part has both a subject (*yo*) and a predicate (*tengo*).

Translation: I have a family.

*Continues*

**BOX 7.5** *Scoring Content at the Earlier Levels of Writing Development (Cont.)*

Haz un dibujo de tu familia. Escríbenos como es tu familia.

mi Familia Jeoɔacomio

Juamoscomisjuetes.

This sample has two ideas, *"mi familia juega conmigo"* and *"jugamos con mis juguetes,"* resulting in a score of 4 on content.

Translation: my family plays with me we play with my toys.

- A sample with a minimum of two ideas will score at least a level 4.
- Beyond a level 4, the reader needs to attend to both the ideas that are shared and how effectively the writer communicates them.
- To receive a 7 or higher, a student must include a clear introduction *and* conclusion.
- The absence of an introduction or conclusion, regardless of the sophistication and voice in the writing, will preclude a score higher than a 6. If a student has more than two ideas, ask yourself if there is a clear introduction and conclusion. If so, you will still want to verify that the descriptors for a 5 and 6 are present. If so, move up from a 6. If not, stay at a 6 or go down to a 5.
- No half scores are allowed, for consistency.

**Structural Elements.** Next, examine the writing for the use of structural elements, the features the writer uses to guide readers through the text. These include the use of capitalization, punctuation marks, and paragraphing. As you evaluate, it is important to note whether the student is experimenting with a feature, or whether he or she controls it. (E.g., see Andrea's Spanish sample—scored at level 3—in Box 7.6.) Advancement within this section of the rubric indicates that a student is gaining control of increasingly more sophisticated guideposts that aid the reader.

### Key Scoring Points

- To earn a 3 on the rubric, a student must control beginning and ending punctuation and experiment with at least a third form of punctuation. The additional punctuation need not be used consistently or correctly.
- By level 4, the writer controls additional punctuation and indicates an understanding of paragraphing through appropriate grouping of ideas and indentation of at least one paragraph.

## BOX 7.6  *Scoring for Structural Elements*

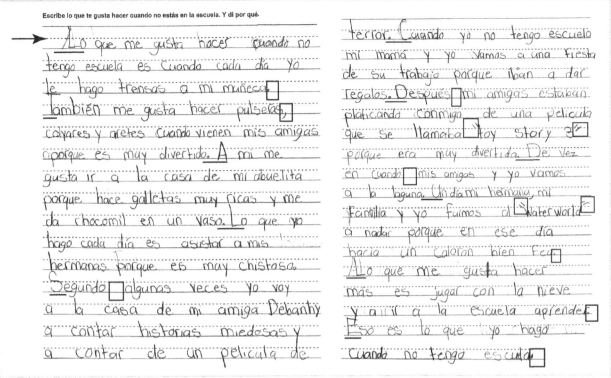

Escribe lo que te gusta hacer cuando no estás en la escuela. Y di por qué.

Lo que me gusta hacer cuando no tengo escuela es cuando cada día yo le hago trensas a mi muñeca. También me gusta hacer pulseras, colyares y aretes cuando vienen mis amigas aporque es muy divertido. A mi me gusta ir a la casa de mi abuelita porque hace galletas muy ricas y me da chocomil en un vaso. Lo que yo hago cada día es asustar a mis hermanas porque es muy chistosa. Segundo algunas veces yo voy a la casa de mi amiga Debanhy a contar historias miedosas y a contar de un pelicula de terror. Cuando yo no tengo escuela mi mama y yo vamos a una fiesta de su trabajo porque iban a dar regalos. Después mi amigas estaban platicando conmigo de una pelicula que se llamaba Toy Story 3 porque era muy divertida. De vez en cuando mis amigas y yo vamos a la laguna. Un dia mi hermana, mi familia y yo fuimos al Waterworld a nadar porque en ese dia hacia un calorón bien Feo. Lo que me gusta hacer mas es jugar con la nieve y a ir a la escuela aprender. Eso es lo que yo hago cuando no tengo escuela.

When scoring for structural elements, identify all punctuation used by students, including those aspects that are controlled and those that are being approximated. In Andrea's Spanish sample, she scored a 3 because she
- Controlled beginning and ending punctuation
- Began composition with paragraph indentation
- Used commas between words in a list (*pulseras, coyares*/bracelets, necklaces)

You would also want to note where you could address improvement in the use of structural elements:
- Use of commas after transition words and adverbial clauses—after *Segundo* (Second) and *De vez en cuando* (Once in a while)

**Translation:** What I like to do when I don't have school is when everyday I braid my doll's hair. Also I like to make bracelets, necklaces and earrings when my friends come over because it is a lot of fun. I like to go to my grandmother's house because she makes delicious cookies and she gives me chocomil (chocolate milk) in a glass. What I do everyday is scare my sisters because it is very funny. Second sometimes I go to my friend Debanny's house to tell scary stories and to tell stories about horror movies. When I don't go to school my mom and I go to a party at her work because they were going to give presents. After my friends were talking with me about a movie that is called "toy story 3" because it is very fun. Once in a while my friends and I go to the lake. One day my sister, my family and I went to "waterworld" to swim because on that day it was miserably hot. What I like to do the most is play with snow and go to school (to) learn. That is what I do when I don't have school.

**Spelling.** Finally, analyze spelling. As you evaluate, bear in mind that because our children live bilingual lives, it is not unusual for them to code-switch. When scoring spelling, do not penalize a student for approximations within the code-switch. For example, if a child wrote: I like to play *futboll* at recess. The code-switch, *futboll* (soccer) for *futból* would not be counted as a spelling error. Do, however, remember this use of language because it will be important during the qualitative analysis.

Again, circle the appropriate score on the left for Spanish and the right for English. (See Box 7.7 for a sample of how to score for spelling.)

---

### BOX 7.7   *Scoring for Spelling*

Draw a picture of your favorite toy. Write about why it is your favorite.

My favorite toy

"My favorite toy is my (tedy) because it is soft. My (tedy's) color is pink and (it's) nose is brown. In my (tedy's) chest there is a (hert). My (tedy's) name is pinky. My (tedy) (well) go (nowere) without me.

To determine a score for spelling, recognize what the child wrote conventionally as well as all approximations in all forms:

- Most high-frequency words are written in standard form: is, toy, my, in, there, without.
- Approximations include
  - tedy/teddy—two instances
  - tedy's/teddy's—three times
  - it's/its
  - hert/heart
  - well/will
  - nowere/no where

This child would score a 4 in English spelling because the majority of high-frequency words are spelled accurately and she is establishing standardization in errors. This means that each time she wrote tedy and tedy's it was written in the same way, instead of writing tedie, tedi, teddies, and so forth.

### Key Scoring Points

- Note which words are spelling approximations; how many times and ways individual words are misspelled; and how many overall words are spelled incorrectly. Most means 85% or more, and majority is over 50%. Accents are considered an aspect of spelling and should be included in this portion of the rubric.
- A message that is unreadable scores a 0.
- The lower end of the rubric (scores 1–3) is used when the writing produced is spelled incorrectly, with some sounds represented, and an emerging knowledge of spelling patterns is demonstrated.
- A sample that has most high-frequency words spelled correctly, with standardization in errors, scores a 4. Standardization in errors means the child is no longer hypothesizing the writing of individual words in multiple ways (e.g., socer, socker, soquer/soccer; *tanbién, tambien, tamben/también*). (See Box 7.7 for an example.) Standardization indicates a more mature understanding of how written language works, and therefore earns the child a higher score.
- To receive a 5 most words (85%) need to be spelled correctly.
- A sample that contains no spelling approximations scores a 6.

## Qualitative Scoring

The qualitative section of the Literacy Squared writing rubric allows for a deeper analysis of emerging bilingual students' writing development. Through this analysis, teachers can identify the linguistic hypotheses and strategies students are using as they develop biliterate writing competencies so that they can better inform their writing instruction. The qualitative side of the rubric calls for the categorization of students' writing strengths and approximations as bilingual strategies or language specific.

### Scoring Bilingual Strategies

It is easiest to complete this section of the rubric if, while reading the samples multiple times during the quantitative evaluation, you have highlighted notable aspects of the child's writing. Record all structures and approximations that can be attributed to biliteracy acquisition in the upper table, bilingual strategies. Note that the table commences with discourse level notation, then proceeds to sentence level observations, and finally has space for word and phonic level comments.

**Discourse Level.** When analyzing student's strategic behaviors, begin globally. Place the Spanish language and English language writing samples side by side in front of you. Note any duplicative features the child is using and record them in the appropriate column. Correct placement within a column requires you to analyze if Spanish is influencing English (Spanish → English), English is influencing Spanish (English → Spanish), or if each language is contributing to certain writing behaviors or writing approximations. For instance, if the child has organized both writing samples by ending with a question, you would indicate this in the upper table at the discourse level. Because "first, then, next, finally" is a rhetorical style attributable to English language discourse, it could be recorded in the "English → Spanish" column. However, when it is used in both samples, we indicate this by recording it as bidirectional (English ←→ Spanish). (See Box 7.8 for some examples of discourse level strategies.)

**BOX 7.8** *Discourse Level Bilingual Strategies*

**Spanish ←→ English: Rhetorical Structure**

In both this student's Spanish and English samples, Diego begins the composition with the same structure: In Spanish—*Un día* (one day), and in English—One Day. He continued each composition to include dialogue (Spanish—La maestra dijo si. English—I tell my dad what's goin on.) However, the dialogue does not include standard punctuation.

Diego's Spanish sample

> Un día mi maestro del gimnasio le dijo a mi
> maestra si se podían quedar seis niños para
> ayudarle. La maestra dijo que si. El maestro

**Translation**: One day my gym teacher told my teacher if six children could stay to help her. My teacher said yes. The teacher

Diego's English sample

> One day, my dad take my sister and I to the
> house of my anty. I tell my dad what's goin on. My
> dad tell me that my mom was goin to have a baby.

**English → Spanish: Punctuation**

This fifth-grader used an exclamation point but did not include one at the beginning of the sentence as is required in Spanish.

> Es muy buena en la escuela. Tuvo
> una calificacion buena en cada clase. Le

**Translation**: She is very good at school. She had a good grade in each class!

**Sentence/Phrase Level.** Next, proceed to the sentence level. Has the child used syntax unique to one language while writing in the other? Does he or she use phrases that are ineffective because they are literal translations that do not carry the same meaning in the partner language? Do they begin a sentence, or series of sentences, in one language, but switch at the phrase or sentence level to the other language? Often, at this level, children will arrange words in an order that would be acceptable in one language but not the other. Also, particular grammatical features (e.g., prepositions, noun phrases) may be included or omitted in ways that are indicative of one language but inappropriate for the other. Copy enough of what the child is doing into the appropriate column so that later you will be able to discern patterns for instruction. (See Box 7.9 for sentence/phrase level examples.)

---

**BOX 7.9**    *Sentence/Phrase Level Bilingual Strategies*

Spanish → English: Word Order
This first-grader is drawing on her knowledge of Spanish syntax when she wrote "ers/ears soft" because in Spanish the adjective comes after the noun.

bear because it is tot and it has ers soft. A... my ....

Spanish → English: Subject Omission
This first-grader omitted the subject is/it's because this is common in Spanish.

I like my toys is prinsses bicause is buyrifou.

Spanish → English: Literal Translation
This third-grader literally translated *doce de la noche* to twelve of the night

stop lafing. And we slep at twelf of the nithe. It was my best day and fu'n day

**Word and Phonetic Level Strategies.** Finally, note what the child is doing with individual words and determine if they are employing a whole word strategy or simply applying phonetic principles cross linguistically. Word level strategies include single word or lexical code-switching (Box 7.10) and word manipulation to "nativize" a word. Manipulating words to make them fit the structure of the partner language indicates a growing and sophisticated metalinguistic awareness of how the two languages interact. In other words, the child who turns the Spanish word *lobo* (wolf) into the English approximation of *lob* knows that sometimes words ending in -o in Spanish can keep their root and drop the –o to communicate the same concept in English (e.g., *carro*/car; *rancho*/ranch). Likewise, students may indicate they know a lot about how letters and sounds are paired by applying phonetic principles specific to one or both languages when encoding words. The use of the letter "w" when writing in Spanish is likely indicative of the application of English language phonetic principles to Spanish. Likewise, the use of the letter "j" to encode the /h/ sound in English is likely indicative of the application of Spanish language phonetic principles to English. Again, note what the student is doing, then analyze what strategies and hypotheses are guiding these behaviors and record them appropriately on the rubric.

---

### BOX 7.10 *Word Level Bilingual Strategies*

**Lexical code-switching:** Bilingual living leads children to write in English about terms and ideas heard in English. In this Spanish composition example, the student is writing about the television cartoon, "Sponge Bob," and how he goes jelly fishing (yalifishing).

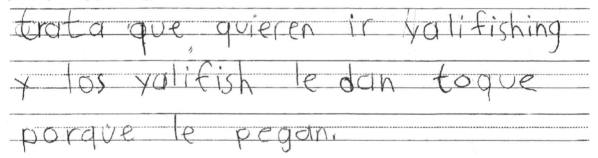

Translation: It is about that they want to go jellyfishing and the jellyfish sting them because they hit them.

**Lexical code-switching:** The child switches codes to express her ideas: teddy bear *de peluche* to express that it is a "stuffed" teddy bear.

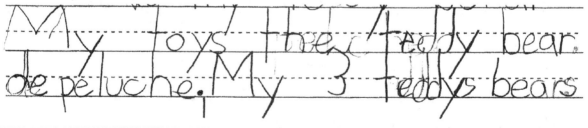

## Scoring Developmental Language-Specific Approximations

Not all approximations and strategic behaviors can be attributed to biliteracy development. In fact, when analyzing students' writing behaviors in the first phase of the study, we noted that many of the students' writing miscues were comparable to those found in the writing of a monolingual child. For example, an emerging bilingual child who writes *baca* for *vaca* (cow) or "wen" for "when" does not yet control the standardized spelling of these words, but the unorthodox spelling cannot be attributed to bilingualism (Box 7.11). Monolingual Spanish-speaking children often substitute the "b" for the "v" because both letters represent the same phoneme. Likewise, monolingual English-speaking children often omit the "h" when first learning to write the word "when." It would be inappropriate, therefore, to record these errors in the upper table of the rubric. Rather, they should be listed on the lower table and sorted by the language in which they occurred. A separate space has been provided so that teachers choose an appropriate instructional approach depending on whether or not the child's writing behaviors are attributable to bilingualism.

---

**BOX 7.11   *Language-Specific Approximations***

**Spanish**: The following spelling approximations can be attributed to Spanish, not bilingualism. In other words, monolingual Spanish speakers would make similar errors: *pero/perro* (dog); *mui/muy* (very); *rason/razón* (reason); *ermanos/hermanos* (brothers); splitting a word into two parts—*con migo/conmigo* (with me); not capitalizing the first letter to begin a sentence.

> Mi animal favorito
> es un pero porque es mu
> bonita. tan bien core mucho
> con migo. otra razon
> es porque mis ermanos

Translation: My favorite animal is a dog because it is very cute. Also it runs a lot with me. Another reason is because my brothers

**English**: The following spelling approximations can be attributed to English, not bilingualism: freinds/friends; jumprop/jumprope

> I like to play with my freinds
> at recess. At recess.a like to
> play jumprope

## Holistic Bilingual Writing Assessment in Action

We have devoted the remaining sections of this chapter to providing a detailed analysis of the writing samples in Spanish and English of five students in grades K–5. (In kindergarten, only Spanish writing samples are collected so there are 11 writing samples in total.) Each analysis begins with an assignment of numeric scores using the quantitative side of the rubric along with a rationale for the numeric assignment in each area of consideration: content, structural elements, and spelling. A description of the qualitative analysis of the rubric follows. Subsequently, a brief discussion of how each student's samples are representative of his or her progress within the hypothesized biliterate writing trajectory is included. Additionally within this discussion, we highlight the writing features, skills, and strategies that each child might attain if appropriate paired literacy instruction, which we have termed "teaching to the biliterate writing potential," is provided. In order to teach to the biliterate writing potential, all of the information gleaned from the quantitative and qualitative analyses are used to inform how paired literacy instruction will accelerate students' trajectory toward biliterate writing development. When this information is known and applied in biliterate writing instruction, students are held accountable for demonstrating certain writing abilities and skills in both languages. Further, teachers make explicit cross-language connections, thus making instruction efficient and accelerating students' biliterate writing development.

The writing samples included herein were selected from hundreds of samples at each grade level. They are neither exceptionally high nor exceptionally low. It is important to note that, although the student writing samples are organized by grade level, we consider them to be demonstrative of emerging bilingual students' biliterate writing development on the hypothesized biliterate writing trajectory. They are a snapshot view of possibilities, and they epitomize trends we have documented over the past decade when students receive planned and consistent paired literacy instruction.

We never look at a student's writing in one language without also looking at the writing in the other. Thus, teaching toward the biliterate potential is based on what a child already knows about writing in both languages. The information gleaned from students' Spanish and English writing is used to form the foundation for paired literacy instruction. Teaching to the potential in writing requires that skills and strategies developed in one language be modeled and used to make explicit cross-language connections while at the same time building oracy skills. In other words, we do *not* have to reteach writing skills in both language environments. Instead, we must demonstrate how such skills are similar in both languages and identify any specific differences, while developing students' metalanguage.

The included samples convey to us the importance of continuity and coherence that can be established by communication across grades and across languages within schools. This includes knowing what students have been taught previously. We recognize that biliteracy growth and development is somewhat idiosyncratic and that an expectation of steady linear growth is unrealistic. However, we believe that it is reasonable to teach students that we expect them to make steady incremental progress in two languages.

## Analyses of Spanish and English Writing Samples, Grades K–5

The following discussion of the student writing samples reproduced in this chapter are organized by grade level and analyzed in two ways: as a summative assessment scored according to the writing rubric (with both quantitative and qualitative measures), and as a formative assessment that provides evidence of biliterate writing potential and thus guides instructional planning. They are included in this assessment chapter to demonstrate how to evaluate biliterate writing using the Literacy Squared writing rubric, and begin developing a biliterate writing trajectory for each child. Remember that these samples represent what each child was able to produce when limited to only 30 minutes. The selected samples, collected in January, are meant to give teachers a broad understanding of emerging bilingual children's biliterate writing potential in grades K–5. Before turning to the writing samples, you may be interested in viewing the prompts and procedures we used to collect them (Box 7.12). Teachers are encouraged to examine these samples and to compare them to the writing their students are producing.

---

### BOX 7.12  *Literacy Squared Writing Prompts and Directions (for summative purposes)*

**Procedures**

1. The Spanish writing prompt should be given the first week in January. The English prompt should be given two weeks later. In kindergarten, English samples are *not* collected.
2. Prompts will be group administered and take no more than *30 minutes*. Students may do a draft and then a final copy if they have time in the allotted 30 minutes.
3. The writing sample should be completed *without* any teacher or peer assistance. The student should do all editing independently. Teachers should not prompt, think aloud, or share examples of how to respond to the prompt.
4. *All students should be provided with a preformatted page with the prompt.* Additional paper may be given to the students for drawing or planning.
5. *Read the prompt to the children.* Tell them that they will have 30 minutes to write to the prompt.

| GRADE | SPANISH | ENGLISH |
|---|---|---|
| K | *Haz un dibujo de tu familia. Escríbenos como es tu familia.* (Draw a picture of your family. Write about your family.) | |
| 1 | *Dibuja el animal que más te gusta. Escríbenos por qué te gusta más.* (Draw your favorite animal and write about why it is your favorite.) | Draw a picture of your favorite toy. Write about why it is your favorite. |
| 2 | *Escríbe lo que te gusta hacer cuando no estás en la escuela. Y dí por qué.* (Write about what you like to do when you are not at school and explain why.) | What do you like to do at recess? Why? |
| 3 | *Dinos por escrito lo mejor que te ha pasado en la escuela este año. ¿Y por qué piensas que fue lo mejor?* (What is the best thing that has happened to you in school this year? Why do you think it was the best?) | Write about the best thing that has ever happened to you. Why was it the best thing? |
| 4 | *¿Quién es tu mejor amigo en todo el mundo? Escríbenos por qué esa persona es tu mejor amigo.* (Who is your best friend in the entire world? Explain why that person is your best friend.) | If you could be someone else for a day, who would you be? Why would you want to be that person? |
| 5 | *Piensa en tu vida personal y escolar, ¿Cómo te ha ayudado saber dos idiomas?* (Think about your personal and school lives. How has knowing two languages helped you in your school and personal lives?) | Think about your experiences learning Spanish and English. What is hard? What is easy? |

## Kindergarten Rubric Analysis

The following rubric scores were given for the Spanish writing sample from a kindergartener we have called Lino, reproduced in Box 7.13. (Note that we assess only Spanish writing in kindergarten; thus an English sample is not included for this grade level.) Let's take a look at the assessment process using the Literacy Squared writing rubric that resulted in these scores.

### Kindergarten: Lino's Rubric Scores

|  | Spanish | English |
|---|---|---|
| Content | 3 | NA |
| Structural elements | 2 | NA |
| Spelling | 5 | NA |
| Overall | 10 | NA |

**Content.** In this writing sample, Lino responds to the prompt by drawing a detailed picture of people positioned in front of a television within a house. His accompanying composition corresponds with the illustration in that he describes what is occurring. He scored a 3 in content because he wrote a complete idea that includes a subject (*Mi papá y enoc*/My dad and enoc) and a predicate (*juegan*/play) along with an object (*conmigo*/with me) and adverb (*siempre*/always).

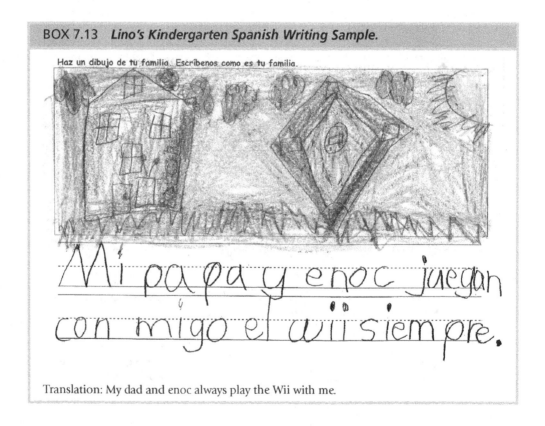

BOX 7.13 *Lino's Kindergarten Spanish Writing Sample.*

Haz un dibujo de tu familia. Escríbenos como es tu familia.

Mi papa y enoc juegan con migo el wii siempre.

Translation: My dad and enoc always play the Wii with me.

**Structural Elements.** As a kindergartner, Lino demonstrates an understanding of and control over beginning and ending punctuation. He uses a capital letter to begin his sentence and a period to end it. Thus, he scored a 2. However, Lino does not apply the use of capital letters when writing proper names—*enoc* is not capitalized.

**Spelling.** Lino encoded almost all of the words in his sentence in standard form, except that he omitted the accent mark in the word *papá*. Additionally, the word *conmigo* is segmented into two distinct parts, which is considered hypersegmentation. It is also important to observe that Lino is still developing his understanding of "wordness." Note that the distances between the words in the first line of text are not as far from each other as the space between *con* and *migo* in line two.

**Developmental Language-Specific Approximations.** Lino's approximations are developmentally specific to acquiring literacy skills in Spanish. Many kindergarten students would display similar writing behaviors.

**Kindergarten Biliterate Potential.** In Spanish writing, Lino

- Understands that writing serves the purpose of conveying a message
- Is able to write a complete thought
- Understands beginning and ending punctuation of a sentence
- Can write some high-frequency words correctly
- Has knowledge of hearing sounds in words in sequence

*For Spanish Writing Instruction*

- Teach capital letters used for proper names
- Expand sentences using descriptive language
- Model and teach the use of varied sentence structures
- Provide opportunities to reinforce and support spelling of words through modeled and shared writing

*For English Writing Instruction*

- Make explicit cross-language connections in drawing and writing ideas to convey a message and teaching similar and different letter sounds
- Reinforce concepts about print through modeling and shared writing opportunities

## Grade 1 Rubric Analysis

Beginning in grade 1, we have both Spanish and English writing samples to evaluate. Here are the set of scores for Gabriella's samples shown in Boxes 7.14 (Spanish) and 7.15 (English).

### Grade 1: Gabriella's Rubric Scores

|                    | Spanish | English |
|--------------------|---------|---------|
| Content            | 5       | 5       |
| Structural elements | 2      | 2       |
| Spelling           | 5       | 4       |
| Overall            | 12      | 11      |

*Text continues on page 118*

## BOX 7.14   *Gabriella's Grade 1 Spanish Writing Sample*

Dibuja el animal que más te gusta. Escríbenos por qué te gusta más.

Mi animal favorito
Mi animal favorito es la
jirafa. Tiene cuello largo
tienen una cola qo cts
corta. Las jirafas comen
hogas y pasto las jirafas
viven en el zolójico. Las
jirafas pueden alcansar

los arboles para comer
hojas. Las jirafas tiene
una lengua larga.

Translation
My favorite animal
My favorite animal is the giraffe. It has a long neck they have a tail that is short. Giraffes eat leaves and grass giraffes live in the zoo. Giraffes can reach trees to eat leaves. Giraffes have a long tongue.

**BOX 7.15   Gabriella's Grade 1 English Writing Sample**

Draw a picture of your favorite toy. Write about why it is your favorite.

My favorite. toy

My favorite toy is a
bear. Because it is
littile. And the ber is
soft. And i like the
bear because it
smals god. I like the

bear because it is
tol and it has ers
soft. A... my ...
name ...

Translation

My favorite toy

My favorite toy is a bear. Because it is little. And the bear is soft. And I like the bear because it smells good. I like the bear because it is toll and has ears soft.

**Content.** Gabriella's Spanish and English content scores are identical because she clearly identified the main idea and provided supporting details in both samples. While Gabriella provides supporting details for why she likes the giraffe in the Spanish sample, she does so by only writing simple sentences, with the exception of one sentence: *Las jirafas pueden alcanzar los arboles para comer hojas* (The giraffes reach the trees to eat leaves). The level of complexity of sentences written in the English sample is a bit higher as compared to the Spanish sample; however, the structure is redundant in that she uses the conjunction "because" three times.

**Structural Elements.** Gabriella received the same score, 2, for structural elements. In both samples, after using a period, she begins the following sentence with a capital letter, thus demonstrating consistent control of one structural element. However, in both samples, Gabriella does not regularly control the concept of a sentence by using a period. For example, in Spanish, she omitted a period between the thoughts, *Tiene un cuello largo* and *tienen una cola que es corta* (They have a long neck/ they have a tail that is short). In the English sample, she placed a period where there should not be one: *My favorite toy is a bear. Because it is littile*. Additionally, Gabriella does not consistently write the pronoun "I" with a capital letter throughout the composition.

**Spelling.** Most of the words in the Spanish sample were spelled conventionally, except for *hogas/hojas, zolojico/zoológico*, and *alcansar/alcanzar*; therefore she scored a 5. Gabriella's spelling score in English, 4, was lower than her Spanish score. The majority of high-frequency words are correct.

**Bilingual Strategies.** Gabriella employed similar rhetorical structures in both samples, writing a main idea followed by details. She also titled each sample; however, she did not capitalize the first letter of each word in the title of the English sample. Instead, she followed the capitalization style of Spanish. Gabriella also drew on her syntactical knowledge of Spanish noun/adjective placement when she wrote "ers (ears) soft" in English.

**Developmental Language-Specific Approximations.** Many of Gabriella's spelling approximations can be considered developmental to both Spanish and English (the use of g/j in *hogas/hojas*, s/z in *alcansar/alcanzar*; the spelling of becuase/because, tol/tall, littile/little). Gabriella's use of a period before the conjunction "because" in English can be considered a language-specific approximation.

**Grade 1 Biliterate Potential.** We find many writing skills and abilities evident in both languages in Gabriella's writing. She seems to control the following writing skills in both languages:

- Writing a main idea with supporting details
- Including a title
- Understanding of beginning punctuation and developing knowledge of how to use periods
- Encoding many high-frequency words accurately in both Spanish and English

In order to teach to Gabriella's biliterate writing potential, we need to create different instructional goals for each language, drawing on the skills she has shown and acknowledging her approximations and bilingual strategies.

*For Spanish Writing Instruction*

- Expand sentences using descriptive language
- Model and teach the use of varied sentence structures
- Introduce and model other punctuation, such as commas, question marks, and exclamation points
- Provide opportunities to reinforce and support spelling of words with s/z and g/j and other sounds represented by varied letters

*For English Writing Instruction*

- Make explicit cross-language connections to identify differences between the use of capital letters in titles in Spanish and English and teach the difference between adjective and noun placement in Spanish and English
- Clarify what a complete sentence is using her knowledge from Spanish
- Model sentences using the conjunctions "because" and "and"
- Provide opportunities to reinforce and support spelling of the approximations made developmentally in English
- Model and teach descriptive language for use in expanding sentence structures

## Grade 2 Rubric Analysis

The set of scores shown here for second-grader, Andrea, apply to the writing samples reproduced in Boxes 7.16 (Spanish) and 7.17 (English).

### Grade 2: Andrea's Rubric Scores

|  | Spanish | English |
|---|---|---|
| Content | 6 | 6 |
| Structural elements | 3 | 3 |
| Spelling | 5 | 5 |
| Overall | 14 | 14 |

**Content.** Andrea scored a 6 in content for both her samples because she developed the main idea in each composition (meeting the requirements for a 5) and wrote multiple ideas with varied sentence structures. While all of the ideas relate to the prompt, and a clear conclusion is evident, Andrea did not write a clear introduction identifying all of the things she likes to do when she is not at school or at recess, which prevented her from scoring a 7.

*Text continues on page 123*

**BOX 7.16** *Andrea's Grade 2 Spanish Writing Sample*

Escribe lo que te gusta hacer cuando no estás en la escuela. Y dí por qué.

Lo que me gusta hacer cuando no tengo escuela es Cuando cada día yo le hago trensas a mi muñeca. También me gusta hacer pulseras, colyares y aretes Cuando vienen mis amigas aporque es muy divertido. A mi me gusta ir a la casa de mi abuelita porque hace galletas muy ricas y me da chocomil en un vaso. Lo que yo hago cada día es asustar a mis hermanas porque es muy chistoso. Segundo algunas veces yo voy a la casa de mi amiga Debanhy a contar historias miedosas y a contar de un pelicula de

BOX 7.16   *(Cont.)*

terror. Cuando yo no tengo escuela
mi mamá y yo vamos a una fiesta
de su trabajo porque iban a dar
regalos. Después mi amigas estaban
platicando conmigo de una película
que se llamaba "toy story 3"
porque era muy divertida. De vez
en cuando mis amigas y yo vamos
a la laguna. Un día mi hermana, mi
familia y yo fuimos al "Waterworld"
a nadar porque en ese día
hacia un calorón bien feo.
A Lo que me gusta hacer
más es jugar con la nieve
y a ir a la escuela aprender.
Eso es lo que yo hago
cuando no tengo escuela.

**Translation**
What I like to do when I don't have school is when everyday I braid my doll's hair. Also I like to make bracelets, necklaces and earrings when my friends come over because it is a lot of fun. I like to go to my grandmother's house because she makes delicious cookies and she gives me chocomil (chocolate milk) in a glass. What I do everyday is scare my sisters because it is very funny. Second sometimes I go to my friend Debanny's house to tell scary stories and to tell stories about horror movies. When I don't go to school my mom and I go to a party at her work because they were going to give presents. After my friends were talking with me about a movie that is called "toy story 3" because it is very fun. Once in a while my friends and I go to the lake. One day my sister, my family and I went to "waterworld" to swim because on that day it was miserably hot. What I like to do the most is play with snow and go to school (to) learn. That is what I do when I don't have school.

## BOX 7.17  *Andrea's Grade 2 English Writing Sample*

**What do you like to do at recess?  Why?**

When I go to recess I play with the jumprope because it is Fun and I get tired. I like to play tag with Naithelith, Lesly Lopez, Lesly Padilla and Yolanda. It is fun to play tag because we get all swetty outsaid. Sometimes I climb In the monkeybars. I allways fall at the monkeybars and my hand herts. I allways like to go at the swings because they go very high. My Friends and I like to talk and walk. We like to make cakes in the mad. Finally That is how I play.

**Structural Elements.** In both the Spanish and English samples, Andrea demonstrated control over beginning and ending punctuation; she consistently started the first letter in every sentence with a capital letter and used periods appropriately. She also indented both compositions. In addition, she utilized commas appropriately to separate items in the Spanish sample, and in English she used them to separate names in a list. She also applied the use of quotation marks around "Water World" to signal a code-switch to the reader. This earned Andrea a score of 3.

**Spelling.** Andrea spelled most words conventionally in both writing samples, resulting in a score of 5 in both languages. (See "Developmental Language-Specific Approximations" for a more in-depth analysis of Andrea's spelling.)

**Bilingual Strategies.** Similar rhetorical structures are used in both samples by remaining on topic, providing supporting details, and including a conclusion. Andrea is signaling to her audience that she is aware that she is code-switching by using quotation marks.

**Developmental Language-Specific Approximations.** While Andrea had very few spelling approximations, those she did have could be attributed to similar errors monolingual writers would make. In Spanish the letters "c," "s," and "z" are often substituted for one another, as Andrea did when writing *pulsera/pulcera* (bracelet) and *trensa/trenza* (braids). Additionally, she omitted accents on the words *película* (movie) and *calorón* (very hot). In English, monolingual students might also mistake the spelling of swetty/sweaty, allways/always, and herts/hurts.

**Grade 2 Biliterate Potential.** In Andrea's writing, we find many shared skills and abilities across languages. She seems to control the following skills in both languages:

- Including supporting details directly related to the prompt
- Utilizing varied sentence structures
- Including a conclusion
- Controlling the use of beginning and ending punctuation and also including commas in a list, quotation marks when code-switching, and use of indention for paragraphs
- Spelling most words in both languages conventionally

It is clear that Andrea is making cross-language connections by distributing her knowledge across languages in her writing and making sense of the similarities and differences across languages. In teaching to the writing potential, Andrea's writing strengths provide us with a focus for instruction that would include the following.

*For Spanish Writing Instruction*

- Teach the purpose of and how to write an introduction
- Use the introduction to serve as an organizational structure to form paragraphs in order to organize ideas and details
- Expand the use of descriptive language (use of adjectives and adverbs)
- Teach additional structural elements, such as exclamation marks and commas to separate adverbial phrases
- Provide opportunities to reinforce and support spelling of the approximations made developmentally in Spanish (e.g., *pulsera/pulcera; trensa/trenza* and accents on the words *película* and *calorón*)

*For English Writing Instruction*

- Model and provide opportunities in both speaking and writing to use and expand descriptive language in English
- Model and reinforce skills being taught in Spanish, such as writing an introduction
- Make explicit cross-language connections to punctuation use by modeling and demonstrating similarities and differences across languages
- Provide ways to reinforce and support spelling of the approximations made in English (e.g., swetty/sweaty, allways/always, and herts/hurts)

In setting foci for instruction, we must limit how many we address so that we are sure to cover them in-depth while also making appropriate cross-language connections.

## Grade 3 Rubric Analysis

The writing scores correspond to third grader, Amanda. Her writing samples can be found in Boxes 7.18 (Spanish) and 7.19 (English).

### Grade 3: Amanda's Rubric Scores

|  | Spanish | English |
|---|---|---|
| Content | 7 | 7 |
| Structural elements | 3 | 3 |
| Spelling | 5 | 5 |
| Overall | 15 | 15 |

**Content.** Amanda's Spanish and English writing samples scored a 7 for content because they both provided many details related to the main idea, included descriptive language and varied sentence structures and had a sense of completeness. Although a clear conclusion was not explicitly written, with rhetorical structures such as "to conclude" or "finally," it could be interpreted that Amanda ends her composition by relating that even though she wants to return and enjoy the experience of riding horses again, she cannot because the horses will be in another place, and she is "OK" with that.

**Structural Elements.** From reviewing both the samples, it is apparent that Amanda had developed control of beginning and ending punctuation and other forms of punctuation in both samples, consequently scoring a 3. In the Spanish sample, she utilized commas for a list of words (*pizza, papitas, pastel*), a hyphen for A-Z, and exclamation points. Amanda used quotation marks in the English sample to mark dialogue. Because she did not use any type of paragraphing, her score could not be considered a 4.

**Spelling.** Most of the words in Amanda's Spanish and English samples were spelled correctly; thus she scored a 5. The majority of the Spanish high-frequency words were written conventionally and her approximations were, for the most part, rule-governed (needed to learn to include accents for the pluperfect and imperfect tense).

## BOX 7.18    Amanda's Grade 3 Spanish Writing Sample

**Dinos por escrito lo mejor que te ha pasado en la escuela este año. Y ¿por qué piensas que fue lo mejor?**

Mi mejor día del año 2008 fue cuando nos hicieron la fiesta de Navidad. Ese día acomodamos las mesas y todo. Despues empezo a llegar la gente con comida para nosotros. Lego Ms. B puso al reno que se llama Rodolfo el Reno. en la pizarra. Primero Ms. B nos dio una hoja de Tic Tac Toe para jugar con campañeros. Cuando nosotros habiamos terminado con esa hoja nos dio otra del abecedario en esa hoja teniamos que escribir nombres de animales de la A - Z. Despues empezamos a comer pizza, papitas, pastel y ensaladas. Al ratito jugamos el juego de rodolfo el reno. Teniamos que estar con los ojos vendados para ponerle la nariz al reno. cuando habiamos terminado con eso nosotros empezabamos a abrir los regalos que nos iban a dar. cuando los abrimos nos pusimos a bailar y cantar ¡Era Fantastico!

### Translation

My best day in 2008 was when they had our Christmas party. That day we rearranged the tables and everything. Later people started to come with food for us. Then Ms. B put a reindeer that is named Rudolf the Reindeer on the board. First Ms. B gave us a paper with Tic Tac Toe to play with our classmates. When we had finished with that paper she gave us another with the alphabet and on that paper we had to write animal names from A-Z. Later we started to eat pizza, chips, cake and salads. A little later we played the rudolf the reindeer game. We had to have our eyes covered to put on the reindeer's nose. when we had finished that we began to open our presents that they were going to give us. when we opened them we started to dance and sing It was fantastic!

---

**BOX 7.19** *Amanda's Grade 3 English Writing Sample*

**Write about the best thing that has ever happened to you. Why was it the best thing?**

The best thing that I have in my life is that I have been ride a horse and that was the best day of my life. The horse was brown whit white. My mom and my dad where proud of me because the horse was so big and I was so little. It was the best thing in my life because it was the first time that I was in a horse. That first time it was because we where in a party. And the guy that was like riding us in the horse tell my dad and mom that we could go sometimes to ride horses whit other people that we now. Then I was saying to my dad " Could we come tomorrow to ride the horses" And he said "No because their not gona have those horses tomorrow because their gonna take them to another place that they should be." And I said "OK dad."

---

**Bilingual Strategies.** Amanda uses a variety of bilingual strategies across languages; see Box 7.20 for a qualitative analysis of her writing. As mentioned in the content section of the analysis, she has an introduction and conclusion in both samples. However, the organization and cohesiveness of ideas across languages is different. In the Spanish sample, Amanda organizes her ideas linearly by providing a sequenced recount of the events of the Christmas party using transitional words and phrases to order them. This type of structure is more consistent with English rhetorical styles than Spanish and is not evident in her English sample. In the English sample, the ideas are not cohesively drawn together. At the sentence level, Amanda draws on her Spanish syntactical knowledge and overgeneralizes the use of "in" for *en* (*en* can be translated as in, at, or on).

**Developmental Language-Specific Approximations.** Many of the spelling approximations in English could be made by monolingual English writers: whit/with, where/were, their/there.

| BOX 7.20   *Qualitative Analysis of Amanda's Grade 3 English and Spanish* | | | |
|---|---|---|---|
| **Bilingual Strategies** | | | |
| | **(Spanish → English)** | **(English → Spanish)** | **Spanish ←→ English (bidirectional)** |
| DISCOURSE<br>☑ *Rhetorical structures* (first, next, last)<br>☐ *Punctuation* (signals awareness of code-switches-*me gusta* "basketball," or ¡Run fast!) | | Organizational structure follows English discourse pattern—*Despues, primero . . . segundo . . .* | Introductory sentence responds to the prompt/Conclusion |
| SENTENCE/PHRASE<br>☑ *Syntax* (subject omission, word order—the bike of my sister)<br>☑ *Literal translations* (*agarré todas bien*/I got them all right)<br>☐ *Code-switching* (*no puedo hablar* in just one language) | Syntax: Brown with white (and); I was in a horse (on a) I was in a party (at a)<br>Literal translation: I have been ride a horse (I went horseback riding) | | |
| WORD LEVEL<br>☐ *Code-switching*<br>☐ *Loan words* (soccer, mall)<br>☐ *Nativized words* (*spláchate*/splashed) | | | |
| PHONICS<br>Spanish → English (japi/happy)<br><br>English → Spanish (awua/*agua*)<br><br>Spanish ←→ English (bihave/behave, lecktura/*lectura*) | | | |
| **Developmental Language-Specific Approximations** | | | |
| **SPANISH** | | **ENGLISH** | |
| **Structural elements, syntax, spelling, hypo/hypersegmentation** | | **Structural elements, syntax, spelling, hypo/hypersegmentation** | |
| HFW: *dia/día, despues/después, fantastico/fantástico*<br>Accents for: Imperfect tense: *teníamos*; pluperfect: *habíamos terminado*<br>Punctuation: Omits commas after transition words: *después, primero*; capitalization of proper nouns: *Rodolfo el Reno* | | Informal language: "the guy that was like riding us in the horse"<br>HFW: where/were, their/there, whit/with, now/know<br>Punctuation: Comma use with quotation marks | |

**Grade 3 Biliterate Potential.** Across languages, Amanda demonstrates competent writing skills for a third-grader, including the following:

- Writing the same amount of text in both languages, controlling beginning and ending punctuation, and including an introduction and conclusion
- Encoding most high-frequency words conventionally in both languages (most spelling approximations would be considered developmentally language specific)

Differences between languages include the following:

- Organization of thoughts and ideas are stronger in the Spanish sample
- Use of quotation marks for dialogue is evident in the English sample

Without looking at Amanda's written abilities in both languages, we would not know all of the writing skills she controls, which could lead to teaching below her potential. As such, to teach to her writing potential we could include the following.

*For Spanish Writing Instruction*

- Teach paragraphing as a way to organize ideas
- Expand her writing by teaching her to include complex sentence structures
- Provide ways to reinforce and support standard spelling of the approximations made in Spanish, focusing on written accent marks

*For English Writing Instruction*

- Model and provide language structures and phrases to express her voice in English as she has done in her Spanish writing
- Model how to organize thoughts more cohesively with effective transitions (drawing on what is done in Spanish) and the use of paragraphing
- Explicitly teach and provide opportunities to read, write, and speak using English prepositional phrases with "in," "on," and "at"
- Provide ways to reinforce and support standard spelling of the approximations made developmentally in English (e.g., whit/with, where/were, their/there)

Amanda's writing skills and abilities are evident in both languages; however, her ability to express herself in using standard grammatical form is in need of explicit instruction. In order to address this, a focus on oracy and explicit instruction in metalanguage needs to be included throughout literacy-based ELD instruction.

## Grade 4 Rubric Analysis

The next two sets of samples—for a fourth-grader (Boxes 7.21 and 7.22) and a fifth-grader (Boxes 7.23 and 7.24)—are from the same child, Gracie, and were chosen to illustrate the cumulative effect of paired literacy instruction from grades 1–5. We have learned from our research that the longer students receive consistent paired literacy instruction, the fewer the differences between their abilities in both languages. This coincides with what we have found in students' biliterate reading development as well. Gracie's samples demonstrate the potential of biliterate writing development because she employs similar writing skills in both Spanish and English.

*Text continues on page 134*

---

**BOX 7.21   *Gracie's Grade 4 Spanish Writing Sample***

¿Quién es tu mejor amigo en todo el mundo? Escríbenos por qué esa persona es tu mejor amigo.

> Mi mejor amiga
>
> Yo tengo muchos amigos. Pero una de ellas es la que es mi mejor amiga. Su nombre es Jenny. Abeses unos niños la llaman Tov, (se ponuncia two). Cada vez cuando voy a recreo jugamos juntas. A ella le gusta irse en los culumpios. No habla español. Nomas habla ingles y un lenguaje que se habla en asia.
>
> Es muy buena en la escuela. Tuvo una calificacion buena en cada clase. Le gusta la escuela mucho como a mi. Tambien

BOX 7.21   *(Cont.)*

es muy buena en la clase de arte. Yo
le pregunte una vez si me da clases de
arte, o porlomenos cómo colorear un pato bien.
Su favorita clase es siencias. En esa clase
amos estado aprendiendo como se va la
electrisidad. Ella normalmente es la primera
en terminar. Es muy inteligente.
   No vive serca de mi casa. Nomas
juego con ella en la escuela. Nunca la veo
por mi casa. Tambien tengo amigos por
donde yo vivo pero no son tan divertidos
como Jenny. Tiene mucha imaginacion. Como cuando
estamos en los columpios dise que estamos en el cielo
volando. Cuando dise eso selramos los ojos
osino miramos arriba y no miramos abajo.
Cuando estamos en el castillito nos
imaginamos que estamos en castillo gigante
del rey y que un dragon nos ataca y
tenemos que escaparnos. Me divierto mucho
con mi mejor amiga y no deseo tener otra
diferente que ella y no creo que algvien
puede ser tan divertida como Jenny.

## Translation

My Best Friend

I have many friends. But one of them is my best friend. Her name is Jenny. Sometimes some kids call her Tou. (it's pronounced two). Every time I go to recess we play together. She likes to go on the swings. She does not speak Spanish. She only speaks English and another language that is spoken in Asia.

She is very good in school. She had a good grade in each class. She likes school very much just like I do. She also is very good in art class. I asked her once if she would give me art instruction, or at least teach me how to color a duck well. Her favorite class is science. In that class we have been learning how electricity works. Normally she is the first to finish. She is very intelligent.

She does not live near my house. I only play with her at school. I never see her around my house. I also have friends that live near me but they are not as fun as Jenny. She has a great imagination. Like when we are on the swings she say we are flying in the sky. When she says that we close our eyes or else we look up and we do not look down. When we are in the little castle we imagine that we are in a king's giant castle and that a dragon is attacking us and we have to escape. I have a lot of fun with my best friend and I do not wish to have a different friend from her and I do not believe anyone can be more fun than Jenny.

**BOX 7.22** *Gracie's Grade 4 English Writing Sample*

If you could be someone else for a day, who would you be? Why would you want to be that person?

Who woud I be?

If I coud be someone else that myself I woud be Diana. She is realy smart. In littersy she always gets no mastackes on her dictado. And she always gets perfect grades, in I think every subject. She went all the way to a black belt in recorder Karaty.

In littersy no matter what we do she is always 1 step ahed of me and my class mates. And in what ever langvage we do dictado (englishand spanish) she gets everything right and no rong. She is very smart and very good with spelling. In her homeroom she is smart too. Even though her first langage is spanish her class is in english. She said she had too learn english because most teachers in our school are american but other are mexican and otters can spick english and spanish.

In other classes like P.E and music she also is very good. In music class we did something called recorder Karaty. That is when you get to play the recorder and the songs are more difficult that the others. Diana made it to the very last song wich was the hardest one wich is the black belt. And in P.E. she is almost the fastest girl runer. I think she does great in every subject in the hole day of school.

BOX 7.23   *Gracie's Grade 5 Spanish Writing Sample*

**Piensa en tu vida personal y escolar, ¿cómo te ha ayudado saber dos idiomas?**

## Ser bilingüe

Siendo bingüe me a ayudado en muchas cosas. Puedo ayudar a mis padres traducir. Tambien les puedo ablar a gente que me pueden ayudar en mi vida en cualquier idioma. El ingles y el español tambien me han ayudado mucho en la escuela.

Mi familia viene de Mexico, y nomas hablan español. Mis padres solo sáben muy poco ingles, entonces cuando ellos no entienden una palabra, me preguntan a mi y les digo la palabra en español y ellos me entienden. Mis padres dicen que soy una ayuda muy grande porque si viene una oportunidad muy buena y no entienden algo saben que pueden confiar en mi.

Yo soy muy buena en la escuela y con eso ya se que vienen oportunidades muy buenas. Me pueden dar una entrevista y puedo ablan en ingles o español, asta puedo ablar los dos para impresinarlos mas. A mucha gente se les hace raro que una mexicana este ablando ingles, sin embargo dice mi máma que es que tienen envidia o estan muy inpresinados.

El ingles me ha ayudado mucho en la escuela. Muchos maestros hablan ingles y no entienden español. Aunque el ingles me sirve mucho en la escuela, tambien nunca sabes cuando vas a necesitar el español. Muchos estudiantes no saben que dice la maestra por no saber el idioma

*Continues*

## BOX 7.23  *Gracie's Grade 5 Spanish Writing Sample* (Cont.)

que estan ablando. Por esa rason
muchos niños no tienen los mejores
grados.
        Siendo biningüe me ayudado
tanto en la vida. Como quisiera que
todos esten bilingües para que nos
entiendamos y no siempre estariamos
peleando.

**Translation**
Being Bilingual
     Being bilingual has helped me in many things. I can help my parents translate. I can also talk to people that can help me in my life in either language. English and Spanish also have helped me a lot in school.
     My family comes from Mexico and they only speak Spanish. My parents only know very little English, so when they don't understand a word, they ask me and I tell them the word in Spanish and then they understand. My parents say that I am great help because if a good opportunity presents itself and they don't understand something they can trust me.
     I am very good in school and I know that with that come very good opportunities. I could be interviewed and I can speak in English or Spanish, I could even speak in both languages to impress them even more. Many people find it strange that a Mexican girl speaks English, however my mom tells me that they are envious or they are very impressed.
     English has helped me a lot in school. Many teachers speak English and they do not understand Spanish. Although English has helped me a great deal in school, you also never know when you may need Spanish. Many students do not know what the teacher is saying because they do not know the language that they are speaking. For that reason many students do not have better grades.
     Being bilingual has helped me a lot in my life. How I wish everyone were bilingual so that we could understand one another and not always fight.

## BOX 7.24  *Gracie's Grade 5 English Writing Sample*

**Think about your experiences learning Spanish and English. What is hard? What is easy?**

            Being Bilingual

     Being able to speak Spanish and
English has helped me alot, but sometimes
it's very dificult to not get comefused. It's
very easy comunacating, but having
all these words in your head is petty
dificult.

**BOX 7.24** *(Cont.)*

One very easy thing I can by speaking two languages is comunicate with almost every body I want. Some people might not speak English nor Spanish, but I can speak with mexicans or with people that are from here, the United States. I like speaking Spanish because many people speak Spanish like in Spain, in Mexico, Perú, and in Puerto Rico. Many people speak English too. They say that English is one of the languages that a lot of people use to comvnacate in the word. Many times I comvnacate with my friends. One of my friends speaks two languages too, but she speaks English and Vietnameas. She tells me "it's very hard to speak with people when you only know English and a language, no one speaks here."

One thing that I think is pretty hard is trying to not get comfused with both the languages. Sometimes, when I am at home, I'm talking to my family in Spanish when all the sudden I just say something in english. For some reason I always get a bit comfused because I have all this vocabulary in my head. My parents just stare at me and say "what did you say?" (but they say it in Spanish) I just say sorry and say that word in Spanish correctly.

I love being able to speak two languages, but sometimes I think it would make my life alot easier if I just speak one language, but then I think again and say "My life is perfect with two languages."

### Grade 4: Gracie's Rubric Scores

|                    | Spanish | English |
|--------------------|---------|---------|
| Content            | 8       | 8       |
| Structural elements | 4      | 3       |
| Spelling           | 5       | 5       |
| Overall            | 17      | 16      |

**Content.** Gracie scored an 8 in content in both Spanish and English. Not only did she have a clear introduction but also, within the introductory paragraphs, she contextualized what she wrote for the rest of the composition and then provided specific details to support her main ideas. She employed a sophisticated and complex use of structure and included descriptive words throughout the compositions.

**Structural Elements.** Gracie earned a 4 in Spanish because she controlled most structural elements. She used parentheses appropriately in both samples and demonstrated beginning control of paragraphing and the use of commas to set off independent clauses from dependent clauses. However, in the English sample, Gracie earned a 3 because she did not control capitalization of proper nouns.

**Spelling.** Gracie scored a 5 for spelling in Spanish because she spelled most words conventionally. Her Spanish spelling approximations were developmental. For example, the substitution of "s" for "c" in words like *siencias*/ciencias and *serca*/cerca are common in Spanish-speaking writers. Interestingly, there were several instances of hyposegmentation in which she did not put appropriate spaces between words: *abeses*/a veces, *porlomenos*/por lo menos, and *nomas*/no más. Gracie also scored a 5 in English spelling; yet she had fewer spelling approximations in English than in Spanish.

**Bilingual Strategies.** (See Box 7.25 for a qualitative analysis of Gracie's writing.) Gracie organized her compositions in both languages in a similar manner. She had a clear introduction and used paragraphs to expand on a topic within the supporting paragraphs. In both Spanish and English, the paragraphs are structurally similar to one another and, while she must have learned to use the three-paragraph structure, the last paragraphs should be split to clearly set apart the conclusion. In the Spanish composition, she utilized English syntax knowledge in *su favorita clase es* (her class favorite is) by placing the adjective before the noun.

| BOX 7.25 *Qualitative Analysis of Gracie's Grade 4 Spanish and English* | | | |
|---|---|---|---|
| **Bilingual Strategies** | | | |
| | **(Spanish → English)** | **(English → Spanish)** | **Spanish ←→ English (bidirectional)** |
| DISCOURSE<br>☑ *Rhetorical structures* (first, next, last)<br>☐ *Punctuation* (signals awareness of code-switches—*me gusta* "basketball," or ¡Run fast!) | | Three paragraph structure. Conclusion should have separate paragraph. | Three paragraph structure. |
| SENTENCE/PHRASE<br>☑ *Syntax* (subject omission, word order—the bike of my sister)<br>☐ *Literal translations* (*agarré todas bien*/I got them all right)<br>☐ *Code-switching* (*no puedo hablar* in just one language) | | *Su favorita clase es* . . . | |
| WORD LEVEL<br>☐ *Code-switching*<br>☐ *Loan words* (soccer, mall)<br>☐ *Nativized words* (*spláchate*/splashed) | | | |
| PHONICS<br>Spanish → English (japi/happy)<br><br>English → Spanish (awua/*agua*)<br><br>Spanish ←→ English (bihave/behave, lecktura/*lectura*) | Spick/speak | | |
| **Developmental Language-Specific Approximations** | | | |
| **SPANISH** | | **ENGLISH** | |
| **Structural elements, syntax, spelling, hypo/hypersegmentation** | | **Structural elements, syntax, spelling, hypo/hypersegmentation** | |
| HFW: *a veces, también*<br>Spelling: s/c: *aveses/veces, siencias/ciencias, serca/cerca, dise/dice, serramos/cerramos*<br>Accents for: *calificación, inglés*<br>Preterite tense: need accent—*pregunté*<br>Hyposegmentation: *aveses, nomas, porlomenos, osino* | | HFW: realy/really, ahed/ahead, wich/which, hole/whole<br>Spelling: littersy/literacy, rong/wrong, runer/runner<br>Punctuation: capital letters for proper nouns: Spanish, English, American, Mexican (cross-language connection)<br>Hypersegmentation: class mates/classmates | |

**Developmental Language-Specific Approximations.** As referenced in the spelling analysis, most of Gracie's Spanish approximations could be attributed to the language. The same can be said about approximations made in English.

**Grade 4 Biliterate Potential.** Across languages, Gracie demonstrates competent writing skills for a fourth grader in the following ways:

- Writing the same amount of text in both languages and including an introduction and conclusion
- Using a variety of sentence structures and descriptive language that give voice to her writing
- Organizing her writing structurally through the use of paragraphs and controlling beginning and ending punctuation
- Spelling most Spanish and English words conventionally

In teaching to the writing potential, we begin by looking at what we need to "introduce and teach in Spanish" and then model and reinforce in English. Setting a focus for instruction may include the following.

*For Spanish Writing Instruction*

- Model and teach how to organize a composition with effective transitions and more vivid examples
- Reinforce the use of paragraphing and provide support in how to organize each paragraph
- Teach how to highlight her conclusion by placing it in a separate paragraph
- Model the use of varied punctuation
- Provide ways to reinforce and support standard spelling of the approximations, focusing on *s/c/z*, *b/v* words, written accent marks, and common or frequent phrasing, such as *por lo menos* and *a veces*

*For English Writing Instruction*

- Model and make cross-language connections by including a conclusion in a separate paragraph
- Provide ways to reinforce and support standard spelling of the approximations, such as woud/would, coud/could, rong/wrong, hole/whole, and wich/which
- Use theDictado to incorporate explicit models and make cross-language connections in teaching

  - The use of capital letters with proper nouns in English
  - Structures for negative statements such as, "she always gets no mistakes/she never makes mistakes" and "she gets everything right and no wrong/she never gets anything wrong"
  - Noun/adjective placement such as, *Su favorito clase/Su clase favorito*

## Grade 5 Rubric Analysis

The writing scores and analysis correspond to fifth-grader, Gracie, whose grade 4 samples and analyses were included previously. Note the progress she has made from grade 4 to grade 5. Her writing development is demonstrative of a positive trajectory.

### Grade 5: Gracie's Rubric Scores

|  | Spanish | English |
| --- | --- | --- |
| Content | 10 | 10 |
| Structural elements | 5 | 4 |
| Spelling | 5 | 5 |
| Overall | 20 | 19 |

**Content.** Gracie scored a 10 in both Spanish and English for content because she fulfilled all the elements of the descriptors for content, and her compositions are focused, engage the reader, and convey emotion.

**Structural Elements.** Gracie has developed a consistent understanding of how to use beginning and ending punctuation and paragraphing to guide the reader in following the progression of her ideas. In both languages she uses commas to separate clauses, but she does so more effectively in English than Spanish. However, she scored a 4 in English and a 5 in Spanish because, even though she used more types of punctuation in the English composition, she demonstrated some errors. For example, she did not include a comma before or after the use of quotation marks to indicate dialogue. Regardless, Gracie demonstrated sophisticated use of structural elements in both Spanish and English.

**Spelling.** Most words were spelled conventionally in both writing samples; thus she scored a 5 in both languages.

**Bilingual Strategies.** Gracie used similar organizational structures for both samples in that she began with a paragraph that introduces her topic and then supports the ideas with subsequent paragraphs. In Spanish, Gracie wrote three supporting paragraphs and, within each, she provided relevant examples and conveyed emotion. While she displayed similar abilities in English, she only wrote two supporting paragraphs, although there seems to be the same amount of text in each language. She also attempted to express complex ideas, and although not standard, it is effective. Take, for example, the last paragraph in the English sample: *I love being able to speak two languages, but sometimes I think it would make my life a lot easier if I just speak one language, but then I think again and say, "My life is perfect with two languages."*

**Developmental Language-Specific Approximations.** Most of Gracie's spelling approximations are specific to the language. In Spanish, she omitted the "h" in many words (*hablar* [to speak] and *hasta* [until]) and omitted accents. There were few English spelling approximations, including "communicate" and "confused," written as many children say it, "comefused." The lack of punctuation before or after quotations marks is developmental and requires explicit instruction.

**Grade 5 Biliterate Potential.** Observing Gracie's writing from grade 4 to grade 5 and across languages, one can see many obvious improvements in both languages, with all aspects of her writing closely paralleling each other. Both compositions demonstrate the following writing abilities:

- Organizing writing comprehensively
- Expressing voice and emotion through figurative language
- Using descriptive language
- Incorporating the use of complex sentence structures
- Utilizing a variety of structural elements within punctuation with some approximations
- Controlling appropriate spelling for most words

At this level, in teaching to the writing potential, much of the teaching is focused on refinement and expansion. Setting a focus for instruction may include the following.

*For Spanish Writing Instruction*

- Assess and teach specific elements and structures to write different genres (informative, persuasive, procedural)
- Model and teach a variety of complex sentence structures that can be used to write the same message
- Explicitly teach structural elements that need refinement (e.g., commas and quotation marks)
- Through theDictado, reinforce and teach explicitly more sophisticated structural elements and refine and review common developmental spelling patterns that continue to appear, such as silent "h" and words with written accent marks

*For English Writing Instruction*

- Make cross-language connections to identify the similarities and differences in sentence structures, vocabulary, punctuation, and spelling in a variety of genres

- Through theDictado, continue to model and reinforce spelling (e.g., confused, communicate, writing "everybody" as a compound word)
- Provide a variety of sentence structures for choices in writing similar ideas

Paired literacy has provided the setting for students like Gracie to take what they have learned in Spanish and apply it to written English. Over time, we see that Gracie has developed an engaging sense of voice in both languages.

## Conclusion

We discussed the need for biliterate writing assessment. The adoption of a holistic bilingual lens makes clear the need to assess emerging bilingual children's Spanish and English biliteracy development simultaneously. This holistic approach to bilingual assessment with emerging bilingual children enables us to approximate a student's trajectory toward biliteracy and to inform instruction. We presented the Literacy Squared writing rubric, an innovative biliterate writing assessment tool that can be used to understand not only children's biliteracy development, but also to inform Spanish literacy and literacy-based ELD writing instruction. Employing a holistic bilingual lens when examining the writing of emerging bilingual children in both Spanish and English respects the notion that children draw on their knowledge and skills in both languages.

## Questions for Reflection and Action

- How might you use the Literacy Squared writing rubric to look at the biliterate writing development of students at your school?
- How could your school use the Literacy Squared writing rubric as a formative assessment in addition to the summative assessments already used?
- How can a holistic bilingual framework assist you in understanding your emerging bilingual students' writing and linguistic strengths? How can this knowledge be applied to your biliterate writing instruction?

# LESSON PLANNING

## Creating Holistic Biliteracy Lessons and Units

Part III presents examples of how the concepts of Literacy Squared described in Parts I and II are put into everyday practice in the classroom. In these final chapters, we demonstrate how the holistic biliteracy framework can be applied to teaching Spanish and English literacy in grades K–5 through the development of biliteracy lessons.

Chapter 8 provides an explanation of the Literacy Squared lesson plan template and the different components within it. We have included a reproducible blank lesson plan template (see next page)* for teachers to use. Note that the lesson plan template is set up bilingually. While we translated the lessons to English for this book (with the exception of oracy elements, which remain in Spanish), we strongly encourage Literacy Squared teachers to write their lesson plans bilingually or in bilingual teams because many of our teachers are stronger in one language or the other. It is important that teachers plan and review the dialogue, vocabulary, language, and so forth that they will need to use in their weaker language to ensure that careful consideration is taken to meet students' language needs.

In Chapters 9 and 10, we present examples of primary and intermediate biliteracy units, to illustrate how the instructional components and strategies of Literacy Squared can blend into a cohesive unit plan. The kindergarten unit in Chapter 9 focuses on connecting language environments by using a different version of the same story in each language. The grade 5 unit in Chapter 10 focuses on doing so by using the same genre of expository text. Each of these chapters includes both a narrative description of the different elements of the lesson plan and the lesson plan itself. Both biliteracy units have been enacted in Literacy Squared classrooms, and we have included various instructional and student artifacts in our discussion of them.

---

*The template can also be found online at casloncommunity.com/Biliteracy-from-the-Start/.

# Literacy Squared Lesson Plan Template

| Teacher/s: | School: | Grade: |
|---|---|---|

| Standards: |
|---|

| Literacy Objectives: |
|---|

| Connections between Literacy Environments: | Cross-language Strategies (if applicable): | Materials: |
|---|---|---|

| Dictado en español: | English Dictado: |
|---|---|
| Enfoque de instrucción: | Teaching Points: |

| Lectoescritura | Literacy-based ELD |
|---|---|
| Objetivo(s) de oralidad: | Oracy Objective(s): |
| Diálogo: | Dialogue: |
| Estructuras lingüísticas: | Language Structures: |
| Vocabulario: | Vocabulary: |
| Evaluación:<br>Expresión oral (hablar y escuchar)<br>Escritura<br>Lectura | Assessment:<br>Speaking<br>Listening<br>Writing<br>Reading |

| Lectoescritura (M = modelado, C = compartido, E = equipos/parejas, I = independiente) | | Literacy-based ELD (M = modeled, S = shared, C = collaborative, I = independent) | |
|---|---|---|---|
| Lectura | Escritura | Reading | Writing |
| **Session 1**<br>Enfoque pedagógico:<br>M C E I<br>Texto:<br>Actividades: | Enfoque pedagógico:<br>M C E I<br>Actividades: | Approach: M C S I<br>Text:<br>Activities: | Approach: M C S I<br>Activities: |
| **Session 2**<br>Enfoque pedagógico:<br>M C E I<br>Texto:<br>Actividades: | Enfoque pedagógico:<br>M C E I<br>Actividades: | Approach: M C S I<br>Text:<br>Activities: | Approach: M C S I<br>Activities: |
| **Session 3**<br>Enfoque pedagógico:<br>M C E I<br>Texto:<br>Actividades: | Enfoque pedagógico:<br>M C E I<br>Actividades: | Approach: M C S I<br>Text:<br>Activities: | Approach: M C S I<br>Activities: |
| **Session 4**<br>Enfoque pedagógico:<br>M C E I<br>Texto:<br>Actividades: | Enfoque pedagógico:<br>M C E I<br>Actividades: | Approach: M C S I<br>Text:<br>Activities: | Approach: M C S I<br>Activities: |
| **Session 5**<br>Enfoque pedagógico:<br>M C E I<br>Texto:<br>Actividades: | Enfoque pedagógico:<br>M C E I<br>Actividades: | Approach: M C S I<br>Text:<br>Activities: | Approach: M C S I<br>Activities: |

# Putting It All Together: Creating Comprehensive Biliteracy Lessons

*The planning aspect of Literacy Squared really makes the teaching of Literacy Squared easy. The template encompasses all the areas we need to cover and incorporates the details down to the learning targets and the Common Core Standards. Starting with the end product and planning backwards makes the whole planning process easy and seamless, for when you have to think of where you want to end up, it's easy to work out where to start.*

Amy Abel, grade 1 Literacy Squared teacher, Auburn Elementary School, Salem, OR

## Key Terms

**Biliteracy units**
**Connecting language environments**

**Cross-language connections**
**Cross-language strategies**

## Guiding Questions

- How might you connect Spanish and English literacy environments as you plan lessons and units?
- How might you plan lessons so as to incorporate the "within and across" language connections between oracy, reading, writing, and metalanguage?

All too often, Spanish literacy instruction and ELD/ESL instruction are disjointed and disconnected, even in dual language programs where the stated aim is to achieve both Spanish and English literacy. This disconnect between Spanish and English occurs as a result of old monolingual paradigms that view bilingual students' languages as separate entities. These paradigms stemmed from theories of sequential bilingualism, arguing that students' languages should be kept separate to avoid confusion between them. However, as discussed in previous chapters, Literacy Squared uses a holistic bilingual lens, acknowledging that the majority of emerging bilingual students are simultaneous bilinguals, and as such, they constantly access both languages even while working in a single language. When students are allowed and encouraged to draw on one language to help them with the other, and when they are explicitly taught about similarities and differences between languages, students develop metalinguistic awareness and biliteracy.

As the instructional framework in Part I illustrates, the theory of holistic bilingualism can be actualized in classrooms where both languages serve as resources for teaching oracy, writing, reading, and metalanguage within both literacy environments. The Literacy Squared lesson plan template was purposefully created to ensure a more holistic and connected approach to paired literacy instruction. Using the lesson plan template ensures that students have opportunities to draw on their experiential and linguistic knowledge in both Spanish and English in either environment. Furthermore, the lesson plan template ensures that teachers include direct and interactive teaching approaches in their lessons, and that as they do so, they gradually release responsibility to the students, beginning with a high level of support and moving to independence. (For more on teaching approaches, see Chapters 3 and 4.) As this chapter illustrates, we use this template to plan instruction that capitalizes on students' rich linguistic resources by **connecting language environments** via genre, theme, literacy objectives, or bilingual texts, and by making explicit **cross-language connections** within each literacy environment. Units should also include personally and/or culturally relevant materials so that students are provided with opportunities for meaningful learning experiences in both languages.

## Literacy Squared Lesson Plan Template

The lesson plan template we have developed allows teachers to plan **biliteracy units** that can last from several days to multiple weeks; and, if completed in its entirety, it ensures that all critical aspects of the holistic biliteracy framework (see Fig. 1.2) are included in a thoughtful and connected manner. The format of the lesson plan is unique, in that it allows for side-by-side planning of instruction in Spanish literacy and literacy-based ELD. It also allows teachers to plan how they will incorporate the recommended grade-appropriate instructional approaches (see Table 1.3), including those that are unique to the framework such as cross-language connections, metalanguage, theDictado, oracy, Lotta Lara, and *así se dice*. Each section of the lesson plan is described in the following section, and a blank lesson template is included with the Part III introduction and online (casloncommunity.com/Biliteracy-from-the-Start/)

### Standards and Literacy Objectives

The lesson plan template begins by having teachers list their standards and literacy objectives for the lesson, thereby enabling diverse districts and states to plan and implement Literacy Squared lessons that address their state and local standards and contexts. Teachers can also align their lessons to the Common Core State Standards and their state's ELD standards. Again, Literacy Squared is not a curriculum; it is a framework for implementing standards-based instruction within a model for biliteracy instruction that emphasizes explicit and interactive work. It can be implemented with a variety of curricula and standards in different types of bilingual programs.

### Connecting Literacy Environments and Using Cross-Language Strategies

After identifying the state and district standards and creating literacy objectives for the lessons, teachers list any connections (e.g., bilingual texts, genre, literacy objective, or theme) they will make between Spanish literacy and literacy-based ELD. **Cross-language strategies** are also highlighted. Planning for these two components is central for implementing Literacy Squared. We believe that planning and instruction must capitalize on the reciprocal and mutually reinforcing nature of how what one learns in one language environment has a direct and instrumental effect on what one learns in the other.

As teachers make connections between the literacy environments, they also need to plan and use explicit cross-language strategies. By connecting the literacy environments in thoughtful ways, we maximize children's opportunities to engage in oracy, reading, and writing instruction in Spanish literacy and literacy-based ELD. Utilizing cross-language strategies allows us to develop children's metalinguistic awareness both within and across languages. While explicit connections between Spanish literacy and literacy-based ELD need to be part of the formal planning of Literacy Squared lessons, cross-language strategies may also be implemented informally through the strategic use of the other language when children need clarifications to ensure their understanding of lessons. (See Chapter 5 for examples of these strategies.)

## TheDictado and theDictado Teaching Points

The lesson plan template includes a place for teachers to write theDictado they will be using for the lesson, as well as the teaching points that accompany it because theDictado should be connected to the biliteracy unit. While theDictado is only presented in one language each week, the lesson plan template includes a space to write Spanish and English Dictados. If the lesson teachers are writing will span only one week, they are advised to write theDictado in that week's language and leave the other space blank. However, most of the biliteracy units we have created have spanned more than one week so Spanish and English Dictados are included because theDictado would be implemented in one language the first week and in the other the second week (except for kindergarten where we only recommend giving theDictado in Spanish). A detailed explanation of theDictado is included in Chapter 4.

## Oracy Objectives

All Literacy Squared lessons have both literacy and oracy objectives and, as explained in Chapter 2, while the literacy objectives drive the reading and writing aspects of the lessons, the oracy objectives focus on the oral language needed to accomplish the literacy tasks. Both can and should be aligned to state and district standards, and teachers should plan specific dialogue, language structures, and vocabulary to ensure that students will have the necessary support to fulfill the oracy objectives.

## Assessment

The assessment section of the lesson plan template is intended for teachers to decide how to assess their students' learning throughout and at the end of the unit. This section should outline how teachers will check for student understanding of the intended literacy and oracy objectives. It should also explain any expected end product. Each biliteracy unit should include classroom-based formative assessment.

## Detailing Biliteracy Instruction

The remainder of the Literacy Squared lesson plan template provides space and opportunity for teachers to write day-by-day plans for their biliteracy units, though what is included in one session often spans more than one day. A space to complete plans for reading and writing is provided for both Spanish literacy and literacy-based ELD. These are side by side so that teachers can continue to plan for both language environments in a connected way. (Part I explains the different approaches teachers should consider when planning instruction.) In addition to identifying the approaches they will use each day, teachers should also include the title of the text(s) that they will be using within their lesson and describe the activities they will use to teach the lesson.

# Creating Biliteracy Units

As a whole, the Literacy Squared lesson plan template was designed to assist teachers' implementation of the holistic biliteracy framework for instruction. The template was originally created to allow teachers to write daily lesson plans for a week at a time. However, many teachers find it easier to use the template to plan complete units that generally last two to three weeks. Thus, as teachers fill in the Spanish literacy and literacy-based ELD reading and writing sessions, one session could include a lesson or lessons that last a few days, and teachers may fill out plans for 10 or more sessions for one unit.

The template has several sections to it and can be time consuming to plan; once completed, however, teachers have a unit that connects Spanish literacy and literacy-based ELD in a cohesive way. It also provides them with a plan for their literacy environments that can last numerous weeks. This could mean that about 12–15 comprehensive biliteracy units covering a variety of genres and topics could span an entire academic year.

## Getting Started

While there is no single way to plan Literacy Squared biliteracy units, many teachers find it helpful to begin by considering the standards that need to be taught and the final product that they would like their students to produce to demonstrate that they have met the standards. From there, teachers consider how the language environments are connected and what instruction will occur in which language to ensure that the Spanish literacy and literacy-based ELD lessons build on one another rather than being duplicative or disconnected.

Generally, we recommend that teachers target the heavier cognitive load in Spanish, knowing that doing so will help students secure a foundation of the content in a deeper way. Then teachers can provide the language necessary to help students transfer and express their new knowledge and understanding in English. This also entails planning literacy and oracy objectives.

Once teachers have established the literacy and oracy objectives in each language, they need to decide on appropriate texts. We recommend the inclusion of texts that are personally and/or culturally relevant. After choosing texts, teachers can use them to determine the specific oracy features (language structures, vocabulary, and dialogue) that students will need to interact with the texts. It is important also to consider the recommended time allocations and grade-appropriate instructional approaches (see Table 1.3). We reiterate our recommendation that instruction be teacher-led and interactive.

## Collaborating for Success

Although time consuming, teachers have found that the collaboration involved in the creation of biliteracy units has been invaluable. Because the lesson plan template requires a high level of detailed planning, the opportunity to collaborate enables teachers to brainstorm ideas, share strategies, and contribute materials to create a better and more complete unit. Furthermore, because some teachers are stronger in Spanish and others in English, planning together allows them to support one another in maintaining a high level of rigor as they plan literacy instruction (especially the components of oracy) in their less dominant language.

In our schools in Salem, Oregon, the district has set up a structure that allows for teachers at each grade level from various schools to come together once every month to plan Literacy Squared lessons. The teachers collaborate throughout the year, creating biliteracy units that they all implement in their classrooms. They have even observed one another teaching their units so that they could provide feedback to one another about what worked and what didn't—which skills needed to be instructed differently—and then revise their units accordingly. The school district also has a venue where teachers can upload units that they have created to share with other teachers, as well as gain access to other teachers' units for use in their classrooms. Such a system has facilitated the successful implementation of Literacy Squared because teachers have access to a multitude of biliteracy units.

# Conclusion

The Literacy Squared lesson plan template helps teachers to include all of the features that make Literacy Squared unique from other bilingual program models. Most importantly, it includes planning space for both Spanish literacy and literacy-based ELD, ensuring that both languages are taught at each grade level, and that English is not delayed and Spanish is not discontinued. While many U.S. instructional models focus on reading alone, the holistic biliteracy framework emphasizes productive (writing and speaking) and receptive (reading and listening) language domains. Thus, in addition to reading, we ask teachers to plan writing lessons and activities that are connected to their reading activities. The lesson plan template also includes space for teachers to plan specific oracy objectives and the language structures, vocabulary, and dialogue necessary to help students achieve such objectives. In planning for their Spanish literacy blocks, teachers are encouraged to use and adapt materials and methods from Spanish-speaking countries; and they are required to plan for and implement theDictado in both languages. Because Literacy Squared is unique compared to other bilingual models, we had to create a way to facilitate teachers' implementation of its features, and the lesson plan template is one way we have done so.

## Questions for Reflection and Action

- Use the Literacy Squared template to create a biliteracy unit appropriate for your grade level. What did you learn in the process?
- How does the lesson plan template facilitate connections across literacy environments?

# 9

# A Kindergarten Biliteracy Unit

*The richer the lessons, the more engaged not only my students are, but I am as a teacher. . . I find that I am teaching in depth. . .and savoring the lessons that I have spent so much effort investing in. Not only that, but instead of planning for a week at a time, I am finding myself teaching the same unit for a month!*

Ingrid Knudson, kindergarten Literacy Squared teacher, Mary Eyre Elementary School, Salem, OR

## Guiding Questions

■ How does multiple week planning across languages enhance student learning while deepening teacher knowledge about biliteracy development?

■ How can biliteracy units be designed to meet and exceed the Common Core standards?

The sample kindergarten unit featured in this chapter, developed by authors Sandra Butvilofsky and Lucinda Soltero-González and implemented in a kindergarten classroom, was created to demonstrate how to connect Spanish literacy and literacy-based ELD instruction via two interpretations of a folktale. It is intended as an illustration of how the process of biliteracy unit planning can be carried to completion for a particular grade level and purpose.

One of the most challenging aspects of creating a comprehensive biliteracy unit is figuring out how to connect the language environments. As we began the planning process with teachers who were just starting to implement Literacy Squared, it became clear that many were unsure about this part of the process, and some of them thought that connecting the two language environments meant teaching the same concepts and skills in Spanish and in English. One teacher described literacy-based ELD instruction as "a mere translation of what we do in Spanish." In order to clarify this misunderstanding, we discussed how Spanish literacy and literacy-based ELD instruction can be connected via bilingual texts, genre, literacy objective, or theme. Throughout the planning and implementation of the unit, we also emphasized two main goals of the Literacy Squared instructional framework: (1) to embed oracy instruction throughout the lessons in both language environments, and (2) to integrate reading and writing instruction.

The end outcomes in Spanish literacy were for children to present to their kindergarten classmates a reenactment of the story using student-created puppets of the main characters in the story and to depict a character using words and symbols. In literacy-based ELD, the final products included a whole-group written retell of a traditional version of the folktale using a cloze structure and an oral and written description of the similarities and differences between the two versions of the folktale.

Following the creation of the unit, we cotaught the unit's lessons with one teacher in her classroom for two weeks; another kindergarten teacher in the building observed us teaching several lessons. We modeled some lessons in their entirety; we cotaught parts of the unit with the teacher; and the teacher had the opportunity to teach some lessons on her own while we observed her.

## Planning the Unit

The planning of this unit began with the understanding that biliteracy instruction should incorporate oracy, reading, writing, and metalanguage as interconnected and reciprocal aspects of language in both literacy settings. This unit connects the literacy environments via a Spanish and English version of the same story. The unit meets state and district standards, as well as the Common Core Standards for English language arts. The literacy objectives in the lesson plan itself and the correspondence between these and the Common Core State Standards are discussed in the section on literacy objectives later in this chapter.

### Connecting the Language Environments

When developing this unit's literacy and language objectives, the general rule was that the "heavy lifting" (e.g., new oral language skills and literacy knowledge that students needed to interact with text, building background knowledge to support understanding of the text) should happen during Spanish literacy instruction. Literacy-based ELD would then build on what children know and can do in Spanish. The texts and topics were familiar to the students so the focus of instruction could be on the language that they needed to engage successfully with the text, accomplish the literacy tasks, and, ultimately, the literacy and oracy objectives.

The language environments were connected via two versions of the folktale, the *Three Little Pigs*: a southwestern version written in Spanish and English, and a traditional version written in English. For Spanish literacy we used the bilingual text, *Los tres cerdos: Tito, Nacho y Miguel* by Bobbi Salinas. Cultural and personal relevance were considered, as was the appropriateness of the textual language. For example, the repetitive nature of certain sentences from the text exposed children to literary language that they needed to understand and talk about the story.

For literacy-based ELD, we selected the version of the *Three Little Pigs* published by Scott Foresman. Because one of the literacy objectives in this lesson was to build oracy and fluency in English, it was critical to pay attention to the appropriateness of the linguistic complexity of the text. Thus, the English version of this folktale was modified, taking into consideration the children's English language proficiency and literacy ability. Text modification included two aspects: linguistic simplification and shortening of the text. The language of the text was simplified to make it comprehensible for students and appropriate to their English language proficiency. In order to accommodate children's emerging reading abilities, text was removed from each page to decrease the overall number of words (e.g., "Little pig, little pig! I'll come down the chimney and eat you up" was changed to: "Little pig, Little pig, here I come to eat you.") Such modifications made the text more developmentally appropriate for kindergartners and provided opportunities for the development of oracy and reading fluency in English.

### Time

The unit was designed as a five-session lesson plan in Spanish literacy and literacy-based ELD. However, the English literacy lessons begin on session 3, after the Spanish literacy lessons have begun. In other words, it was staggered because we expect to build students' cognitive knowledge around the text in Spanish before moving into the English version. However, this does not mean that literacy-based ELD would not be taught during this time; instead, it might consist of finishing up the previous unit or reinforcing other skills based on students' needs. Note that if your school's goal is to ensure full Literacy Squared implementation, teachers should be following the minimum time allocations (see Table 1.3) and teaching Spanish literacy and literacy-based ELD every day. In full-day kindergarten, Spanish literacy is scheduled for a minimum of 2 hours (1 hour for half-day kindergarten) and literacy-based ELD is scheduled for a minimum of 45 minutes (30 minutes for half-day kindergarten). We intended for each session of this unit to last no more than 20–30 minutes, as the lessons in both Spanish and English are a smaller part of the entire biliteracy block, which lasts 2.75 hours in full-day kindergarten classrooms.

# The Lesson

## Literacy Objectives

The literacy objectives for this unit are in the lesson plan at the end of the chapter. They were developed using the district's language arts standards and are compatible with the Common Core English language arts standards, which can also be found in the lesson plan. The literacy objectives include developing students' reading comprehension skills, paying particular attention to making predictions and inferences and analyzing characters.

## Spanish Dictado

This unit contains only a Spanish Dictado because we do not recommend an English Dictado in kindergarten. TheDictado's content is related to the text that the students will be using to ensure that it is meaningful for the children. The teaching points reinforce the concept of a word and use of periods and capital letters, extend the writing of simple sentences to more complex ones, and include more sophisticated vocabulary. (For a more detailed explanation of theDictado, see Chapter 4.)

## Oracy Objectives

The oracy objectives directly relate to the literacy objectives in that students will learn vocabulary and language structures to comprehend and discuss the stories, make predictions and inferences, and analyze characters using descriptive language. Oracy instruction is an essential element of interactive read aloud, which is used in the lesson, because it allows for language acquisition through explicit vocabulary instruction and opportunities to learn and rehearse meaningful language structures. Thus, in providing opportunities for students to meet the oracy objectives, the teacher is supplying vocabulary and language structures to support the students as they talk about the stories.

The oracy objectives in literacy-based ELD build on children's knowledge of the Spanish interpretation of the folktale, *Los tres cerdos: Tito, Nacho y Miguel*. This familiarity enables them to retell and identify similarities and differences with the more traditional version of the *Three Little Pigs* read in English. Oracy instruction focuses on teaching children specific book language related to the text, language structures to compare and contrast, and descriptive vocabulary related to the different characters' demeanors.

**Language Structures.** Language structures are used as a scaffold to ensure that students can understand and interact with the texts and one another. When planning for language structures, it is important to consider the ways in which students will need to use language to understand and talk about the texts. In both Spanish literacy and literacy-based ELD, the children are provided with language structures to support them in expressing their ideas about the similarities and differences in the two stories. Although some of this dialogue will occur in Spanish, even within literacy-based ELD, it is important for the teacher to move the dialogue into English, to provide students with the language structures and practice they need.

**Vocabulary.** Vocabulary is a critical component of oracy; children need to learn vocabulary to help them understand, interact with, and discuss the text. The Spanish and English vocabulary in this unit was chosen specifically to ensure that students would understand the most beneficial words for thinking and talking about the stories and participate successfully in all of the activities throughout the unit.

**Figure 9.1** Illustration comparing and contrasting different versions of the *Three Little Pigs* in literacy-based ELD.

**Dialogue.** This is an important component of the lesson. Engaging in dialogue provides students with ample opportunities to use and hear new language that helps them interact with the text and take part in metalinguistic discussions to help them meet the literacy and oracy objectives. (For a more in-depth discussion on oracy, see Chapter 2.) Dialogue questions and strategies should be preplanned to ensure that the teacher can help guide the students in producing the necessary language to further their language development.

During Spanish literacy, students talk about their predictions and inferences regarding the book. During literacy-based ELD, while engaging children in discussion to compare and contrast the different versions of the folktale, both Spanish and English are used to ensure children's receptive and productive understanding. For this reason, the compare/contrast dialogue questions are presented in Spanish, even though the dialogue is taking place during literacy-based ELD. Illustrations are used to record students' contributions (Figure 9.1). Because the majority of the children can make the appropriate cognitive connections in Spanish, the teacher should ensure that those are communicated before adding on the English language load.

Once the children have discussed the similarities and differences between the story interpretations in Spanish, explicit instruction is provided in English about the language structures needed for comparing and contrasting the texts (Figure 9.2). Additionally, children are provided with multiple opportunities to use English meaningfully in structured dialogue. Children first compare the stories and then subsequently compare and contrast character traits to more fully appropriate the language.

## Assessment

Throughout the unit, several indicators help the teacher to assess the students. In both language environments, speaking and listening assessments are anecdotal so that the teacher can observe whether or not students are participating in the dialogue and using the new language structures and vocabulary. Additionally, during Spanish literacy, the teacher assesses the students during readers theater. In literacy-based ELD, students have to

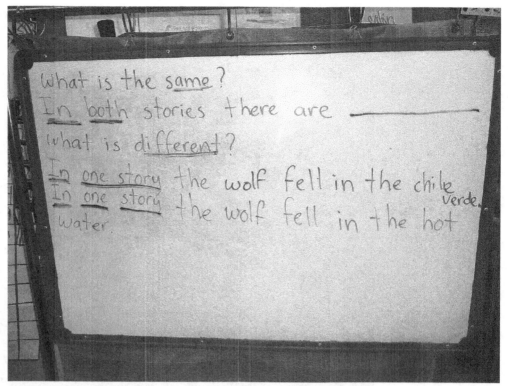

**Figure 9.2** Language structures for comparing and contrasting different versions of the *Three Little Pigs* in literacy-based ELD.

describe and compare/contrast two characters using the newly learned language structures. In Spanish, reading and writing are assessed through students' character analyses, theDictado, and their participation in the interactive read aloud. Student reading and writing are assessed in English as they complete a cloze retell of the text that they read.

## Session Plans for the Unit: Detailing Biliteracy Instruction

The unit plan is broken into seven sessions, though there are only five in each language. As previously mentioned, the unit has a staggered start so that students have two sessions of Spanish literacy before beginning the literacy-based ELD unit. This format allows the teacher to frontload some information in Spanish so that when students begin the English unit, they already have some background knowledge and experiences to transfer to their learning in English. As can be seen in the following description of the sessions, throughout the unit the different teaching approaches outlined in Chapters 3 and 4 were used to provide support to students in obtaining the unit objectives. Shared and interactive methods and direct instruction are used to support children's English literacy and language learning. Additionally, students are given the opportunity to reenact the story through a drama, which reinforces comprehension through retelling. Through dramatic play, students develop a deeper understanding of the story and have the opportunity to use literary language in an engaging and amusing way.

**Sessions 1 and 2.** To begin the unit, the teacher introduces the text, activates background knowledge and explains the textual structure. She then does a picture walk of the book to begin introducing the children to the vocabulary and repetitive phrases of the book. Students participate in a dialogue to make predictions about the book. Following the predictions, the teacher leads the students in an interactive read aloud of the Spanish text. This approach helps to develop students' comprehension while also providing them the opportunity to enjoy the text. Interactive read aloud provides further oracy support because the instructor can explicitly teach new vocabulary and provide students with multiple opportunities to practice the predetermined meaningful language structures. After the read aloud, the teacher leads the students in a dialogue about their predictions and whether or not they were confirmed.

**Session 3.** In this session, the teacher continues the interactive read aloud in Spanish literacy, leading students in a dialogue about character analysis. As students talk about different characters in the story, the teacher conducts a shared writing with the students about one of the characters. Shared writing involves the co-construction and negotiation of a written text between students and teacher. This approach demonstrates how writing fulfills a communicative act and also provides students with an opportunity to learn and apply various writing skills and conventions. Within this unit, shared writing is used to teach students to describe a character from the story. As the teacher encodes the message, she can invite students to share the pen with her as she reinforces certain skills.

After students have multiple exposures to the story and conversations about the characters in their shared writing experience, they are invited to write about and draw symbols related to a character (Boxes 9.1 and 9.2). Incorporating various semiotic representations, such as the use of drawing and dramatization, in the classroom promotes students' active participation in the construction of meaning and learning (Genishi, Stires, & Yung-Chan, 2001; Short, Kauffman, & Kahn, 2000). Drawing allows students to explore other symbol systems beyond the written word to creatively express their thoughts, ideas, and perceptions. The session ends with students sharing their character representation with the class.

This session marks the beginning of the literacy-based ELD part of the unit. The teacher begins by reminding students of their Spanish knowledge and explains that they will be reading a different version of the same story in English so that they can talk about the similarities and differences between the two stories. The teacher then introduces the text and guides the students through a picture walk of the story, introducing, clarifying, and practicing vocabulary and language structures. After the picture walk, the teacher does an interactive read aloud of the text.

---

**BOX 9.1   *Andrea's Character Analysis of the Wolf***

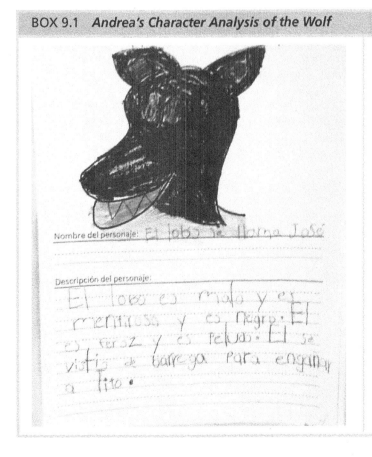

Nombre del personaje: El lobo se llama José

Descripción del personaje:
El lobo es malo y es mentiroso y es negro. El es feroz y es peludo. El se vistió de barrega para engañar a Tito.

**Translation**
Character's name: The wolf's name is José.
Character description: The wolf is mean and he is a liar and he is black. He is ferocious and he is hairy. He dressed himself as a lamb to trick Tito.

**BOX 9.2** *Andrea's Character Analysis of Tito*

**Translation**
Character's name: The little pig's name is Tito.
Character description: Tito likes to paint pictures and he likes to build his house with wood. He likes to wear a colorful vest and he has brown spots.

**Session 4.** In session 4 in Spanish literacy, the teacher begins with an interactive read aloud of the text, teaches the children the repetitive lines, and invites them to join in when reading those sections of the text. This type of reading differs from shared reading because students are not held responsible for tracking text. In anticipation of the dramatization of the story, the teacher uses shared writing to help students create an invitation to the performance for students in another classroom. Each student creates his or her own invitation to give to another student (Box 9.3).

During literacy-based ELD, shared reading is used to engage children in reading and to assist in their appropriation of English literary language. Because the text is long, various scaffolds are utilized to ensure children's success. Children are held accountable for reading the repetitive parts of the text and the characters' dialogue. The scaffolds include the rehearsal of the repetitive text structures, echo reading of characters' dialogue, and the use of icons within the text to cue students' attention to the text they are expected to read.

Shared writing is also used to reinforce both the literacy and language objectives, and to explicitly teach cross-language connections and metalanguage. A cloze structure (Figure 9.3) is used to retell the traditional version of the *Three Little Pigs*, and specific metalanguage strategies are used to draw children's attention to similarities and differences between Spanish and English rhetorical structures, orthography, and punctuation. This jointly constructed text is used in a shared reading format to promote fluency. Because children become familiar with the story over the course of the unit, they also copy the written retell (Figure 9.4).

**Session 5.** In Spanish literacy in session 5, the teacher continues with an interactive read aloud, this time reading and participating with students in a dialogue to identify a favorite part of the story. The teacher models how to draw and write about an event from the story and then, through shared and interactive writing, the children help the teacher write about an event from it. Students then try it themselves and share their work with the class. During literacy-based ELD, students practice reading different characters' dialogue.

BOX 9.3  *Karina's Invitation to the Dramatization*
**of Los tres cerdos *(Three Little Pigs)***

Invitació...vi tr

Teinvto al show de los Y

tres cerdos Y el lobo

may malo.

Fecha: Lunes

del 2011 Hora 8:45.

Lugar: Salón 111

Karina

**Translation**
Invitation: I am inviting you to the performance of the three little pigs and the very mean
wolf. Date: Monday 2011. Time 8:45. Place: Room 111.

**Figure 9.3**  Sharing the pen to complete a cloze
structure of the *Three Little Pigs.*

**Figure 9.4** Lulú copying the English retell of the *Three Little Pigs.*

**Sessions 6 and 7.** The Spanish literacy part of this unit is finished, but because literacy-based ELD begins after Spanish literacy, more time is needed to complete the English portion of the unit. During these sessions, the teacher reads the text while the students read the character dialogue that they have been rehearsing. The teacher leads the students in a dialogue of character analysis. Students take part in a shared writing to describe a character and create a word bank of descriptive words. To extend students' knowledge of comparing and contrasting, the teacher models how to compare characters by demonstrating the transformation "was/was not": The third little pig was smart. Transformation: The wolf was not smart. The unit culminates with the teacher and students comparing the characters from the text.

## Conclusion

Children's bilingualism and biliteracy can be strategically and effectively developed when careful consideration is given to Spanish and English language and literacy instruction. The children who participated in this particular study unit demonstrated great success because of the use of direct and interactive instructional methods, a gradual release of responsibility structure, the personally and culturally relevant materials, and the opportunities to learn and use both languages meaningfully and purposefully. Literacy Squared is not intended to be a curriculum, but rather is a framework for developing biliteracy in connected and coordinated ways. In implementing the Literacy Squared model, we recommend that schools consider how to align and articulate curricular goals and expectations across grade levels to ensure continuity and expansion of students' biliterate and bilingual development.

## Questions for Reflection and Action

- How is the biliteracy unit included here different from the ways in which you are planning and teaching Spanish and/or English literacy now?
- How could you use this sample lesson plan to help create your own biliteracy unit, in which Spanish and English literacy are connected without being duplicative?
- What would you consider when choosing texts for your unit?

# Literacy Squared Kindergarten Lesson Plan: *Los tres cerdos/Three Little Pigs*

**Common Core English Language Arts Standards:** Literacy.RL.K.2: with prompting and support retell familiar stories and key details; Literacy.RL.K.3: with prompting and support identify characters, settings, and major events in the story; Literacy.RL.K.5: recognize common types of texts (e.g., storybooks and poems); Literacy.W.K.2: use a combination of drawing, dictating, and writing to compose informative/explanatory texts in which they name what they are writing and supply some information about the topic; Literacy.SL.K.1.b: continue a conversation through multiple exchanges.

**Objetivos de lectoescritura:** Students will understand the structure of a fairy tale; students will make and confirm predictions about the story; students will respond to the story by making a character analysis.

**Literacy-based ELD Objectives:** Students will understand the structure of a fairy tale; students will make and confirm predictions about the story; students will respond to the story by making a character analysis.

**Connections between Literacy Environments:** The lesson is based on a Spanish and an English version of the *Three Little Pigs*.

**Cross-Language Strategies (*if applicable*):**

**Materials:**
Salinas, B. (1998). *The three little pigs, los tres cerdos: Nacho, Tito y Miguel.* Oakland, CA: Piñata Publications.
Scott Foresman (1971). *The three little pigs.* England: Scott, Foresman & Co. Chart paper, markers, crayons, outline of pig and wolf, sentence strips, paper plate, drama center, paper.

---

**English Dictado:** Not recommended in kindergarten.

**Teaching Points:**

---

## Literacy-based ELD

**Oracy Objective(s):** Develop vocabulary and literary language to discuss the similarities and differences between the two stories and the characters; develop literary language to participate in the shared reading of the text.

**Dialogue:**
Talk about the similarities and differences between the two stories (in Spanish or in both languages). *¿En qué se parecen las dos historias? ¿En qué son diferentes? ¿Las dos historias pasan en el mismo lugar? ¿Cómo es diferente el lugar donde se desarrolla cada historia? ¿Por qué son diferentes las casas de los cerditos en ambas historias? ¿Las dos terminan igual o tienen un final diferente?* (How are the two stories the same? How are they different? Do both stories have the same setting? How is the setting different in each story? Why are the three little pigs' houses different in each story? Do the stories have the same or different endings?) Talk about the similarities and differences between the two characters' *language structures:* Book language—Once upon a time. ...; "Little pig, little pig, let me in;" "Not by the hair of my chinny chin chin" "Then I'll huff and I'll puff and I'll blow your house down!"

Discuss similarities and difference between characters: The first (second) little pig was _____. Transformation: The third little pig *was not* _____. He was _____. The wolf was _____.

**Vocabulary:** Angry, mean, hungry, scared, afraid, happy

---

## Lectoescritura

**Dictado en español:** *El lobo*
*El lobo José es malvado porque quería comerse a los tres cerdos.* (The Wolf. José the wolf is wicked because he wanted to eat the three pigs.)

**Enfoque de instrucción:** Description of a character using a conjunction; sophisticated vocabulary—*malvado*; concept of word; beginning and ending punctuation; and capital letter to write name of a character.

---

**Objetivo(s) de oralidad:** Develop vocabulary and language structures necessary for students to: predict, dis/confirm predictions, describe characters using adjectives, and analyze characters.

**Diálogo:**
Making predictions: *¿Qué piensan que va a pasar después? ¿Cómo lo saben? ¿Qué piensan de lo que dijo _____? ¿Quién tiene otra idea diferente?* (What do you think will happen next? How do you know? What do you think of what _____ said? Who has a different idea? What is it?)
Making inferences: *¿De qué harías tu casa? Por qué? ¿Qué harías si tú fueras uno de los tres cerdos y viniera el lobo a tu casa a quererte comer?* (What would you make your house out of? Why? What would you do if you were one of the three pigs and the wolf came to your house to eat you?)

**Estructuras lingüísticas:**
Repetitive book language: *Por las barbas de mi abuela no entrarás aunque te duela"* (I won't let you come in—not by the hairs on my chinny-chin-chin) *"Entonces bufaré, soplaré, y tu casa tiraré"* (Then I will huff, and I will puff, and I will blow your house in.)
Making predictions: *Yo pienso que _____ porque _____.* (I think _____ because ___.)
Making inferences: *Yo haría mi casa de _____ porque _____.* (I would make my house with _____ because ___.)
**Vocabulario:** *Paja* (straw), *adobe, chiquero* (pigsty)

## Lectoescritura

**Evaluación**

**Expresión oral (hablar y escuchar):** All students will participate in dialogues, use language structures, participate in the readers theater, and use literary language in the drama center.

**Escritura:** Students will use words and symbols to analyze a character from the story; for theDictado, students will use spaces between words and beginning and ending punctuation.

**Lectura:** Students will understand how to analyze characters, join in the shared reading for readers theater, and reenact parts of the story in the drama center.

## Literacy-based ELD

**Assessment**

**Speaking and Listening:** Students will describe two characters using descriptive language and compare and contrast them using appropriate language structures.

**Reading and Writing:** Students' comprehension of the story will be assessed through completing a cloze retell of the *Three Little Pigs* utilizing a word bank.

---

### Lectoescritura
(M = modelado, C = compartido, E = equipos/parejas, I = independiente)

| | Lectura | Escritura |
|---|---|---|
| **Session 1** | **Enfoque pedagógico: M** <br> **Texto:** *Los tres cerdos: Nacho, Tito y Miguel* <br> **Actividades:** <br> Interactive read aloud. Introduce text: Activate background knowledge and explain the text structure (characteristics of a folk tale; this is a different version; explain the author is Mexican American). <br> Picture walk: Introduce vocabulary and repetitive phrases of the text (see oracy). <br> Dialogue: Making predictions. | **Enfoque pedagógico: M, C, E, I** <br> **Actividades:** <br> Dictado |
| **Session 2** | **Enfoque pedagógico: M** <br> **Texto:** *Los tres cerdos* <br> **Actividades:** <br> Interactive read aloud. Dialogue: Confirming/disconfirming predictions. | **Enfoque pedagógico: M, C, E, I** <br> **Actividades:** <br> Dictado |
| **Session 3** | **Enfoque pedagógico: M** <br> **Texto:** *Los tres cerdos* <br> **Actividades:** <br> Interactive read aloud. Dialogue: Character analysis ¿Qué observan en. . . ? ¿Qué cosas le gusta hacer? ¿Por qué creen que ___ hizo su casa de ___? ¿Qué pasó cuando vino el lobo? (What do you notice about ___? What does he like to do? Why do you think ___ made his house with ___? What happened when the wolf came?) | **Enfoque pedagógico: C, I** <br> **Actividades:** <br> Dictado <br> Reading response. Describing a character: Teacher will engage students in a dialogue related to the different characters in the story. Selecting one of the characters, teacher and students will negotiate a description of the character as part of shared writing. Students will select a character from the story and use pictures and words to describe him/her. Students will then share their character representation with the class. |

### Literacy-based ELD
(M = modeled, S = shared, C = collaborative, I = independent)

| | Reading | Writing |
|---|---|---|
| **Session 1** | | |
| **Session 2** | | |
| **Session 3** | **Approach: S** <br> **Text:** *Three Little Pigs* <br> **Activities:** <br> Explain the purpose for reading the English version: We will talk about how the two stories are the same and different <br> Introduce the text: Explain that this is the traditional version <br> Picture walk: Introduce, clarify, and practice vocabulary and language structures <br> Read the story aloud for pure enjoyment | **Approach: M, S, C, I** <br> **Activities:** |

| | | | | |
|---|---|---|---|---|
| **Session 4** | **Enfoque pedagógico: M, C**<br>**Texto:** *Los tres cerdos*<br>**Actividades:**<br>Interactive read aloud. Extension activity: Shared reading and dramatization. Students will reenact the story with the teacher narrating and the students reciting the dialogue between José the wolf and each of the three pigs. Students can make masks to use during the dramatization (see activities at the end of the text—place materials in the drama center for students to revisit). | **Enfoque pedagógico: C**<br>**Actividades:**<br>Dictado<br>Shared writing of an invitation. Teacher will discuss inviting students from another class to see the dramatization of the story of the *Three Little Pigs*. Essential elements of the invitation will be included: Description of the event, date/time, and place. Each student will write/copy the invitation to give to a student in another class. | **Approach: S**<br>**Text:** *Three Little Pigs*<br>**Activities:**<br>Reading with the students: Invite children (whole group) to join you in reading the characters' dialogue. Tell them that when they see a little icon next to the text they should read with you.<br>Use echo reading as way to scaffold their involvement with the text.<br>Responding to the story: Talk about similarities and differences in the two stories (in Spanish or in both languages—see oracy dialogue section). | **Approach: M, S**<br>**Activities:**<br>Through modeled and shared writing, identify and record similarities and differences using pictures and words on a T-chart graphic organizer. |
| **Session 5** | **Enfoque pedagógico: M**<br>**Texto:** *Los tres cerdos*<br>**Actividades:**<br>Interactive read aloud: Purpose for reading today is for students to identify their favorite part of the story, orally and then via writing and drawing.<br>Dialogue: Talk about your favorite part of the story. In pairs, students share their favorite part with one another. | **Enfoque pedagógico: C, I**<br>**Actividades:**<br>Dictado<br>Model how to illustrate and write about an event from the story. Through shared writing, invite children to encode the message on the board. Provide explicit instruction around conventions (use of beginning and ending punctuation, spaces between words)<br>Students will then illustrate and write about their favorite part of the story and share their work with the class. | **Approach: M, S**<br>**Text:** *Three Little Pigs*<br>**Activities:**<br>Reading with the students.<br>Character reading: Teacher will be the narrator and different students will read one character's dialogue.<br>Group students according to the character they chose.<br>Tell students to pay attention to the icon next to the text. | **Approach: M , S, C, I**<br>**Activities:** |
| **Session 6** | | | **Approach: M, S**<br>**Text:** *Three Little Pigs*<br>**Activities:** Teacher reads the text and students read the dialogue parts of the text. | **Approach: M, S**<br>**Text:** Text for cloze activity<br>**Activities:** Cloze shared writing activity: Retell of the story. Focus on repetitive language from the text. (e.g., Once upon a time there were three _____. The first little pig made a house with _____.) |

*Continues*

| Lectoescritura (M = modelado, C = compartido, E = equipos/parejas, I = independiente) | | Literacy-based ELD (M = modeled, S = shared, C = collaborative, I = independent) | |
|---|---|---|---|
| Lectura | Escritura | Reading | Writing |
| | | **Approach: M, S**<br>**Text:** *Three Little Pigs*<br>**Activities:**<br>Teacher reads the text and students read the dialogue parts of the text.<br>Character analysis: Preteach vocabulary—mean, angry, hungry, happy, afraid, scared<br>Dialogue: How do you think the first little pig felt? The first little pig was _____. | **Approach: S**<br>**Activities:**<br>Shared writing: After discussion and dialogue about the characters' similarities and differences, the teacher will create a word bank of different characteristics (e.g., scared, excited, hungry) Through shared writing, the characters will be described using the language structure: The _____ was _____. The characters will be compared by using transformations.<br>Transformation: was/was not.<br>Language structures: The _____ was _____. The _____ was not _____. |

Session 7

158

# 10 Grade 5 Expository Text Unit

*I see the looks on my students' faces as they're learning, and so for me it's worth it to put the time into it. It helps to have coworkers that are supporting me and helping me figure out lesson plans that will be effective.*

Stephanie Griffith, grades 4 and 5 Literacy Squared teacher, Lamb Elementary School, Salem, OR

## Guiding Questions

▪ How is the role of Spanish literacy different in the intermediate grades from the goals of Spanish literacy in the primary grades?
▪ How can one create a unit that both values authentic Spanish literacy methods and materials and remains compatible with U.S. curricula?

The grade 5 expository text lesson featured in this chapter was created by Sandra Butvilofsky and Wendy Sparrow. The lesson was cotaught between Sandra and a grade 5 classroom teacher in Denver, Colorado. Throughout the unit, Sandra implemented the lessons with the teacher and the students, modeling some of the lessons for the teacher and supporting the teacher's implementation for the rest of them. This biliteracy unit was part of a larger unit on expository text, with the eventual outcome in Spanish literacy for students to work in collaborative groups to research and write an expository text on a group-selected topic, while in literacy-based ELD, they would do so independently.

## Planning the Unit

This lesson plan is part of a larger literacy unit that explores reasons for reading and writing expository text in grade 5 as mandated by both state and district standards, as well as the Common Core State Standards for English language arts (see lesson plan at the end of the chapter for the specific standards addressed). In accordance with the holistic biliteracy framework, which includes the implementation of oracy, writing, reading, and metalanguage in both Spanish and literacy-based ELD, the unit presented herein connects the literacy environments via the genre of expository text, as stated in the connections between literacy environments section of the lesson plan.

### Connecting the Language Environments

We utilized the curriculum materials set forth by the *Secretaría de educación pública (SEP) de México*, which is the federally mandated curriculum (http://basica.sep.gob.mx/reforma integral/sitio/index.php?act=buscadorlibros) to address the authenticity of Spanish instruction and the importance of including culturally and personally relevant topics, materials, and themes. The particular expository unit from the SEP materials addresses the topic of obesity, which is especially relevant because childhood obesity is a pervasive public health problem in both Mexico and the United States.

After reviewing the expository unit in the grade 5 SEP materials and considering the Literacy Squared time allocations, we identified the aspects of the unit that would address the state standards of reading and writing expository texts, and also assist in developing the cognitive load in Spanish. Because only 45 minutes are allocated to Spanish literacy in grade 5 each day, it is important to use it as efficiently as possible, building the depth of knowledge in Spanish and then working to connect that knowledge to English. We also recognize the challenge teachers face in finding authentic Spanish materials to use during Spanish literacy; the use of the SEP materials fulfills such a need.

To ensure that the lesson would not be duplicative across languages when planning for literacy-based ELD, we drew on our Spanish plan and thought about how to extend that knowledge in English via the use of different materials, objectives, and end products. For example, in considering the structures of expository text such as defining, describing events/processes, expressing cause/effect relationships, comparing/contrasting, and stating problem/solution relationships (Fountas & Pinnell, 2001), we chose to focus on different structures in each language. In attending to these different structures of expository text, students not only had the opportunity to read and write as they learned about these structures, they also used language specific to each structure and made cross-language connections to identify the rhetorical and grammatical structures specific to expository text across languages.

More specifically, we thought about the end products we expected students to produce from exploring the different text structures. In both languages, students would produce a five-paragraph essay exploring different aspects of obesity and utilizing different text structures with varying levels of support. In Spanish, the essay defines obesity and identifies the characteristics of an obese person, describes the processes of why obesity occurs, and provides the detrimental effects of obesity. In English, students identified the problems related to obesity, but the primary focus was to provide the reader with solutions for preventing obesity in a persuasive manner. This biliteracy unit was part of a larger unit on expository text, with the eventual outcome in Spanish literacy to have students work in collaborative groups to research and write an expository text on a group-selected topic; in literacy-based ELD they would do so independently.

## Time

This biliteracy unit was planned to span two to three weeks. As noted in the unit plan, we established the purpose and cognitive concepts to be developed in Spanish literacy for a couple of sessions before beginning the unit in literacy-based ELD. This is not to say that literacy-based ELD should not occur during those first couple of days, but rather that the teacher would be finishing up a different unit in literacy-based ELD or reviewing past knowledge based on students' needs. As a reminder, for Literacy Squared to be effective teachers must adhere to minimum time allocations in Spanish literacy and literacy-based ELD each day, with no exceptions. In addition, it is important to keep in mind that in grade 5, literacy-based ELD is scheduled for a minimum of two hours and Spanish literacy is scheduled for a minimum of 45 minutes. The following plan encompasses the entire Spanish literacy block. However, the duration of the literacy-based ELD lessons linked to this unit should only be between 45–60 minutes a day so that time is still available for teaching other aspects of literacy using different pedagogical approaches.

## The Lesson

### Literacy Objectives

The literacy objectives for this unit are in the unit plan at the end of the chapter. While the topic of obesity is culturally and personally relevant to fifth graders, the unit's objective was not for students to study about obesity in-depth. Instead, it was for students to understand the structures of expository text so that they could access information from other expository texts and produce them in other content areas. In this way, both reading and writing are integrally related, thus re-emphasizing the holistic and comprehensive nature of the framework. Literacy Squared biliteracy units can have the same literacy objectives for both languages. However, in this particular unit, while most of the literacy objectives overlap in both languages, the objective of taking a position on an issue and writing persuasively to convince readers is unique to literacy-based ELD.

## Cross-Language Strategies

This unit uses the cross-language strategies of *así se dice* and cognate identification to increase comprehension. While in-depth use of *así se dice* is provided in this particular lesson, for more information on the strategy itself see Chapter 5. Throughout the unit many cognates arise and explicit attention should be given to their reinforcement. Recognizing cognates can help students understand unknown words in one language that they know in the other one, further developing their vocabulary and reinforcing how their bilingualism serves as a valuable resource.

Direct/explicit and interactive methods were utilized in both language environments (see Chapter 1 for grade-appropriate instructional approaches). However, because of time constraints in Spanish literacy, the primary pedagogical approaches we selected for this particular biliteracy study unit included modeled, shared, and collaborative approaches. Because more time is allocated to literacy-based ELD in grade 5, we included those approaches addressed in Spanish literacy and also created opportunities for students to work independently. As noted in the lesson plan, modeled and shared experiences provide scaffolding for students before they are released to work collaboratively and independently, providing them with higher levels of support as they are introduced to the main objectives of the lesson.

## Spanish and English Dictados

This unit presents a Spanish and an English Dictado that are meaningful to the topic and the genre of the unit. The Spanish Dictado is for the first week of the unit and the English Dictado for the second. TheDictado always includes attention to spelling and punctuation. However, theDictado also serves as a means of teaching metalinguistic awareness. Notice that in both Dictados, specific attention is given to the rhetorical nature of expository text. For example, the first sentence of the English Dictado begins with a question—a rhetorical device that is common to expository text. In addition, language structures are specific to the function of compare and contrast (e.g., on the other hand, as well as). Vocabulary was also strategically chosen to expand students' linguistic repertoires. TheDictado should not only be used to teach basic writing skills, but also as an essential tool in assisting students in appropriating literary language.

The Spanish and English Dictados for this biliteracy unit reinforce the unit's text and language structures taught in both languages. In Spanish, the structure of cause/effect was used [*El resultado de __ es__* (As a result of ___, ___)], while in English, the structure of compare/contrast (___, on the other hand___; ___, as well as ___) was reinforced. In both languages, students were learning appropriate spelling, punctuation, and high-utility and technical vocabulary. (See Chapter 2 for more information on selecting vocabulary.) In Spanish, the focused vocabulary words included: *esencial* (essential), *requiere* (requires), *longevidad* (longevity), and *rutinario* (daily), some of which are also cognates. Words with "c," "s," and "z" were strategically chosen for the Spanish Dictado because in some words these letters represent the same phoneme [*alimentación* (nutrition), *esencial* (essential), *aparezca* (appear), *ejercicio* (exercise), *física* (physical), and *balanceada* (balanced)]. In English, different suffixes were used ("ly," "er," and "ing") to teach morphology and spelling.

On the first day, theDictados appeared too challenging for the majority of the class. However, through explicit instruction accomplished via the talk-through, students demonstrated the appropriation of the targeted teaching points. Box 10.1 shows an example of a student's Spanish Dictado over the course of three days. On day 1, Marisol's Dictado

BOX 10.1  *Marisol's Spanish Dictado*

On the first day of the Spanish Dictado, Marisol had many approximations, but with practice she appropriated the teaching points. On day 1, she omitted the accent marks in the words *alimentación* and *física*; however by day 2, she learned the standard forms. As was the focus of the spelling aspect of theDictado, on day 1 Marisol approximated many of the words with "c," "s," and "z": *esencial, aparezca, ejercicio,* and *balanceada.* By day 3 she learned to spell all words accurately, except for *aparezca* and *esencial.* It is important to note that on day 2 she did not self-correct her approximation of *aparezca,* which then resulted in the same approximation on day 3. After two days of practice, Marisol appropriated the use of the comma after the dependent clause.

shows that she needed more practice differentiating between "c," "s," and "z," as well as using a comma after a dependent clause. However, by day 3, as seen in Marisol's work, students mastered the teaching points.

## Oracy Objectives

When determining the oracy objectives for each language, it was important to take into account the literacy objectives and the levels of prior knowledge that students had about those particular concepts. In recognizing that fifth-graders would have already been exposed to the concept of compare/contrast and problem/solution, we determined that the focus of oracy instruction in literacy-based ELD would be for students to learn the language used to express compare/contrast and problem/solution relationships, In Spanish it would be more helpful for them to learn the language of defining, cause/effect, and describing processes.

**Language Structures.** To guarantee that students can meaningfully understand and interact with texts and each other, the teaching of specific language structures is offered as a support. As is illustrated in the lesson plan, when creating language structures, we addressed varying levels of complexity for these oracy objectives to account for students' differing levels of language proficiency. When planning for language structures, it is important to consider how language is used in speaking, reading, and writing. Explicit attention needs to be given to the language authors/texts used to identify problem/solution relationships because this may be different from how you teach students to communicate problem/solution. In other words, we expand students' repertoires by attending not only to what they encounter in texts, but by also providing them with alternative structures. In one of the texts the students read in English, the author states the solution in the following manner: "The main solution is. . . ," while the structure we selected for students' proposed solutions is: "___ proposes ____ (to solve the problem)." It is important to keep an integrated approach to understanding and using language, which can only be accomplished when all language domains are taken into consideration.

**Vocabulary.** For this biliteracy unit, we selected both technical and high-utility words so that students can interact with the text and learn new vocabulary they are likely to encounter in other contexts. In Spanish literacy, specific attention was given to morphology because this skill provides students with strategies to apply such knowledge to other words. For example, the prefix *sobre* means over [(e.g., *sobrepeso* (overweight), *sobrevivir* (to survive), *sobrecargar* (to overload)]. Thus, if students understand this meaning and encounter other words with the same prefix, they will be more strategic at deciphering the meaning of the new word. When providing explicit instruction for vocabulary, it is unnecessary to teach all the words at once. Instead, we suggest providing students with an understanding of the terms necessary to understand the texts, and then teaching other words as they are encountered in context. Of course, students will need multiple exposures to the words; this can be facilitated throughout the unit and in all language domains.

**Dialogue.** Engaging students in dialogue is a critical aspect of teaching oracy. Because activities for dialogue provide students with opportunities to interact meaningfully with the text and to engage in a metalinguistic discussion that is particular to the literacy and oracy objectives, it is important for teachers to preplan dialogue questions and strategies so that student talk is productive and serves the purpose of expanding oracy skills. Such opportunities are especially important in the intermediate grade levels. For this lesson we embedded topics and questions to elicit dialogue within the specific sessions. Some of the questions are to elicit connected discourse to prepare students to read or expand their understanding of the text, while other questions are more specific to ensure that as they talk the oracy objectives are met. For session 3 in literacy-based ELD, we planned for both types of dialogue. To expand students' understanding of the text, we ask them to think of ways they might help an obese friend or family member. While the students are free to think about how they might help, they are required to use the targeted language structure of providing a solution: "I propose to help my obese friend/family member by _____." As mentioned in Chapter 2, an effective dialogue involves students taking turns talking to each other, rather than only responding to the teacher's questions. To ensure that a dialogue takes place, students need to listen and respond to their classmates by confirming and/or expanding on what is said. Although such interactions may seem difficult to create, with careful planning and practice, students will understand and undertake such roles.

## Assessment

We had several indicators to assess student learning in this biliteracy unit. In Spanish literacy and literacy-based ELD, the speaking assessment was collected anecdotally, with the teacher observing that all students were taking part in dialogue and appropriately using the newly learned language structures. In Spanish literacy, student writing was assessed on whether or not students could find information and take notes related to the key questions. In addition, the end product of the unit was a five-paragraph expository essay using the text structures of defining, describing processes, and cause/effect relationships. In literacy-based ELD, writing was assessed on whether or not students could write the newly learned language structures with the related information from readings in their notebooks. They were also required to take notes successfully based on solutions to obesity. The end product was a five-paragraph expository essay using the text structures of compare/contrast and problem/solution, as well as using persuasive writing to propose a solution to obesity. This essay also provided the teacher with information regarding the students' understanding of the texts read. In Spanish literacy, students take a quiz to see if they can identify defining, describing processes, and cause/effect relationship text structures within the texts that they read. While not stated explicitly in the lesson plan, the teacher should gain an idea of the students' listening skills by observing their answers as they respond to their classmates during dialogues and when they provide feedback as their peers share their writing.

## Session Plans for the Unit: Detailing Biliteracy Instruction

The plan is broken into 12 sessions or lessons detailing the activities for how we structured the teaching and learning in this biliteracy unit. The first three sessions in Spanish literacy are intended to access and build students' background knowledge around both the genre of expository text and the topic of obesity. This work contextualizes and sets the stage for the intended learning. Directed questions guide students through understanding the structures of expository text and elicit dialogue related to their understanding. We elected to use direct and interactive approaches for reading and writing to facilitate a collective understanding of the purposes for which expository texts are read and written. More specifically, such approaches provide scaffolding to students to help them reach the unit objectives. By using direct and interactive approaches for reading and writing, students have teacher and peer support as they are learning and practicing the language needed to interact successfully with the text and meet the unit objectives. Furthermore, as students have multiple opportunities to hear, say, read, and write the new language and vocabulary, they gain command over the language and are able to transfer their new skills to other contexts.

For students to truly understand that expository texts are read to gather information, we decided to create questions (see writing section of session 2) that would focus our reading. We also wanted students to write their own expository text that related their understanding to a wider audience and served as the end product of this unit. The process for preparing the end product involved reading and the note-taking abilities. These skills are modeled for the students and gradually completed using a shared approach as students become comfortable with the process. These three sessions provide students with a clear example of what to do when reading and writing expository texts and, more significantly, why it is important to know how to do so.

As the foundation of reading for specific information and taking notes is being practiced in Spanish literacy, the purpose for reading and writing expository texts in literacy-based ELD is introduced in session 3. While students are gaining the knowledge from Spanish literacy to guide them through expository text, in literacy-based ELD we guide them through the text structures of problem/solution and compare/contrast because they will be reading to find solutions for obesity, proposing written solutions, and comparing and contrasting such solutions. A graphic organizer (Table 10.1) is used in both language environments to categorize and define the various structures of expository text. It includes key words (connectives) that are used in such structures and relevant samples for students to reference as the unit progresses. Note that the English focus is different from the Spanish one. In Spanish literacy, students will define, describe, and establish cause-and-effect relationships of obesity. Learning how and why to read and write expository texts and about the theme of obesity are common to both environments. As students learn about them in one language, they draw on that knowledge and transfer it to their work in the other language environment.

**Session 1.** To begin the unit, students are introduced in Spanish literacy to expository text via the SEP article, *"Textos expositivos"* (Expository texts). During this session, students' prior knowledge of expository text is activated through dialogue. Then students engage in a shared reading of various examples of text structures from the SEP materials (Box 10.2) and discuss purposes for reading and writing expository texts. The teacher records students' understanding of expository text structures in the graphic organizer (see Table 10.1).

**Session 2.** In the following session, students are reminded of the importance of understanding how to read expository texts, regardless of the topic. The text, *"Lo que conozco"* (What I know) (Box 10.3), establishes the questions that are used to find relevant information on obesity and include information on how certain features and structures of expository text help in finding relevant information. After conducting a shared reading of the text, students work collaboratively in small groups to activate their prior knowledge regarding obesity (Box 10.4) and record their understandings. Subsequently, groups report their understandings of the topic. This provides the teacher with valuable information related to students' understanding of the topic and insight into their linguistic skills.

**Sessions 3 and 4.** In the next two sessions in Spanish literacy, students learn how to analyze the specific expository text structures of defining, establishing cause-and-effect relationships, and describing events. Simultaneously, students find the information needed to answer the guiding questions established in the previous session: defining obesity,

**TABLE 10.1**

Graphic Organizers for Defining Expository Text Structures in Spanish Literacy
and Literacy-based ELD

*Nombre:* _____

| Estructuras de textos expositivos | | | |
|---|---|---|---|
| **Estructura del texto** | **Definición/preguntas** | **Nexos** | **Ejemplos** |
| *Definir* | | | |
| *Describir eventos o procesos* | | | |
| *Causa-efecto* | | | |

| Patterns of Text Structure in Expository Texts | | | |
|---|---|---|---|
| **Text Structure** | **Definition** | **Key Words** | **Examples** |
| Compare/contrast | | | |
| Problem/solution | | | |

## BOX 10.2 *Definition of Expository Texts and Text Structures with Example from the SEP Materials*

**Un dato interesante**

Plutón, que durante 76 años fue considerado un planeta del Sistema Solar, en 2006 dejó de serlo; ahora es sólo un cuerpo celeste que está en órbita alrededor del Sol.

El resultado de dos años de debates tuvo como consecuencia la nueva definición de planeta que dio la Unión Astronómica Internacional. Actualmente el Sistema Solar cuenta con ocho planetas.

No hay verdades absolutas, están en constante cambio por el avance de la ciencia y la tecnología.

**Textos expositivos**

En un texto expositivo se muestran de forma neutra y objetiva determinados hechos o realidades. Por esa razón, no basta con lo que un autor crea o suponga sobre un tema; es necesario recopilar información sobre el hecho, asegurarse de que es veraz para divulgar conocimientos ciertos y confiables.

Los textos expositivos están organizados por medio de títulos y subtítulos con la finalidad de presentar la información de manera clara, ordenada y ágil para que el lector pueda ubicarla con mayor facilidad.

Para responder las preguntas, elaboren pequeños textos que buscarán:

- definir algo.
- establecer relaciones de causa-efecto.
- describir eventos o procesos.

**Textos para definir**

Cuando la pregunta sea ¿qué es? o ¿cómo se define?, responde con sencillez y claridad las características del concepto, por ejemplo.

### ¿Qué es un ciclón?

Un ciclón es una concentración anormal de nubes que gira en torno a un centro de baja presión atmosférica, cuyos vientos convergentes rotan en sentido contrario a las manecillas del reloj a grandes velocidades. Sus elementos principales son lluvia, viento, oleaje y marea de tormenta. Se clasifican de tres modos de acuerdo con la fuerza de sus vientos: depresión tropical, tormenta tropical, y huracán, el cual tiene cinco categorías.

"¿Qué hacer en caso de... ciclones?" en *Desastres. Guía de prevención.* México, Secretaría de Gobernación-Conapred, 2006, pág. 14.

**Textos para establecer relaciones de causa-efecto**

Cuando las preguntas sean ¿por qué ocurre?, ¿qué provoca?, ¿a causa de qué?, contesta mencionando las causas de un suceso y cómo están relacionadas con sus efectos. Ejemplo:

### ¿Por qué se producen los incendios forestales?

Los incendios forestales son producidos principalmente por quemas de limpia para uso del suelo en la agricultura, quemas de pasto para la obtención de 'pelillo' que sirve como forraje, con el objeto de combatir plagas y otros animales dañinos; fogatas en los bosques; lanzamiento de objetos encendidos sobre la vegetación herbácea; tormentas eléctricas, desprendimiento de las líneas de alta tensión y acciones incendiarias intencionales.

"¿Qué hacer en caso de... incendios?", en *Desastres. Guía de prevención.* México, Secretaría de Gobernación-Conapred, 2006, pág. 36.

**Textos para describir eventos o procesos**

Cuando tienes que responder a las preguntas: ¿cómo se produce?, ¿qué características tiene?, ¿cuál es el origen?, debes redactar la descripción del proceso, suceso o fenómeno, enfatizando lo que ocurre, paso a paso. Lee el siguiente ejemplo:

### ¿Cómo se origina un tsunami?

Para que un terremoto origine un tsunami, el fondo marino debe ser movido abruptamente en sentido vertical, de modo que el océano es impulsado fuera de su equilibrio normal. Cuando esta inmensa masa de agua trata de recuperar su equilibrio, se generan las olas. El tamaño de las olas del tsunami estará determinado por la magnitud de la deformación vertical del fondo marino. En la gran mayoría de los casos, el movimiento inicial que provoca la generación de los tsunamis es una dislocación vertical de la corteza terrestre en el fondo del océano, ocasionada por un sismo.

"¿Qué hacer en caso de... tsunami?" en *Desastres. Guía de prevención.* México, Secretaría de Gobernación-Conapred, 2006, pág. 49.

Courtesy of Secretary of Public Education in Mexico (SEP).

## BOX 10.3 Lo que conozco. *Introduction to Obesity with Focus Questions for Research*

### MENTE SANA EN CUERPO SANO

### Lo que conozco

En la actualidad, uno de los temas más preocupantes es el de la adecuada alimentación, ya que la desnutrición o los trastornos de la alimentación, como la obesidad, la anorexia y la bulimia, son fenómenos que van en aumento.

¿Conoces alguna persona con alguno de estos problemas de alimentación? ¿Has leído textos que presenten información sobre este tipo de enfermedades? ¿Cuáles son las características de los textos expositivos? ¿En qué fuentes de información puedes encontrar este tipo de textos?

Lee el siguiente texto relacionado con los trastornos de la alimentación; sigue las instrucciones de tu maestro.

Courtesy of Secretary of Public Education in Mexico (SEP).

**BOX 10.4** *Activating Prior Knowledge*

**Collaborative Work: Activating Prior Knowledge of Obesity through Dialogue and Writing**

Structuring the dialogue
1. To activate students' prior knowledge on the topic of obesity, students work in groups of four
2. Each member of the group is assigned a role
   - Person 1: Asks the questions
   - Person 2: Task master—timekeeper and messenger who keeps the group on task
   - Person 3: Recorder—records student responses on the appropriate sheet (see following example)
   - Person 4: Reporter—reports the group's responses to the larger group
3. At the end of 15 minutes, reporters share their group's answers to the four questions.

---

1. ¿Qué es la obesidad (sobrepeso)?

Obesidad es que cuando estas gordo.
La Obesidad es cuando alguin no deja de comer chucherias.

2. ¿Qué características tiene una persona obesa?

Una persona obesa no pueda caminar y levantarse.
Una persona floja aue come chucherias.

3. ¿Por qué es un problema?

Es un problema por que se puede morir por tanta grasa.
Es un problema por que no puede hacer lo que tiene que hacer.

4. ¿Por qué ocurre la obesidad? ¿Qué provoca?

Ocurre la obesidad por que no hacen ejercicio. eso lo provan
la grasa.

describing how individuals become obese, and relating effects for obesity. In writing, the teacher models how to take notes in response to the guiding questions (Figure 10.1). As the lesson progresses, students take on more of the note-taking responsibility, first through shared and then through collaborative writing.

While students learn about note-taking in Spanish, they are introduced to the unit's purpose in English. In the first two literacy-based ELD sessions (3 and 4), students are reminded of what they learned about expository text in Spanish and they are introduced to a new expository text in English. As in Spanish literacy, students' prior knowledge is activated through planned dialogue, and they participate in a shared reading of an article about fighting obesity (*Let's Move! to Fight Obesity*, www2.scholastic.com/browse/article .jsp?id=3753544), continuing to a postreading dialogue. Students learn the text and language structures for expressing problems and solutions and the teacher models written examples from the text in the graphic organizer that demonstrate the structure of expressing problem/solution relationships. In the next session, the class talks about their learning

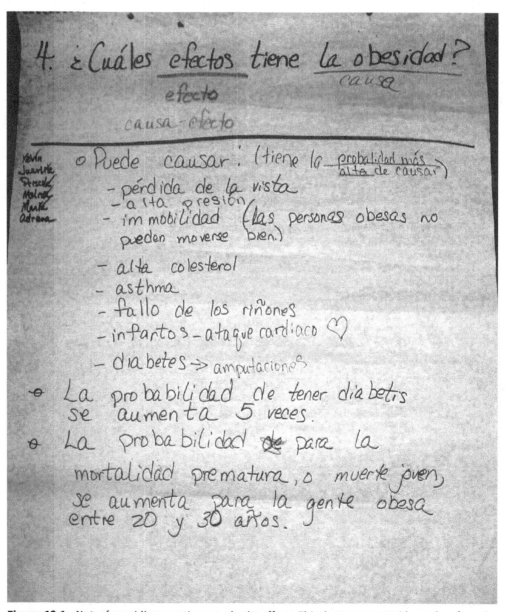

**Figure 10.1** Notes for guiding questions on obesity effects. This chart represents ideas taken from the various expository texts the students and teacher read to find answers for the guiding questions around obesity. The teacher modeled taking notes and, as students learned the process, they also kept notes for each guiding question.

from the previous day and does a shared reading of another article about obesity ("What Is Obesity?" www2.scholastic.com/browse/article.jsp?id=3754039). This time, students work collaboratively to express problem/solution relationships.

**Session 5.** Next, during Spanish literacy, the teacher reviews key aspects of expository text (e.g., key words, table of contents) and leads the students in a dialogue about how such aspects help us understand and find information in expository texts. In collaborative groups, students use different sources the teacher has gathered from the library and internet to read and take notes on. This information helps them answer the key questions. As groups report on the information they find, the teacher records it for the class, reminding them also to record references for their bibliographies. During literacy-based ELD, students provide the teacher with information about their prior knowledge regarding comparing and contrasting and what language they know to express such relationships. The teacher writes these, as well as new, more complex language structures on the graphic organizer, and the class begins to identify similarities and differences between the two articles they had read, adding examples to the graphic organizer. The teacher records all of the similarities and differences they find on a T chart so that students can use them to practice the new language structures for comparing and contrasting text. After they have sufficient practice, students work in collaborative groups to identify and write two similarities and two differences from the articles in their notebooks using the new language structures. Table 10.2 provides an example of how the T-chart looked.

**Session 6.** In the following session in Spanish literacy, students take part in a shared reading (Box 10.5) about using specific transitions in expository text and they begin planning how to organize the information they found into an expository piece. The piece includes an introductory paragraph and a paragraph that answered each key question they had been working to answer: What is obesity? What are the characteristics of an obese person? Why is obesity a problem? and What causes obesity? Using modeled and shared approaches, the teacher helps students create a graphic organizer and write titles and subtitles for their text. She also guides their thinking about considering text structure, audience, and the language that they want to use in their written product.

While students are beginning to prepare their expository writing piece in Spanish literacy, in literacy-based ELD they begin outlining their expository English text, which is to include an introductory paragraph, a paragraph defining obesity, two paragraphs of two different solutions for obesity, and a final persuasive paragraph explaining which recommended solution the author prefers or believes is more feasible. Note how these paragraphs require students to use the skills of comparing/contrasting and expressing problem/solution relationships that they have been practicing. Considering the outline students are following, the teacher leads the class in a shared writing of the introductory text paragraph.

---

**TABLE 10.2**

## Comparing and Contrasting: "Let's Move! to Fight Obesity" and "What Is Obesity?"

| Similarities | Differences |
| --- | --- |
| • The "Let's Move! to Fight Obesity" article, *as well as* the "What Is Obesity?" article are about obesity. | • One article explains the First Lady's campaign, *while* the other article answers kids' questions about health. |
| • Both articles are *alike* because they are about Michelle Obama's "Let's Move!" campaign. | • The "Let's Move! to Fight Obesity" article was aimed at an audience that included parents, *whereas* the "What Is Obesity?" article was targeted towards children. |
| • The "Let's Move! to Fight Obesity" article provided facts about childhood obesity in America. *Similarly,* the "What Is Obesity?" article provided facts about how many children are overweight. | • In one article, the First Lady said that we already know the cure for obesity, *as opposed to* the other article, where she explained that "Let's Move" was a cheap and easy initiative. |
| • Both articles explained possible solutions to childhood obesity. *Likewise,* they both mentioned that the First Lady planted a garden at the White House. | |

BOX 10.5 **El uso de los nexos** *Use of Transition Words in Expository Texts from the SEP Materials*

## El uso de nexos

Lee los siguientes textos y revisa su redacción:

- Una de las causas por las que se presenta la anemia en la infancia es la insuficiencia de hierro en la dieta, por lo tanto, hay que procurar que los niños consuman alimentos que contengan este mineral.
- El sobrepeso es un factor que acorta la vida de las personas porque puede provocar diabetes mellitus o enfermedades cardiovasculares.
- Las estadísticas de salud en nuestro país muestran una tendencia cada vez mayor al desarrollo de trastornos alimenticios, por ejemplo, la obesidad, la anorexia y la bulimia.

### Fichero del saber

Los textos expositivos están organizados por medio de títulos y subtítulos, con la finalidad de presentar la información de manera clara, ordenada y ágil para que el lector pueda ubicarla con más facilidad.

Enriquece esta información y elabora la ficha correspondiente.

En los textos expositivos se utilizan un tipo palabras que tienen como función unir palabras o enunciados para explicar o dar ejemplos, para señalar un orden, una causa o una consecuencia. Estas palabras se llaman nexos, entre ellas podemos encontrar: *por ejemplo, por lo tanto, cuando, entonces, porque,* etcétera.

Localiza los nexos en las oraciones anteriores y después elabora la ficha correspondiente para el Fichero del saber.

Courtesy of Secretary of Public Education in Mexico (SEP).

**Sessions 7 and 8.** For the next two Spanish literacy sessions, students continue writing their expository essays, beginning with a shared writing of the introduction and working on their essays in collaborative groups. The teacher then leads the class in a shared writing of their conclusion and students work independently to revise and edit their essays, expanding on them as necessary and making sure that their bibliography is included.

During this time in literacy-based ELD, students look through various texts that the teacher has gathered from the library and internet for information on solutions for obesity. The teacher reminds students of their Spanish literacy knowledge (e.g., using text features to answer key questions, taking notes, keeping a list of references) and models them in English. The teacher then reviews language structures and vocabulary for expressing problem/solution and compare/contrast relationships and models writing a paragraph about a solution for obesity, making sure to include some of the new structures. This flows into sessions 9 and 10, during which students work collaboratively to choose a solution to obesity and write a paragraph about it. Students then independently choose a second solution and write a paragraph about it.

**Sessions 9 and 10.** While students are writing their paragraphs in literacy-based ELD in session 9, during Spanish literacy groups share their essays with one another and, through a structured dialogue (see questions in Spanish reading, session 9), they discuss the essays and provide one another with feedback for improvement. As students continue writing during literacy-based ELD, session 10 of Spanish literacy consists of a collaborative *así se dice* activity where students use their Spanish expository text to write an English paragraph that defines obesity. The rationale for using students' Spanish texts and *así se dice* to write the English paragraph is that the students have already done all of the work to research and define obesity in Spanish and they do not need to repeat it in English. However, for their English essays to make sense, they need to include such a paragraph after their introductory paragraph. Thus, rather than providing them with duplicative work, students engage in a complex and sophisticated translation activity to transfer the knowledge they gained and the work they did in Spanish into English. Using their Spanish texts, students use the *así se dice* strategy to define obesity, identify its characteristics, categorize it, and explain its causes and effects. While this information extends throughout their Spanish essays, they need to choose strategically the necessary information for one paragraph within their English texts. Student success with *así se dice* depends on their experience from previous exposure to this cross-language strategy.

**Sessions 11 and 12.** In the last two sessions, students finish their essays on expository text in literacy-based ELD. They read the two paragraphs they wrote about solutions to obesity and decide which one they thought was better or more feasible. The teacher models writing a persuasive paragraph that includes the new language structures for comparing and contrasting. After modeling the paragraph, the teacher rewrites it as a cloze structure with blank spaces so that students who need more support can use the structure to complete their paragraphs. Students take a stance and, independently, write a persuasive paragraph to convince their reader which solution was the stronger one and why. Students are expected to use the structures they learned to compare and contrast the different solutions within their paragraphs.

In the final session, the teacher models combining the paragraphs they had written to create a five-paragraph essay. As the teacher does this, she models how she needs to edit (e.g, to ensure that the paragraphs transition smoothly). Students then edit their texts, making sure they include all of the necessary components. (See Box 10.6 for a sample of a student's final expository text.) As students finish their expository pieces, they share them with the class and the teacher leads them in a dialogue about the similarities and differences between their essays (specifically, the paragraphs from the *así se dice* and where they wrote their solutions). Students then consider what they and their peers wrote and choose a solution to obesity that they can use as a goal for themselves and/or their families. They use the language structure in literacy-based ELD writing session 12 to write their goal independently and how they plan to achieve it. During this time in Spanish literacy, they read about public service announcements in an SEP article and, based on their knowledge of obesity, nutrition, and eating disorders, they create their own public service announcement to inform the community on how to lead a healthier lifestyle.

BOX 10.6  *Teresa's Expository Essay on Obesity*

Obesity is a problem in the United States especially for children. Obesity is defined in various ways. Excercise is one solution to childhood obesity. Another way to solve the problem is to eat healthy food. These are some answers to the dilemma of childhood obesity. Th The following is a definicion of obesity the biggest enemy of the hummanity. Obesity is the overweight that is caused by medical problems and by eating alot of oil and sugar of for not burning calories with excerrsixe. One person that is obese has the characteristics of not eating enough of fruits and vegetables and being sedentary. Obesity is a problem for 15 " of the boys and girls of the U.S.A are obese if they continue they will have medical problems. Obesity has strong effects for the obese people for example probability to have diabetetes, sicknesses mortabilyty of being young. For these reasons, obesity is dangerous for human beings.

## Conclusion

As with the primary lesson we shared in Chapter 9, this biliteracy unit on expository texts exemplifies our commitment to the holistic biliteracy framework. This unit purpose-fully connects Spanish literacy and literacy-based ELD; includes reading, writing, oracy, and metalanguage; and uses direct and interactive approaches before releasing students to independence. It is our sincere hope that the lessons presented in Chapters 9 and 10 offer a model that teachers can use as they enact Literacy Squared in their schools and class-rooms. Our experience has shown us that emerging bilingual students develop high levels of biliteracy and thrive academically when their schooling includes thoughtful paired lit-eracy beginning in kindergarten and continuing throughout elementary school.

BOX 10.6    *(Cont.)*

Eating heathy food is a solution to childhood obesity. If kids eat heathy food they will be heal thy. If they put heal thier food in lunches and in vending machines that will help alot. The kids shouldn't be the ones calling the shots at our dinnertime. That is how eating healthy helps decrease obesity.

The excercise helps also to decrease obesity. You should play 60 minutes a day. Yo can go to washinto or the internet to the Lets Move program and excercise. This solution will help you decrease obesity.

To conclude, those are some ideas to prevent obesity. You can define obesity in various ways. One solution is to excercise often. Eating healthy food is another solution to this problem. The dilemma of childhood obesity can be solved by these ideas.

## Questions for Reflection and Action

- Inventory the texts in your classroom/school. How might you identify and pair texts for connected teaching and learning within Spanish literacy and literacy-based ELD?
- Examine an intermediate level unit you teach. Are the expectations for students comparable across languages?
- You have just finished reading this book. Can you develop an action plan that identifies a timeline for implementing the elements of the holistic biliteracy framework into your biliteracy instruction?

# Literacy Squared Grade 5 Lesson Plan

## *Buscar información en fuentes diversas para escribir textos expositivos*/Search for information in various sources to write expository texts

**Common Core English Language Arts Standards:** Literacy.RI.5.1: Quote accurately from a text when explaining what the text says explicitly and when drawing inferences from the text. Literacy.RI.5.8: Integrate information from several texts on the same topic in order to write or speak about the subject knowledgeably. Literacy.W.5.1: Write opinion pieces on topics or texts, supporting a point of view with reasons and information. Literacy.W.5.2: Write informative/explanatory texts to examine a topic and convey ideas and information clearly. Literacy.SL.5.1: Engage effectively in a range of collaborative discussions (one-on-one, groups, and teacher-led) with diverse partners on *grade 5 topics and texts*, building on others' ideas and expressing their own clearly.

**Literacy Objectives:** Write expository texts based on different sources. Identify and understand the characteristics and language used in expository texts. Look for information and select pertinent information that can be used to relate information in writing.

**Literacy-based ELD Objective/s:** Take a position on an issue and write persuasively to convince readers; create an organizing structure appropriate to purpose and audience

| Connections between Literacy Environments: | Cross-language Strategies (If applicable): *Así se* | Materials: Grade 5 SEP materials from 2010 and 2011 (see |
|---|---|---|
| Genre: expository texts | *dice;* cognates when applicable | Boxes 10.2, 10.3, and 10.5); * Scholastic articles: "Let's Move! to Fight Obesity" (www2.scholastic.com/browse/article.jsp?id =3753544) and "What Is Obesity?" (www2.scholastic.com/ browse/article.jsp?id=3754039): graphic organizer; various Spanish and English resources from library and internet on obesity/nutrition/health; chart paper; markers; sentence strips |

### Dictado en español: *La alimentación*

*La adecuada alimentación es esencial para impedir que aparezca la obesidad. Para asegurar que no haya trastornos de la alimentación, se requiere una dieta equilibrada y ejercicio rutinario. El resultado de una dieta balanceada y actividad física es la longevidad.* (Nutrition: Proper nutrition is essential in preventing the onset of obesity. Establishing a balanced diet and a regular exercise routine can thwart the appearance of eating disorders. The result of a balanced diet and physical activity is longevity.)

**Enfoque de instrucción:** *Estructuras lingüísticas: cláusula dependiente (uso de la coma); Nexos de causa y efecto (El resultado de___ es___); Vocabulario (esencial, requiere, longevidad, rutinario); Ortografía (palabras con la c/s/z)* (Teaching points: Language structures: dependent clauses (comma use); Transition words for cause/effect relationships (The result of ___ is ___); Vocabulary (essential, requires, longevity, routine); Spelling (words with c/s/z))

### English Dictado: Obesity

Are you aware that obesity is an increasing problem in our communities? When people are obese, they are more likely to develop health problems. People who have healthier lifestyles and maintain a healthy weight, on the other hand, have fewer health risks, as well as more energy and a longer lifespan.

**Teaching Points:** Rhetorical structure of beginning with a question/hook; Transitional words for compare/contrast (on the other hand, as well as); Vocabulary (maintain, aware, develop, lifestyles); Spelling (suffixes—increasing, likely, healthier/healthy, fewer, longer)

---

## Lectoescritura

**Objetivos de oralidad:** Define, establish cause and effect relationships, describe processes

**Diálogo:** See questions and discussion points throughout lesson

**Estructuras lingüísticas:** ___ *se caracteriza por/con ___. Por ejemplo ___. Una de las causas de ___ es ___. Por lo tanto ___. El resultado de ___ es ___; a causa de, por lo tanto ___.* (___ is characterized by ___. For example ___. A cause of ___ is ___; therefore ___. As a result of ___. Because of ___, therefore ___)

**Vocabulario:** *obesidad, prefijo—sobre (sobrepeso, sobrealimentarlos, sobrecargan), veraz, nexos, requiere, esencial, rutinario, trastornos* (obesity, prefix—over (overweight, overeat, overload), feat, maintain, aware, develop, lifestyles truthful, requires, essential, routine, disorder)

---

## Literacy-based ELD

**Oracy Objective(s):** Express compare/contrast relationships, describe problem/ solution relationships

**Dialogue:** See questions outlined throughout lesson

**Language Structures:** ___ is a problem. A reason for ___ is ___ proposes ___ (to solve problem). ___ as well as ___, describe ___. Similarly/ likewise, ___. The ___ article was ___, whereas/on the other hand, the ___ article was ___. In one article ___ as opposed to the other article where ___.

**Vocabulary:** disturbing, pursue, essentially, recommend(ed), "stroke of genius," feat, maintain, aware, develop, lifestyles

---

*The online repository of SEP materials is updated periodically. Materials are often placed in a different year.

**Evaluación**

**Expresión oral (hablar y escuchar):** Anecdotal—All students should take part in dialogue and use newly learned language structures.

**Escritura:** All students will take notes related to the key questions/topics of the unit and write a five-paragraph expository text incorporating appropriate language structures related to process, cause/effect relationships, and description.

**Lectura:** Students will take a test to identify the different expository text structures to define, describe a process, and establish cause/effect relationships.

**Assessment**

**Speaking:** Anecdotal—All students should take part in dialogue and use newly learned language structures.

**Writing:** Write newly learned language structures with related information in notebooks. Take notes based on solutions to obesity. End product will be a five-paragraph expository essay using the text structures of compare/contrast and problem/solution, as well as persuasive writing.

## Lectoescritura
(M = modelado, C = compartido, E = equipos/parejas, I = independiente)

| Lectura | Escritura |
|---|---|
| **Enfoque pedagógico\*: M, C**<br>**Texto:** *"Textos expositivos"* (SEP materials, pp. 44–45)<br>**Actividades:**<br>Introduction to expository texts.<br>Dialogue: Activating background knowledge: *¿Cuáles son las características de los textos expositivos?* (What are the features of expository texts?) *¿En qué fuentes de información puedes encontrar este tipo de textos?* (In which sources of information can you find these texts?) Shared reading of text: Discussion about purpose of these texts. | **Enfoque pedagógico: C**<br>**Actividades:** Teacher and students will write a definition of and features of expository texts. A graphic organizer will be used to identify different expository text structures (Define/describe, cause/effect relationships, describing events/processes, problem/solution, compare/contrast) |
| **Enfoque pedagógico: C**<br>**Texto:** *"Lo que conozco"* (SEP materials p. 41)<br>**Actividades:** Explain purpose for the unit for Spanish literacy and literacy-based ELD is to search for information in various sources to write an expository text related to obesity as an eating disorder. | **Enfoque pedagógico: M, E**<br>**Actividades:** Dialogue: Begin with questions that will guide the investigation around obesity and activate background knowledge. Having such questions helps focus the search for information. Before reading texts, in collaborative groups, students will answer the following questions and one member of each group will serve as the note-taker and another person will report the ideas discussed to the whole group. *¿Qué es la obesidad? ¿Qué características tiene una persona obesa? ¿Por qué es un problema? ¿Por qué ocurre? ¿Qué provoca?* (What is obesity? What characteristics does an obese person have? Why is obesity a problem? Why does it occur? What are the effects of it?) |

## Literacy-based ELD
(M = modeled, S = shared, C = collaborative, I = independent)

| Reading | Writing |
|---|---|
| **Approach: M, S , C, I**<br>**Text:**<br>**Activities:** | **Approach: M, S, C, I**<br>**Activities:** |
| **Approach: M, S, C, I**<br>**Text:**<br>**Activities:** | **Approach: M, S, C, I**<br>**Activities:** |

Session 1

Session 2

| | Lectoescritura (M = modelado, C = compartido, E = equipos/parejas, I = independiente) | | Literacy-based ELD (M = modeled, S = shared, C = collaborative, I = independent) |
|---|---|---|---|
| | **Lectura** | **Escritura** | **Reading** |

| | Lectura | Escritura | Reading | Writing |
|---|---|---|---|---|
| **Session 3** | **Enfoque pedagógico: M**<br>**Texto:** *"Kilos de mas: muerte de cerca"* y *"Un dato interesante"* (SEP materials pp. 41–42)<br>**Actividades:**<br>Review that purpose of lesson is for students to learn about various expository text structures. Text will be introduced as will key vocabulary. Texts that define, identify problems related to obesity, and those that establish cause/effect relationships are read (refer to graphic organizer). Identify key questions such text structures answer and identify key words used within them.<br>Dialogue related to questions answered from the use of the three text structures and on the following questions: *¿Cuáles son algunas de las consecuencias del sobrepeso? ¿Qué les sucedió a los ratones sobrealimentados?* (What are some of the consequences of being overweight/obese? What happened to the laboratory rats that were overfed?) | **Enfoque pedagógico: M, S**<br>**Actividades:** Model how to take notes from text read that answer key questions related to obesity. Emphasize difference between copying and taking notes. Teacher models how key words help identify/create the expository text structures of cause/effect (*A causa de la obesidad uno tiene el riesgo de la mortalidad prematura*/Because of obesity people run the risk of premature death); and to define and describe (*la obesidad se caracteriza con el tener demasiada grasa en el cuerpo*/A characteristic of obesity is having too much body fat). | **Approach: S**<br>**Text:** *"Let's Move! to Fight Obesity"*<br>**Activities:**<br>Discuss purpose of unit in English: Reading/writing expository texts, specifically researching and proposing solutions to problem of obesity. Introduce magazine article with structure of problem/solution. Michelle Obama is on a campaign to fight obesity.<br>Dialogue: What do you know about obesity? What are some reasons for childhood obesity? How do you think you can stop it? Introduce vocabulary/language structures. (___ is a problem. A reason for [the problem] is ___. ___ proposes ___ [to solve problem].)<br>Shared reading of text.<br>Postreading dialogue: What can you do to prevent childhood obesity? How might you help an obese friend or family member? I propose to help my obese friend/family member by ___. | **Approach: M, S**<br>**Activities:**<br>Shared writing of key words for problem/solution in graphic organizer. Teacher model writes example of text identifying the patterns that demonstrate the text structure of problem/solution. (The fact that children consume half of their daily calories at school is a problem. A reason for this problem is that the standards for school meals are low. Mrs. Obama's program proposes to update the Child Nutrition Act and increase the standards of those meals.) |
| **Session 4** | **Enfoque pedagógico: C**<br>**Texto:** *"Trampas del comedor compulsivo"* (SEP materials, p. 42)<br>**Actividades:**<br>Review questions related to topic. Introduce text to be read and review expository text structure of describing events/processes (refer to graphic organizer).<br>Shared reading of text.<br>Dialogue: *¿Cuáles son los hábitos de alimentación de las personas obesas?* (What are an obese person's eating habits?) The following question will serve as the main topic in literacy-based ELD. *¿Qué solución recomendarías a una persona obesa con problemas de alimentación?* (What solutions would you recommend to an obese person with poor eating habits?) | **Enfoque pedagógico: E**<br>**Actividades:** Collaborative groups will read and take notes on the text titled, *"Comedor compulsivo."* Afterwards, students will compare the notes taken and discuss how to only use essential words when taking notes. | **Approach: S**<br>**Text:** *"What Is Obesity?"*<br>**Activities:**<br>Reinforce/review text structure of problem/solution through shared reading. Introduce magazine article and vocabulary.<br>Dialogue: What do you remember about the Let's Move! campaign? What were the problems and solutions identified yesterday? Make sure Students use targeted language structures from yesterday.<br>Read article.<br>Discuss/dialogue about article focusing on problem/solutions. How can we reduce childhood obesity? | **Approach: C**<br>**Activities:** In pairs or small collaborative groups, students identify one of the problems in the article and provide a reason for the problem and a solution. Students need to use the sentence structures and write sentences in their notebooks. (Childhood obesity is a problem. A reason for this problem is that children eat too many calories at school. Mrs. Obama proposes more recess time to solve this problem.) |

Continues

| | | | | |
|---|---|---|---|---|
| **Session 5** | **Enfoque pedagógico: M, E**<br>**Texto:** *"Identifica contenidos"* (SEP materials p. 44) and a variety of other texts related to obesity and nutrition.<br>**Actividades:**<br>Review expository text features that help the reader find relevant information (key words, table of contents, index, illustrations/photos, titles, headings, and subheadings).<br>Engender dialogue on how these features help with comprehension and to more efficiently find information within such texts. | **Enfoque pedagógico: E**<br>**Actividades:**<br>Using a variety of other texts related to obesity and nutrition, students will read and take notes in collaborative groups to answer unit's key questions. A student from each group will report information found and teacher will add all relevant information to the class notes.<br>Teacher will model how to record all references for the bibliography. | **Approach: S**<br>**Text:** "Let's Move! to Fight Obesity" and "What Is Obesity?"<br>**Activities:** Purpose is to compare/contrast the overall structure of events, ideas, concepts, or information in the two articles read. Ask students what key words they know to compare/contrast. Teacher provides new key words to establish compare/contrast relationships with similarities and differences (as well as; likewise; whereas; as opposed to) and adds to graphic organizer. Together, identify similarities and differences using appropriate language structures that students already know and introduce new ones to elevate language and add to graphic organizer. | **Approach: S, C**<br>**Activities:** Record similarities/differences in note form on T-chart. Students practice language structures in whole group. In pairs/collaborative groups students will compare and contrast articles and write two similarities and two differences in their notebooks using the new language structures. |
| **Session 6** | **Enfoque pedagógico: C**<br>**Texto:** Notes answering unit's key questions and *"El uso de nexos"* (SEP materials p. 47)<br>**Actividades:** In collaborative groups, students will read about the function of key words in expository texts. Students will apply these key words with their appropriate texts. | **Enfoque pedagógico: M, C**<br>**Actividades:** As all necessary information has been collected to answer the unit's key questions, the expository text will be written through modeled and shared writing. First, an organizational structure will be determined using a graphic organizer. Headings and subheadings are used to organize information logically. Students and teacher will negotiate how to organize the various expository text structures and use appropriate key words. | **Approach: S**<br>**Text:** "Let's Move! to Fight Obesity" and "What Is Obesity?"<br>**Activities:** Shared reading to reread articles. Tell students about expository text that they're going to write (five paragraphs—intro, identifying problem, characteristics, two solutions, conclusion that includes persuasive paragraph on best solution). Today we're going to write an intro together and outline the text. Ask them what they know about introductions and the structure of expository text (connect this to Spanish —e.g., titles/subtitles). | **Approach: S**<br>**Activities:** Shared writing of intro and subtitles. (Subtitles can change later, but get structure set so students know how the essay will develop.) (Intro: Obesity is a growing problem in our communities today. Unlike other diseases, we already have a cure for obesity, so we should be doing everything we can to stop it. There are many solutions to obesity, and this essay will offer some easy ways to help solve this growing epidemic.)<br>Title: "Obesity, We Can Fight It!"<br>Subtitles: Intro, What is it? How can we solve it? What should we do? |

| | Lectoescritura (M = modelado, C = compartido, E = equipos/parejas, I = independiente) | | Literacy-based ELD (M = modeled, S = shared, C = collaborative, I = independent) | |
|---|---|---|---|---|
| | Lectura | Escritura | Reading | Writing |
| Session 7 | **Enfoque pedagógico: C**<br>**Texto:** Notes<br>**Actividades:** | **Approach: C, E**<br>**Actividades:**<br>Via shared writing, an introduction to obesity will be written by answering and explaining: *¿Qué es la obesidad? Y ¿Qué características tiene una persona obesa? (definir y describir).* (What is obesity? What are the characteristics of an obese person? Text structures of defining and describing).<br>The rest of the text will be written in collaborative groups and answering the following questions: *¿Por qué ocurre? ¿Por qué es un problema?* (Why does it occur? Why is obesity a problem? What are the effects of it?) Each question will have its own paragraph that includes a topic sentence, appropriate key words, and supporting details. | **Approach: M**<br>**Text:** Various texts related to the solution of exercise<br>**Activities:** Tell students they are going to write about a possible solution for the problem of obesity. Remind students of list of solutions to obesity that they generated in Spanish. Show students variety of resources/texts. | **Approach: M**<br>**Activities:** Model with student help how to read sections of the text and take notes that answer the key questions. Remind students of what they learned in Spanish—text features (TOC, index) to find answers to key questions without reading entire text; note taking: questions to guide their search (What is it? What are the characteristics? What are the causes/effects?); keep list of references. Review language structures/ vocabulary for expressing problem/ solution relationships from days 3 and 4 and compare/contrast to days 5 and 6. |
| Session 8 | **Enfoque pedagógico: C**<br>**Textos:** Group texts | **Enfoque pedagógico: C, E, I**<br>**Actividades:** Through shared writing, a concluding paragraph will be written. Students will edit, revise, and publish their final drafts. A bibliography with appropriate references will be included. | **Approach: M**<br>**Text:** Various texts related to the solution of exercise<br>**Activities:** Continue from yesterday, using notes/answers to questions to model writing paragraph for expository essay. Include some of the practiced language structures. | **Approach: M**<br>**Activities:** Model writing paragraph (continue from reading) |

**Session 9**

**Enfoque pedagógico: C**
**Textos:** Group texts (SEP materials, p. 48)
**Activities:**
Once the groups' texts are published, texts will be exchanged amongst groups for review. Each group will comment and give feedback to improve them.
Dialogue: Guiding questions for group review ¿*Qué tan importante es el cuidado de la salud a través de la alimentación? ¿Qué utilidad tienen los textos expositivos para la investigación de un tema? ¿Piensas que tu texto expositivo cumple con su función? ¿por qué?* (How important is it to maintain healthy nutrition? What function do expository texts serve? Did the text read serve its function? How?)

**Approach: C**
**Text:** Various texts depending on student solutions
**Activities:** In collaborative groups, students will choose a solution from the list they generated in Spanish, research it, take notes on it, and write a paragraph about it.

**Approach: C**
**Activities:** Continue writing solutions (from reading).

**Session 10**

**Enfoque pedagógico: E**
**Texto:** Group texts
**Actividades:** *Así se dice*

**Enfoque pedagógico: E**
**Actividades:** Using the *así se dice* strategy, in collaborative groups, students will translate the first paragraph from their Spanish expository texts, which will be used as the introductory paragraph for their English expository text. This paragraph needs to define obesity, identify its characteristics, problems associated with it, and cause/effect relationships

**Approach: I**
**Text:** Various texts depending on student solutions
**Activities:** Students independently choose a second solution to research, take notes, and write a paragraph about.

**Approach: I**
**Activities:** Continue writing solutions (from reading).

*Continues*

# Literacy-based ELD

| Lectoescritura (M = modelado, C = compartido, E = equipos/parejas, I = independiente) | | Literacy-based ELD (M = modeled, S = shared, C = collaborative, I = independent) | |
|---|---|---|---|
| **Lectura** | **Escritura** | **Reading** | **Writing** |
| **Assessment:** Students will need to identify the five expository text structures covered in the unit.<br><br>Next unit of study in literacy will be: *"Elaborar y publicar anuncios publicitarios de bienes o servicios proporcionado por su comunidad"* (Develop and publish advertisements of goods and services provided by the community) (SEP materials, pp. 26–39)<br>Purpose of the unit is to write advertisements and disseminate them.<br>Students will learn to identify the structure, function, and graphic organization of advertising to develop a poster that promotes ways to stay healthy.<br>This activity serves as an extension for students to share the knowledge learned about proper nutrition and the effects of obesity. The posters/advertisements created will be shared with the school community. | | **Approach: M, I**<br>**Text:** Student-generated paragraphs on solutions<br>**Activities:** Students will read the two paragraphs they have written on solutions to obesity, take a stance, and write a persuasive paragraph to tell their reader which solution they think is the stronger one and why. They should use the structures they practiced for comparing/contrasting to write about why one solution is better or more feasible than the other. This will also be their concluding paragraph. | **Approach: M, I**<br>**Activities:** Model writing persuasive paragraph with language structures for compare/contrast. Provide structure students can use to fill in blanks if they need the support. Then students write their concluding paragraphs independently. |
| | | **Approach: M, C, I**<br>**Text:** Student-generated texts on obesity<br>**Activities:**<br>Teacher models combining paragraphs for the essay with her own version of the text (e.g., edit, ensure subtitles, smooth transitions b/n paragraphs). Students edit and revise their texts, making sure they have subtitles and transition well between paragraphs.<br>Students share expository text they have written.<br>Teacher leads dialogue about similarities and differences from *así se dice* section and solution paragraphs (using compare/contrast structures from days 5 and 6). | **Approach: M, C, I**<br>**Activities:** Using what they heard as their peers read expository texts aloud, students choose one solution to obesity that they can make as a goal for themselves and/or their families. Students write the goal and how they plan to achieve it in their notebooks. My goal is to ____. I think I will be able to achieve this by ____. |

Session 11

Session 12

# Glossary

## A

**Analytic reading approaches:** A method to teach reading that starts with the reading of whole texts and words. The focus is on meaning. The method then breaks down sentences to words and words into syllables and letters. The point of departure for teaching children to read is first to read for meaning as well as to learn to decode.

**Anchor charts:** These are used to record and display student thinking, key concepts, and essential skills, which help students to see the connections across literacy environments. They are a stable reference that students can return to when in need of clarification.

**Approximation:** An approximation is a more positive term used in place of misspellings, miscues, or errors. It is not an exact representation but it is close enough to be useful.

*Así se dice* (that's how you say it): This is a cross-language strategy that we developed to validate translation as a constructive and worthwhile endeavor that engages students in a complex, sophisticated scrutiny of language and emphasizes the subtleties and nuances of communicating messages across cultures and languages.

**Authentic Spanish literacy instruction:** Approaches to teaching reading and writing in Spanish that are grounded in the internal structure of Spanish and in Central and South American methods, as opposed to translated instructional models designed for monolingual English speakers. Equal amounts of instructional time during Spanish literacy are devoted to oracy, reading, writing, and metalanguage. It incorporates culturally and personally relevant texts that, to the extent possible, are originally written in Spanish, as well as Spanish-English bilingual texts.

## B

**Bidirectional transfer:** The application of features of one language to another.

**Bilingual strategies:** Observable cross-linguistic strategies that emerging bilingual writers demonstrate as they transfer knowledge and abilities from one language to the other.

**Bilingualism:** The ability to use two languages along a continuum that includes variations in proficiency in expressive (speaking and writing) and receptive (listening and reading) language; differences in proficiencies between the two languages; variations in proficiency between the two languages, according to the functions and purpose of use of each language; and changes in proficiency of each language over time.

**Biliteracy:** The ability to read and write with high levels of proficiency in two languages through the appropriate and effective use of grammatical, syntactic, graphophonic, semantic, and pragmatic systems of the two languages.

**Biliteracy unit(s):** Units that highlight the importance of purposefully connecting the four core instructional elements: reading, writing, oracy, and metalanguage using authentic Spanish literacy and literacy-based ELD.

**Biliteracy zones/Biliterate reading zones:** Numeric representations that capture a holistic picture of a child's Spanish and English reading levels. The zone represents a progressive relationship for instruction in and development of Spanish and English literacy based on Literacy Squared research findings. Each zone is comprised of an expected range of Spanish reading levels matched to an expected range of English reading levels.

**Biliterate benchmark:** A number used to represent realistic end-of-year benchmark goals for Spanish and English literacy development for grades K–5.

**Biliterate reading:** The process used to make sense of texts in two languages. It involves using a reservoir of bilingual competencies, strategies, and knowledge in interaction and collaboration with others to comprehend texts.

In Literacy Squared, biliterate reading instruction in K–5 bilingual classrooms includes interactive and explicit teaching of a variety of reading skills and strategies, including: foundational reading skills (e.g., concepts of print, decoding, fluency), reading comprehension skills (e.g., describe main ideas or major events in a text and central lesson, including key supporting details; distinguish elements and structure of literary and informational texts), comprehension strategies (e.g., activate prior knowledge, make predictions, make personal and intertextual connections, cognate study), and reading of a range of text types of grade-level appropriate complexity. Children are taught how to apply these skills and strategies across languages and to see similarities and language-specific differences.

**Biliterate writing:** A complex process to develop and produce texts that involves bilingual competencies, strategies, and knowledge in two languages.

**Biliterate writing potential:** The understanding of what emerging bilingual students can do in writing in both languages in order to inform writing instruction within paired literacy.

**Biliterate writing trajectory:** A framework for documenting patterns of development and growth in Spanish and English writing for emerging bilingual children who are receiving paired literacy instruction. Children's writing achievement is expressed in terms of biliterate development rather than by grade levels or other monolingual norms that separate the two languages. It is also hypothesized that students' Spanish writing will be ahead of their English writing; however each child's writing development is unique.

## C

**Choral reading:** A method that involves students and teacher reading aloud in unison.

**Code-switching:** The alternation of languages within one linguistic context. This may take place within sentences (intrasententially) or in alternating sentences (intersententially). It is rule-governed behavior that requires a high degree of understanding of each of the languages being inserted into the communication.

**Cognates:** Words in different languages that share an etymological root resulting in similar spelling, meaning, and pronunciation.

**Collaborative reading:** A reading approach wherein the teacher creates opportunities for children to read *with peers* and monitors their work for the purpose supporting a deeper understanding of the text.

**Collaborative writing:** An approach to teaching writing in which children write with their peers and the teacher monitors their work, providing further assistance as needed. It encourages greater student involvement in the actual encoding, revising, editing and publishing processes. It is also an opportunity for students to talk about what they intend to write.

**Concurrent translation:** A method of teaching in which every statement the teacher makes is directly translated into a second language. Research has concluded definitively that it is a poor method because it teaches students that they only need to pay attention when information is offered in their more proficient language.

**Connecting language environments:** Within the Literacy Squared lesson plan template (via genre, theme, literacy objectives, or bilingual texts), students capitalize on their resources in one language to help them understand in the other.

**Cross-language connections:** The ability to use one language to analyze and understand a second language. Cross-language connections enable children to develop metacognitive abilities and knowledge about their two languages and how they are the same and different. Cross-language connections are bidirectional. This project uses two types of cross-language connections. The first cross-language connection refers to specific methods that the model has adapted from Mexico and modified for use in U.S. English/Spanish literacy programs. The second focuses on teaching children the metacognitive linguistic skills of cross-language expression in reading and writing.

## D

**Dialogue:** An *oracy* component meant to ensure meaningful student participation in literacy-related discussions.

**Dual language program:** An additive bilingual education model that consistently uses two languages for instruction and communication. It has a balanced number of students for two language groups who are integrated for instruction for at least half of the school day. The goals of dual language programs are bilingualism, biliteracy, and biculturalism.

## E

Early-exit transitional bilingual program: A subtractive transitional bilingual education model that provides native language instruction for one to three years while students acquire sufficient English language proficiency to function in classrooms where English is the sole instructional medium.

Echo reading: The teacher reads a short segment of text fluently and the students reread it using expression and intonation.

Emerging bilingual: Emerging bilinguals are defined as children (ages 3 and above) who speak a native language other than English and who are in the dynamic process of developing bilingual and biliterate competencies (in this case in English and Spanish), with the support of their communities (e.g., parents, school, neighbors). This term is used interchangably with the term *emergent bilinguals*.

English language learner (ELL): The term used to describe students who are acquiring English as a second language. ELL is a more developmental and positive term that is replacing the traditional and more commonly used deficit-oriented term *limited English proficient (LEP)*.

## F

Funds of knowledge: Those skills, concepts, bodies of knowledge, and ways of knowing that students acquire in their families and communities; they include language and ways of conveying meaning.

## G

Gradual release of responsibility model: A model of explicit and interactive instruction in which the teacher initially provides extensive scaffolding, primarily through whole groups and shared literacy and language opportunities. Gradually, the teacher removes the scaffolds providing increased opportunities for students to read and write text, to develop oracy, and to apply metalinguistic analyses in collaborative or independent contexts.

## H

Holistic bilingualism: The coexistence of two or more languages within a person whose experiences and knowledge can never be measured or understood as independently constrained by each language separately. It considers the totality of the bilingual experience as a unique and unified whole.

Holistic biliteracy framework: A framework that includes recommended teaching approaches and time allocations across the grades intended to foster development and learning in two languages through *paired literacy instruction*. This instructional framework is unique in that it intentionally and purposefully connects Spanish and English literacy environments.

## I

Independent reading: A reading approach where the students read by themselves without direct teacher support. Its purpose is to offer sustained and expanded opportunities for children to read self-selected materials, enjoy reading, and refine their comprehension strategies and literacy skills.

Independent writing: An approach to writing instruction in which children write by themselves across a variety of genres and there is little or no teacher support. The teacher provides feedback through individual writing conferences.

Interactive read aloud: A reading approach in which the teacher reads aloud *for* children, thus modeling the reading process and comprehension strategies. In Literacy Squared, this also includes directing students' attention to cross-language connections. An essential feature of this approach is active student engagement in conversations about the text in order to support both literacy skills and oral language development.

Intersentential code-switching: Code-switching (switching from one language to the other) that occurs between sentences.

Intrasentential code-switching: Code-switching that occurs within the boundaries of a sentence.

**L**

Language-specific approximation: This occurs when children encode text in nonstandard but rule-governed ways that are appropriate to each of the languages.

Language structures: An *oracy* component intended to expand the grammatical complexity of students' speech.

Late-exit transitional bilingual program: A program that uses a child's native language as a medium of instruction for all or part of a school day while the child is learning English. As the child acquires English, less of the native language is used for instruction and, eventually (usually after grade 5), English becomes the dominant or only medium of instruction. Both early- and late-exit programs are considered to be subtractive education models because their goal is English acquisition rather than biliteracy. Late-exit programs offer bilingual instruction for five to six years.

Limited English proficient (LEP): A deficit-oriented term used to describe students who are acquiring English as a second language. It is being replaced by the more positive term, *emerging/emergent bilingual*.

Literacy-based ELD instruction: A Literacy Squared text-based innovation that is especially designed to promote English literacy development in Spanish-English emerging bilingual students. Instruction builds on and refines the literacy skills and strategies as well as the conceptual knowledge that students are developing in Spanish and does not re-teach them. Instead, it teaches children how skills and knowledge can be applied to reading, writing, speaking, and listening in English. Literacy-based ELD instruction further develops students' awareness of the similarities and differences between English and Spanish literacy skills. Equal amounts of instructional time are devoted to oracy, reading, and writing that are specific to English and to metalanguage to help children make cross-language connections.

Literacy Squared writing rubric: A rubric designed for the analysis of biliterate writing for the purposes of informing and measuring growth.

Literal translations: Verbatim phrases that have been converted from one language to another.

**M**

Metalanguage: Thinking and talking about language and, in the case of biliteracy, understanding the relationships between and within languages. It is the language used to talk about language, and its mastery allows students to analyze how language can be leveraged to express meaning. The development of metalanguage includes the ability to identify, analyze, and manipulate language forms and to analyze sounds, symbols, grammar, vocabulary, and language structures between and within languages. It has been identified as one of three fundamental skills, along with the psycholinguistic abilities, necessary to decode and comprehend.

Model: Explicit and interactive instruction where student responsibility for learning is gradually released from teacher modeling and explanation, to guided practice, and then to independent practice.

Modeled writing: A teaching approach where the teacher demonstrates for students the process of writing a text and multiple uses of writing as a communicative and learning tool. In modeled writing, the teacher encodes the message and students watch as they participate orally in the composition of the written piece. The teacher writes the text produced, which is at a higher level than what the students would be able to compose independently.

**O**

Oracy: The development of oral skills in formal education. Oracy is an important form of communication between human beings. It has many purposes and functions, including talking to learn and the capacity to understand speech and use it to express oneself. Oracy skills assist children in expressing their reading and writing comprehension. Oracy has three main components: language structures, vocabulary, and dialogue.

## P

Paired literacy instruction: A holistic approach to teaching reading and writing where students learn to read and write in two languages simultaneously, beginning in kindergarten. Paired literacy practices are not duplicative and do not involve concurrent translation.

Partner reading: Pairs of students take turns reading aloud to one another.

## S

Shared reading: A reading approach in which the teacher reads *for* and *with* the children. It calls for more direct student involvement in the actual reading of the text. Teachers engage children in guided dialogue to extend their understanding of texts and to enrich their oral language repertoire. They also encourage students to articulate (not only observe) cross-language connections.

Shared writing: An instructional approach in which the teacher and students take turns constructing a written text together. All the students in the class participate in the writing of the text by sharing the pen with the teacher, copying from the board, or encoding the text in their own notebooks.

Simultaneous bilinguals: Children who develop two languages at the same time. Definitions of simultaneous bilingualism vary, but it is generally thought to be exposure to and acquisition of two languages before the age of 5. Simultaneous bilinguals can be circumstantial (those who learn a second language because of their circumstances, such as immigrants or children of foreign students in universities) or elective (those whose parents choose to teach them two languages).

Strategic use of language: The planned use of both languages to maximize learning and to achieve the greatest efficiency in the classroom environment. Do not confuse this method with *concurrent translation*.

Synthetic reading approaches: A method to teach reading that moves from part to whole. These methods start with teaching children parts of words, such as letters and letter sounds. They commonly use letters, syllables, and letter sounds to build up to words.

## T

Teacher-led small groups: A reading approach where the teacher addresses specific students' needs with regard to reading skills, comprehension strategies, and interests. Small reading groups are formed based on students' areas of interest rather than reading levels.

Teaching to the potential: Understanding what emerging bilingual students are capable of doing in both languages in order to inform paired literacy instruction. Students are held accountable for using and accessing all of their knowledge, regardless of the language of the environment. Teachers use their knowledge of a student's entire linguistic repertoire to plan explicit instruction and make cross-language connections to accelerate biliterate development.

TheDictado: A method to teach content, conventions, grammar, and spelling in an integrated way. It involves having the teacher dictate a series of phrases or sentences to the students. The students and teacher then collaborate to create a corrected model of the focus text. Students amend their sentences using a two-color system to draw attention to errors. The same phrases or sentences are repeated throughout the week, giving students multiple opportunities to practice and learn the targeted content, conventions, grammar, and spelling. TheDictado is adapted from Latin American schools and provides multiple opportunities for within-language and cross-language metalinguistic development.

Trajectory toward biliteracy: A framework for documenting patterns of development and growth in Spanish and English for emerging bilingual children who are receiving paired literacy instruction. Children's achievement is expressed in terms of biliteracy development rather than by grade levels or other monolingual norms that separate the two languages. Spanish literacy outcomes may be slightly ahead of the English literacy outcomes in this trajectory.

## V

Vocabulary: An *oracy* component used to refine and expand students' word and concept range.

# LITERACY SQUARED OBSERVATION PROTOCOL*

Circle the teaching approach used (M, S/C, C/E, I), and identify the implementation level for each domain/indicator (–, ✓, +). Include evidence, comments, or questions about implementation in the empty columns. Review the protocol with the teacher to identify strengths and focal areas for professional development.

Date _____     School _____     Observer _____
Time _____     Teacher _____     Grade _____ Subject _____

| **SPANISH LITERACY**<br>Scheduled _____ min<br>Observed _____ min<br><br>Reading<br>M  C  E  I<br><br>Writing<br>M  C  E  I | **Domain/Indicators**<br>– = Developing/Not evident<br>✓ = Evident<br>+ = Exceptional<br>N/A = Not applicable (Only possible for *italicized* indicators) | **LITERACY-BASED ELD**<br>Scheduled _____ min<br>Observed _____ min<br><br>Reading<br>M  S  C  I<br><br>Writing<br>M  S  C  I |
|---|---|---|
| | **Text Selection or Production**<br>__ Relevant to teaching objective<br>__ Appropriate linguistic aspects of text (e.g., syntax, vocabulary)<br>__ Appropriate literary aspects (e.g., genre, contextualized)<br>__ *Culturally and personally relevant* | __<br>__<br><br>__<br><br>__ |
| | **Literacy Objective**<br>__ Standards based (✓ = teaches to standard; + = includes all language domains)<br>__ Authentic to language environment | __<br><br>__ |
| | **Oracy**<br>__ Matches literacy objective<br>__ Students likely to encounter or use target vocabulary (from text and objectives)<br>__ Opportunities to dialogue are purposeful<br>__ Student participation in dialogue is scaffolded to ensure their success<br>__ Meaningful selection of language structures<br>__ Multiple opportunities for students to rehearse, appropriate, and respond to target language structures<br>__ Teacher talk vs. student talk<br>  (✓ = 40%–60% student talk; + = ≥61% student talk)<br>__ Multiple opportunities for connected discourse<br>__ *Specifically address register and language variation*<br>__ *Structured student talk (e.g., think-pair-share, inside outside circles)* | __<br>__<br><br>__<br>__<br><br>__<br>__<br><br><br>__<br><br><br>__<br>__<br>__ |
| | **Accountability**<br>__ Teacher has high and clear student expectations<br>__ All students are held accountable for actively participating in the activity/lesson<br>__ Teacher checks for student understanding<br>__ Teacher provides appropriate feedback to enhance student learning<br>__ *All students are held accountable for completing their work* | __<br>__<br><br>__<br>__<br><br>__ |

M = *modelado*/modeled; C/S = *compartido*/shared; E/C = *equipos-parejas*/collaborative; I = *independient*/independent.
*Not all indicators are present at each observation, but teachers should strive to incorporate as many as possible.

*Continues*

| SPANISH LITERACY | Domain/Indicators | LITERACY-BASED ELD |
|---|---|---|
| Scheduled _____ min<br>Observed _____ min | – = Developing/Not evident<br>✓ = Evident<br>+ = Exceptional<br>N/A = Not applicable (Only possible for *italicized* indicators) | Scheduled _____ min<br>Observed _____ min |
| Reading<br>M  C  E  I | | Reading<br>M  S  C  I |
| Writing<br>M  C  E  I | | Writing<br>M  S  C  I |

### Cross-Language Connections

— *Connection between literacy environments (e.g., theme, genre, standards)* —
— *Visual side-by-side analysis of languages (e.g., cognates, anchor posters)* —
— *Metalanguage* —
— *Strategic translation (e.g., así se dice, homonym translation)* —
— *Teacher uses languages strategically to enhance student learning (e.g., clarification, preview/review, instructions)* —
— *Teacher flexibly responds to student's language alternations (e.g., response to code-switching)* —

### Student Involvement

— Students are actively engaged in activity/lesson —
— Students actively use language related to the lesson —
— Students communicate in whole groups or w/peers in a way that is relevant to the lesson objective —
— *Reading* —
— *Writing (or text-related drawing)* —
— *Listening* —
— *Speaking* —
— *Students share prior knowledge or personal connections* —
— *Students demonstrate understanding of objectives or new learning* —
— *Students take pride in their work/learning* —

### Lesson Delivery

— Teacher clearly communicates literacy objective to students (How) —
— Teacher clearly communicates literacy objective to students (Why) —
— Teacher clearly communicates oracy objective to students —
— Teacher fosters safe environment for risk taking —
*Language specific metalanguage*
— *Teacher successfully scaffolds students literacy learning based on their needs* —
— *Teacher explicitly models literacy and language objectives* —
— *Teacher gradually releases responsibility to students in an appropriate way, allowing them to successfully meet the learning/language objective(s)* —

### TheDictado

— Students skip lines —
— Students use colored pen to self-correct —
— Students make self-corrections —
— TheDictado is comprehensible and contextualized —
— Same Dictado 3x/week —
— Clear teaching points —
— Explicit talk through is metalinguistic —
— TheDictado is between 15–20 minutes —
— TheDictado has a title —
— Teacher reads entire Dictado for meaning —

# References

Adams, M.J. (1990). *Beginning to read: Thinking and learning about print.* Urbana-Champaign, IL: University of Illinois, Reading Research and Education Center.

Ammon, P. (1985). *Helping children to write in ESL: Some observations and hypotheses.* Norwood, NJ: Ablex.

August, D., Carlo, M., Dressler, C., & Snow, C. (2005). The critical role of vocabulary development for English language learners. *Learning Disabilities Research & Practice, 20*(1), 50–57.

August, D., & Hakuta, K. (Eds.). (1997). *Improving schooling for language-minority children: A research agenda.* Washington, DC: National Academy Press.

August, D., & Shanahan, T. (2006). *Developing literacy in second-language learners: Report of the National Literacy Panel on language-minority children and youth.* Mahwah, NJ: Erlbaum.

Avila, E., & Sadoski, M. (1996). Exploring new applications of the keyword method to acquire English vocabulary. *Language Learning, 46*(3), 379–395.

Baker, C. (2001). *Foundations of bilingual education and bilingualism* (3rd ed.). Clevedon, UK: Multilingual Matters.

Bauer, E. B., & Gort, M. (2011). *Early biliteracy development: Exploring young learners' use of their linguistic resources.* Florence, KY: Routledge, Taylor & Francis Group.

Beeman, K., & Urow, C. (2013). *Teaching for biliteracy: Strengthening bridges between languages.* Philadelphia: Caslon.

Benjamin, R. (1996). The functions of Spanish in the school lives of Mexican bilingual children. *Bilingual Research Journal, 20*(1), 135–163.

Bernhardt, E. (2003). Challenges to reading research from a multilingual world. *Reading Research Quarterly, 38,* 112–117.

Bialystok, E. (2007). Cognitive effects of bilingualism: How linguistic experience leads to cognitive change. *International Journal of Bilingual Education and Bilingualism, 10*(3), 210–223.

Buhrow, B., & Garcia, A.U. (2006). *Ladybugs, tornadoes, and swirling galaxies.* Portland, ME: Stenhouse.

Butvilofsky, S.A. (2010). *Towards the development of a biliterate pedagogy: A case study of emerging biliterate writing* (Doctoral dissertation). Available from ProQuest Dissertations and Theses. (UMI No. 3419442).

Campbell, R., & Sais, E. (1995). Accelerated metalinguistic (phono-logical) awareness in bilingual children. *British Journal of Developmental Psychology, 13,* 61–68.

Canagarajah, S. (2011). Codemeshing in academic writing: Identifying teachable strategies of translanguaging. *The Modern Language Journal, 95*(3), 401–417.

Capp, R., Fix, M., Murray, J., Ost, J., Passel, J.S., & Herwantoro, S. (2005). *The new demography of America's schools: Immigration and the No Child Left Behind Act.* Washington DC: Urban Institute.

Cappellini, M. (2005). *Balancing reading and language learning: A resource for teaching English language learners, K–5.* Portland, ME: Stenhouse.

Celebration Press. (2007a). *Evaluación del desarrollo de la lectura.* Parsippany, NJ: Celebration Press.

Celebration Press. (2007b). *Developmental reading assessment.* Parsippany, NJ: Celebration Press.

Clay, M.M. (1993). *An observation survey of early literacy achievement.* Portsmouth, NH: Heinemann.

Cooper, P.J., Collins, R., & Saxby, M. (1992). *The power of story.* Melbourne, Australia: MacMillan.

Cornwell, L. (2012). *What is reader's theater?* Retrieved from www.scholastic.com/librarian/programs/whatisrt.htm

Coxhead, A. (2000). A new academic word list. *TESOL Quarterly, 34*(2), 213–238.

Creese, A., & Blackledge, A. (2010). Translanguaging in the bilingual classroom: A pedagogy for learning and teaching? *The Modern Language Journal, 94*(1), 103–115.

Creese, A. & Blackledge, A. (2011). Separate and flexible bilingualism in complementary schools: Multiple language practices in interrelationship. *Journal of Pragmatics, 43*(5), 1157–1160.

Cummins, J. (1986). Empowering minority students: A framework for intervention. *Harvard Educational Review, 56*(1), 18–37.

Cummins, J. (2008). Forward. *AILA Review, 21,* 1–3.

Cummins, J., Bismilla, V., Chow, P., Cohen, S., Giampapa, F., Lioni, L., . . . Sastra, P. (2005). Affirming identity in multilingual classrooms. *Educational Leadership, 63*(1), 38–43.

Díaz, S., Moll, L.C., & Mehan, H. (1986). Sociocultural resources in instruction: A context-specific approach. In California Office of Bilingual Bicultural Education (Ed.), *Beyond language: Social and cultural factors in schooling language minority students* (pp. 197–230). Los Angeles: Evaluation, Dissemination, and Assessment Center, California State University.

Dutro, S., & Kinsella, K. (2010). English language development: Issues and implementation in grades 6–12. In *Improving education for English Learners: Research based approaches.* Sacramento: California Department of Education.

Dyson, A.H. (1991). Viewpoints: The word and the world: Reconceptualizing written language development or do rainbows mean a lot to little girls? *Research in the Teaching of English, 25*(1), 97–123.

Dyson, A.H., & Genishi, C. (Eds.). (1994). *The need for story: Cultural diversity in classroom and Community.* Urbana, IL: National Council of Teachers of English.

Elley, W.B. (1991) Acquiring literacy in a second language: The effect of book-based programs. *Language Learning, 41,* 375–411.

Elley, W.B., & Mangubhai, F. (1983). The impact of reading on second language learning. *Research Reading Quarterly, 19,* 53–67.

Ernst-Slavit, G. (1997). Different words, different worlds: Language use, power, and authorized language in a bilingual classroom. *Linguistics and Education, 9,* 25–47.

Escamilla, K. (2000). Bilingual means two: Assessment issues, early literacy and two language children. In *Research in literacy for limited English proficient students* (pp. 100–128). Washington, DC: National Clearinghouse for Bilingual Education.

Escamilla, K. (2006). Semilingualism applied to the literacy behaviors of Spanish-speaking emerging bilinguals: Bi-illiteracy or emerging biliteracy? *Teachers College Record, 108,* 2329–2353.

Escamilla, K., Andrade, A.M., Basurto, A.G.M., & Ruíz, O. A. (1996). *Instrumento de observación: De los logros de la lecto-escritura inicial.* Portsmouth, NH: Heinemann.

Escamilla, K., & Coady, M. (2001). Assessing the writing of Spanish-speaking students. In S. Hurley & J. Tinajero (Eds.), *Literacy assessment of second language learners* (pp. 43–63). Boston: Allyn & Bacon.

Escamilla, K., Geisler, D., Hopewell, S., Sparrow, W., & Butvilofsky, S. (2009). Using writing to make cross-language connections from Spanish to English. In C. Rodriguez-Eagle (Ed.), *Achieving literacy success with English language learners: Insights, assessment and instruction* (pp.143–158). Worthington, OH: Reading Recovery Council of North America.

Escamilla, K., & Hopewell, S. (2007, April). *The role of codeswitching in the written expression of early elementary simultaneous bilinguals.* Paper presented at the Annual Conference of the American Educational Research Association, Chicago, IL.

Escamilla, K., & Hopewell, S. (2010). Transitions to biliteracy: Creating positive academic trajectories for emerging bilinguals in the United States. In J. Petrovic (Ed.), *International perspectives on bilingual education: Policy, practice, and controversy.* Charlotte, NC: Information Age.

Faltis, C. (1996). Learning to teach content bilingually in middle school bilingual classrooms. *Bilingual Research Journal, 20*(1), 29–44.

Ferreiro, E. (2002). *Relaciones de (in)dependencia entre oralidad y escritura.* Mexico City: Gedisa Editorial.

Ferreiro, E. (2003). *Past and present of the verbs to read and to write. Essays on literacy.* (Mark Fried, Trans.) Toronto: Groundwood Books.

Fisher, D., Rothenberg, C., & Frey, N. (2007). *Language learners in the English classroom.* Urbana, IL: National Council of Teachers of English.

Fountas, I.C., & Pinnell, G.S. (1996). *Guided reading: Good first teaching for all children.* Portsmouth, NH: Heinemann.

Fountas, I.C., & Pinnell, G.S. (2001). *Guiding readers and writers grades 3–6: Teaching, comprehension, genre, and content literacy.* Portsmouth, NH: Heinemann.

Francis, D., Carlson, C., Foorman, B., Goldenberg, C., Iglesias, A., Miller, J., . . . ,Vaughn, S. (2006). *Oracy/literacy development of Spanish-speaking children.* Washington DC: National Institute of Child Health and Human Development and the Institute of Educational Sciences.

Freeman, Y.S., & Freeman, D.E. (2006). *Teaching reading and writing in Spanish and English in bilingual and dual language classrooms.* Portsmouth, NH: Heinemann.

Gajo, L. (2007). Linguistic knowledge and subject knowledge: How does bilingualism contribute to subject development? *International Journal of Bilingual Education and Bilingualism, 10*(5), 563–581.

García, E.E., Bravo, M.A., Dickey, L.M., Chun, K., & Sun-Irminger, X. (2002). Rethinking reform in the context of cultural and linguistic diversity: Creating a responsive learning community. In L.I. Minaya-Rowe (Ed.), *Teacher training and effective pedagogy in the context of student diversity.* Greenwich, CT: Information Age.

García, O. (2009). *Bilingual education in the 21st century: A global perspective.* West Sussex, UK: Wiley-Blackwell.

García, O. (2011). Educating New York's bilingual children: constructing a future from the past. *International Journal of Bilingual Education and Bilingualism, 14*(2), 133–153.

Genesee, F., Lindholm-Leary, K., Saunders, W., & Christian, D. (Eds.). (2006). *Educating English language learners: A synthesis of research evidence.* New York: Cambridge University Press.

Genesee, F., & Riches, C. (2006). Literacy: Instruction issues. In F. Genesee, K. Lindholm-Leary, W. Saunders, & D. Christian (Eds.), *Educating English language learners: A synthesis of research evidence* (pp. 109–176). New York: Cambridge University Press.

Genishi, C., Stires, S.E., & Yung-Chan, D. (2001). Writing in an integrated curriculum: Prekindergarten English language learners as symbol makers. *The Elementary School Journal, 101,* 399–416.

Gentile, L. (2004). *The oracy instructional guide.* Carlsbad, CA: Dominie Press.

Gersten, R. (1996). Literacy instruction for language-minority students: The transition years. *The Elementary School Journal, 96,* 227–244.

Gersten, R., & Baker, S. (2000). What we know about effective instructional practices for English-language learners. *Exceptional Children, 66,* 454–470.

Goldenberg, C. (2008). Teaching English language learners: What the research does—and does not—say. *American Educator, 32*(2), 8–44.

González, N., Moll, L., & Amanti, C. (2005). Funds of knowledge: Theorizing practices in households, communities, and classrooms. Mahwah, NJ: Erlbaum.

Gort, M. (2006). Strategic code-switching, interliteracy, and other phenomena of emergent bilingual writing: Lessons from first grade dual language classrooms. *Journal of Early Childhood Literacy, 6,* 323–354.

Grant, R., & Wong, S. (2003). Barriers to literacy for language minority learners: An argument for change in the literacy education profession. *Journal of Adolescent & Adult Literacy, 46,* 386–394.

Greene, J. (1997). A meta-analysis of the Rossell and Baker review of bilingual education research. *Bilingual Research Journal, 21,* 103–122.

Grosjean, F. (1989). Neurolinguists, beware! The bilingual is not two monolinguals in one person. *Brain and Language, 36,* 3–15.

Grosjean, F. (2006). Studying bilinguals: Methodological and conceptual issues. In T.E. Bhatia & W.C. Ritchie (Eds.), *The Handbook of Bilingualism* (pp. 32–63). Oxford: Blackwell.

Gutiérrez, K.D., Baquedano-López, P., Alvarez, H.H., & Chiu, M.M. (1999). Building a culture of collaboration through hybrid language practices. *Theory Into Practice, 38*(2), 87–93.

Hickman, P., Pollard-Durodola, S., & Vaughn, S. (2004). Storybook reading: Improving vocabulary and comprehension for English language learners. *The Reading Teacher, 57,* 720–730.

Hopewell, S. (2011). Leveraging bilingualism to accelerate English reading comprehension. *International Journal of Bilingual Education and Bilingualism, 14*(5), 603–620.

Izquierdo, E. (2010, November). *Biliteracy: What is it?* Paper presented at La Cosecha Conference, Santa Fe, NM.

Jennings, C. (1991). *Children as story-tellers.* Melbourne, Australia: Oxford University Press.

Jiménez, R. (1997). The strategic reading abilities of five low-literacy Latina/o readers in middle school. *Reading Research Quarterly, 32,* 224–243.

Kenner, C. (2004). Living in simultaneous worlds: Difference and integration in bilingual script-learning. *Bilingual Education and Bilingualism, 7*(1), 43–61.

Kimbell-Lopez, K. (2003). Just think of the possibilities: Formats for reading instruction in the elementary classroom. *Reading Online, 6.* Retrieved from http://www.readingonline.org/articles/art_index.asp?HREF=kimbell-lopez/index.html

Klingner, J.K., & Vaughn. S. (2000). The helping behaviors of fifth graders while using collaborative strategic reading during ESL content classes. *TESOL Quarterly, 34*(1), 69–98.

Koda, K., & Zehler, A. (2008). *Learning to read across languages: Cross-Linguistic relationships in first- and second-language literacy development.* London: Routledge.

Kuhn, M. (2004). Helping students become accurate, expressive readers: Fluency instruction for small groups. *The Reading Teacher, 58*(4), 338–344.

Lachtman, O. (1995). *Pepita talks twice/Pepita habla dos veces.* Houston: Arte Publico.

Lesaux, N.K., & Geva, E. (2006). Synthesis: Development of literacy in language minority students. In D. August & T. Shanahan (Eds.), *Developing literacy in second-language learners. Report of the National Literacy Panel on Language-Minority Children and Youth* (pp. 53–74). Mahwah, NJ: Erlbaum.

Lubliner, S., & Hiebert, E. (2011). An analysis of English-Spanish cognates as a source of general academic language. *Bilingual Research Journal, 34,* 76–93.

MacLure, M., Phillips, T., & Wilkinson, A. (1988). *Oracy matters.* Milton Keynes, UK: Open University.

Manyak, P. C. (2002). "Welcome to salon 110": The consequences of hybrid literacy practices in the primary-grade English immersion class. *Bilingual Research Journal, 26*(2), 213–234.

Martin-Beltrán, M. (2010). The two-way language bridge: Co-constructing bilingual language learning opportunities. *The Modern Language Journal, 94*(2), 254–277.

Martínez-Roldán, C., & Sayer, P. (2006). Reading through linguistic borderlands: Latino students' transactions with narrative texts. *Journal of Early Childhood Literacy, 6,* 293–322.

McCarrier, A., Pinnell, G.S., & Fountas, I.C. (2000). *Interactive writing: How language & literacy come together, K–2.* Portsmouth, NH: Heinemann.

Miller, J.F., Heilmann, J., Nockerts, A., Iglesias, A., Fabiano, L., & Francis, D.J. (2006). Oral language and reading in bilingual children. *Learning Disabilities Research & Practice, 21,* 30–43.

Moll, L. C. (1988). Some key issues in teaching Latino students. *Language Arts, 65*(5), 465–472.

Moll, L.C., & Diaz, S. (1985). Ethnographic pedagogy: Promoting effective bilingual instruction. In E.E. Garcia & R.V. Padilla (Eds.), *Advances in bilingual education research* (pp. 127–149). Tucson: University of Arizona.

Mooney, M. (1990). *Reading to, with, and by children.* New York: Richard C. Owens.

Nagy, W., Garcia, G., Durgunoglu, A., & Hancin-Bhatt, B. (1993). English-Spanish bilingual students' use of cognates in English reading. *Journal of Reading Behavior, 25*(3), 241–259.

Naqui, R., Thorne, K., McKeough, A., & Pfitscher, C. (2010). *Building bridges: Acknowledging children's first languages: Final report May, 2010.* Alberta, CA: Alberta Centre for Child, Family & Community Research.

Nation, I.S.P. (2001). *Learning vocabulary in another language.* Cambridge, UK: Cambridge University Press.

National Institute of Child Health and Human Development. (2000). *Report of the National Reading Panel: Teaching children to read: An evidence based assessment of the scientific research literature on reading and its implications for reading instruction* (NIH Publication No. 00-4769). Washington DC: U.S. Government Printing Office.

Norman, C. (1992). *Thinking voices: The work of the national oracy project.* London: Hodder & Stoughton.

O'Day, J. (2009). Good instruction is good for everyone—or is it? English language learners in a balanced literacy approach. *Journal of Education for Students Placed at Risk, 14*(1), 97–119.

Orellana, M.F., Martínez, D.C., and Montaño, E. (2013, November). *Leveraging translation for writing and the expansion of linguistic repertoires.* Paper presented at the Literacy Research Association Conference, San Diego, CA.

Pappamihiel, N.E. (2001). Moving from the ESL classroom into the mainstream: An investigation of English language anxiety in Mexican girls. *Bilingual Research Journal, 25*(1-2), 31–38.

Pearson, P.D., & Gallagher, M.C. (1983). The instruction of reading comprehension. *Contemporary Educational Psychology, 8,* 317–344.

Phillips, L. (1991). *The role of storytelling in early literacy development.* Retrieved from http://www/australianstory telling.org.au/txt/chidhd.php

Pikulski, J.J., & Chard, D.J. (2005). Fluency: Bridge between decoding and reading comprehension. *The Reading Teacher, 58*(6), 510–519.

Pollard-Durodola, S., Mathes, P.G., Vaughn, S., Cardenas-Hagan, E., & Linan-Thompson, S. (2006). The role of oracy in developing comprehension in Spanish-speaking English language learners. *Topics in Language Disorders, 26,* 365–384.

*Programa Nacional para el Fortalecimiento de la Lectura y la Escritura Básica.* (PRONALEES). (2002). Mexico D.F: Secretaria de Educación Pública.

Reyes, I. (2006). Exploring the connections between emergent biliteracy and bilingualism. *Journal of Early Childhood Literacy, 6*(3), 267–292.

Reyes, M. (1991). A process approach to literacy using dialogue journals and literature logs with second language learners. *Research in the Teaching of English, 25,* 291–313.

Reyes, M. (1992). Challenging venerable assumptions: Literacy instruction for linguistically diverse students. *Harvard Educational Review, 62,* 459–466.

Rodríguez-Valls, F. (2011). Coexisting languages: Reading bilingual books with biliterate eyes. *Bilingual Research Journal, 34*(1), 19–27.

Rolstad, K., Mahoney, K., & Glass, G.V. (2005). The big picture: A meta-analysis of program effectiveness research on English language learners. *Educational Policy, 19,* 572–594.

Ruiz, R. (1988). Orientations in language planning. In S. McKay & S. Wong (Eds.), *Language diversity: Problem or resource?* (pp. 3–25). Cambridge, MA: Newbury House.

Said, E. W. (2000). *Out of place: A memoir.* New York: Vintage.

Saunders, W., Foorman, B., & Carlson, C. (2006). Is a separate block of time for English language development in programs for English Learners needed? *The Elementary School Journal, 107,* 181–198.

Saunders, W. & Goldenberg, C. (1999). The effects of instructional conversations and literature logs on limited and fluent English proficient students' story comprehension and thematic understanding. *The Elementary School Journal, 99,* 277–301.

Saunders, W., O'Brien, G., Lennon, D., & McLean, J. (1998). Making the transition to English literacy successful: Effective strategies for studying literature with transition students. In R.M. Gersten & R.T. Jiménez (Eds.), *Promoting learning for culturally and linguistically diverse students* (pp. 99–134). Belmont, CA: Wadsworth.

Schmoker, M. J. (2011). *Focus: Elevating the essentials to radically improve student learning.* Alexandria, VA: ASCD.

Short, K.G., Kauffman, G., & Kahn, L.H. (2000). "I just need to draw": Responding to literature across multiple sign systems. *The Reading Teacher, 54*(2), 160–171.

Simich-Dudgeon, C. (Summer 1998). Classroom strategies for encouraging collaborative discussion. In *Directions in Language and Education* (ED 435 188). Washington, DC: National Clearinghouse for Bilingual Education.

Slavin, R.E., & Cheung, A. (2005). A synthesis of research on language of reading instruction for English language learners. *Review of Educational Research, 75*(2), 247–284.

Smith, P.H., Jiménez, R.T., & Martínez-León, N. (2003). Other countries' literacies: What U.S. educators can learn from Mexican schools. *The Reading Teacher, 56,* 772–781.

Sneddon, R. (2008). *Bilingual books-biliterate children: Learning to read through dual language books.* London, UK: Trentham.

Snow, C.E., & Tabors, P.O. (1993). Language skills that relate to literacy development In B. Spodek & O. Saracho (Eds.), *Yearbook in early childhood education* (Vol. 4, pp. 1–20). New York: Teachers College Press.

Soltero-González, L., Escamilla, K., & Hopewell, S. (2010). A bilingual perspective on writing assessment: Implications for teachers of emerging bilingual writers. In G. Li & and P.A. Edwards (Eds.), *Best practices in ELL instruction* (pp. 222–244). New York: Guilford Press.

Soltero-González, L., Escamilla, K., & Hopewell, S. (2011). Changing teachers' perceptions about the writing abilities of emerging bilingual students: Toward a holistic bilingual perspective on writing assessment. *International Journal of Bilingual Education and Bilingualism.* DOI: 10.1080113670050.2011.604712

Sparrow, W., Butvilofsky, S., & Escamilla, K. (2011). The evolution of biliterate writing through simultaneous bilingual literacy instruction. In E.B. Bauer & M. Gort (Eds.), *Early biliteracy development: Exploring young learners' use of their linguistic resources.* New York: Routledge.

Sparrow, W., Butvilofsky, S., Wiley, E., & Escamilla, K. (2012, April). *Assessing fidelity of implementation of an instructional model: Targeting student trajectories toward biliteracy.* Paper presented at American Educational Researchers Association, Vancouver, Canada.

Sparrow, W., & Escamilla, K. (2012). Literacy Squared phase II: Oregon replication study technical report, 2009–2012. Boulder, CO: BUENO Center for Multi-cultural Education.

Taberski, S. (2000). *On solid ground: Strategies for teaching reading, K–3.* Portsmouth, NH: Heinemann.

Ulanoff, S.H., & Pucci, S.L. (1999). Learning words from books: The effects of read aloud on second language vocabulary acquisition. *Bilingual Research Journal, 23*(4), 409–422.

Valdés, G., & Anloff Sanders, P. (1999). Latino ESL students and the development of writing abilities. In C. Cooper & L. Odell (Eds.), *Evaluating writing: The role of teachers' knowledge about text, learning, and culture* (pp. 249–278). Urbana, IL: National Council of Teachers of English.

Valdés, G., & Figueroa, R.A. (1994). *Bilingualism and testing: A special case of bias.* Norwood, NJ: Ablex.

Vernon, S., & Ferreiro, E. (1999). Writing development: A neglected variable in the consideration of phonological awareness. *Harvard Educational Review, 69,* 395–415.

Vygotsky, L. (1978). *Mind in society: The development of higher psychological processes.* Cambridge, MA: Harvard University Press.

Walker, L. (2012). *Readers theater scripts for schools.* Retreived from www.LiteracyConnection.com/Reader'sTheater .php

Wei, L., & Wu, C. (2009). Polite Chinese children revisited: Creativity and use of code-switching in the Chinese complementary school classroom. *International Journal of Bilingual Education and Bilingualism, 12*(2), 193–211.

West, M. (1953). *A general service list of English words.* London: Longman, Green.

Zentella, A. (1997). *Growing up bilingual: Puerto Rican children in New York.* Boston: Blackwell.

# Index

Page numbers followed by b, f, or t refer to boxes, figures, or tables, respectively.